Hertford County North Carolina

Guardian Accounts
- 1830-1832 -

Complied by:
Raymond Parker Fouts

Southern Historical Press, Inc.
Greenville, South Carolina

Please direct all correspondence and book orders to:
SOUTHERN HISTORICAL PRESS, Inc.
PO Box 1267
Greenville, SC   29602-1267

ISBN #978-1-63914-195-1
Printed in the United States of America

CONTENTS

(1) [Column #1]

Burrell WHITLEY 1 + 29
David _ WHITLEY 1+ 29.74.1⁻3/149.177./
Sarah M WILLIAMS 1.31
Jenkins NEWSOM 1
Martha D ASKEW 2
Emmeline A ASKEW 2
Ann _ BRITT _2.83
Mary BRITT 3.83.152/182/
Permelia BRITT _ 3.83.153 .182)
Elizabeth BRITT 3.83.154. ??/183/
Martha BROWN 4.65
Elizabeth PARKER ___4
Julia Ann BRITT 4
Rebeckah BRITT 5.43.76. 80
Margaret BRITT 5+44.81 122
Martha BEVERLY 5.82
Wm BEVERLY _5.81
James H BRITT 6.45.80. 121)
Alexander BRITT 6.44.81 121)/154.181/
Martha BRITT _ 6.
Rebecca P BRITT 7.119
William BOON 7.72
John BARKER 9.45
George BARKER 9.45
Polly CLARK 10
Watson COLSON 10.46
Henry COTTON 11.84
Peggy CURL 11.66
Richard DUNSTUN 11
Mary DARDEN 12+13+14
James DEANES 15 128.156
Thomas J DEANES 15.47
Daniel DEANES 15.47.84. 124.155
Pennina EVANS 15.85.144
Lawrence FELLS 15
Cecelia GREEN 16.48
Jesse Y HARRELL 16.67. 86.128.159
Heirs of Jesse VANN 17. 107.141.170

Column #2]

Sid
Sindy, Reany & Malicha HOLLOMON 17.49.87
William HOLLOMON 17. 87.129

Jacob HOLLOMON 18.87. 129
Anthony IRVIN 18.67
Mary JORDAN 18
Casten JORDAN 19
Barsha JEGETTS 19.111. 145
Winborn JENKINS 19.50. 89.130.161
Penelope JENKINS 20.49. 89.129.160
Mary Jane MONTGOMERY 21.51. 109.131/163./
John MAGETT 21+22.113. 119
Amon OVERTON 23.52. 95
Dossey OUTLAW 23.51. 14?3
Sarah PORTER 23
Dauson William and Bryant RALEIGH 23)
Nancy REA _ 24.70
Hannah P REA 24.70
Thomas ROBERTS 25
Esther L ROBERTS 25
Mary A. W. RAMSAY 25
Elisha SESSOMS Children 26.58.106.136.170
John B SHARP _ 26.56
Jacob SHARP _26.57.100
Elizabeth SHARP 26.57. 100
Sarah SIMONS 27.115
Newet? VICK 27.73.118. 148.177
Cordia VICK 28.73.117. 148.176
Rebecah VICK 28.73.118. 149.177.
Etney VICK 28.74.118. 149.177
William VICK 28.74.118. 148.176
Elizabeth VANNPELT 28. 71.107.142.171
Orphans of David WILLIAMS 29
Margaret WHITLEY _29. 74.112.149.177
William WILLSON 30
Wm WORD _31.63.78
Sally M?
Sabry WHEELER 32

(2) [Duplicate of previous page.]

(3) [Column #1]

Joseph BENTHALL 32
Martha BOON 34
Peterson BOON 34
Wm M DAUGHTERRYS Heirs 34-5-6-7
Starkey L HARE 37-8-9-40-1-6
Inventory of the amt. Rec/d/.. of John WINBORN as Admr. of Joseph PERRY dec/d/ due 41 Charles SKINNER 41
Levina ASKEW 43.79.121. 151.
Emily ASKEW 43.79.120. 151.
Charles S KENKINS 49.89. 131.161.
Wm P. JENKINS 49.88.131
Hartwell, Aidement Martha LIVERMAN 3?7.90.131
Aron OUTLAW 52.96.132. 163.
Mary Jane PERRY 53.136. 165.
Wm PERRY 53-4.96. 99.132.134/164./
James PERRY 55.98.135. 163.
Joseph PERRY 55.69.99. 110.133.146.163./185/
Levina SIMONS 58.102
Mary SIMONS 59.102.137. 167
Elizabeth SIMONS 59.104. 138.146.168
John SIMONS 60.105.140. 167.
Edward SIMONS 61.103. 138.166
Sarah SIMONS 62-3.104. 139
Hilliry SOWELL 63.141. 170
Sally M WILLIAMS 64. 108.142
Wm WATSON 64
Elva BEST 65
Timothy BEST 65
Robert FLYNN 66.144.173
William HOLLOMON 66.

159
Jacob HOLLOMON 67. 158
Peston PERRY 68.109.146. 174
Mary PERRY 68.96.110. 147.174
Patrick PERRY 69.111.147. 175
Elizabeth PERRY 69.110. 175
John D. PERRY 70.111. 146.176
William H SMITH 70
Elizabeth VANPELT 71

[Column #2]

Joseph YEATES 71.108. 143.172
Martha WIGGINS 71
Elizabeth WIGGINS 72
James WIGGINS 72
Mary WIGGINS 72
Jabez B. WHEELER 75. 112
Wm H WILLSON/s/. (Recpt.) 75
Saml. F MAGET 76
James MAGET 77
Wm PARKERs Recpt 78
John MAGET 78
George BAKER 82.122
John BAKER 82 123
orphans of Wm Mills DAUGHTRY} 84
Alfred J GRIFFITH 86. 157.185
Starkey HARRELL 88.128. 157.185 (end)
Mary HARRELL 88.158
Charles E KNIGHT 90.131. 161
Richard MOORE 91.179
A W MOORE 92
Ad. E. MOORE 92.178
Mary Ann MOORE 93.179.
Elizabeth P. C. MOORE 93
Heirs of John MOORE in a/c cur. 94
Wm PERRY 96
Jane PARKER 97
Lemuel PARKER 97.135. 166
Robert PARKER 98.166
Hillery SCULL 106
Melvill WISE 108.142.171.

(12) (Cont.)
157.184.224.254.308.330.
363.393.426.462.497.524.
DOUGHTEY Celia heirs
148.176.212.242.276.303.
324.357.422.456.464.465.
499.500.
DARDEN Samuel 155.307.
328.361.
DUKES James 155.184.
224.239.rect.
DUKES Charles E. 156.
185.186.
DICKINSON Joseph 224.
275.364.394.428.464.500.
DICKINSON Mary 224.
274.362.425.
DICKINSON John 275.
DOUGHTRY Henry
Mills 300.
DOUGHTEY John heirs
389.
DAVIS David 427.463.500.
DAVIS Henry 428.463.500.
DOUGHTIE James 465.
DOUGHTIE Jordan 465.
DOUGHTIE Napolian
466.
DOUGHTIE Franklin 466.
DARDEN Harriet 524.528.
DARDEN William 525.529
DARDEN James 526.530.
DARDEN Lenny 531.

(13)
EVANS Penina 15.85.144.
173.rec/t/.
EVORITT Julia F. 492.
EVORITT Lewis F. 493.

(14)
FELLS Sumner 15
FLYNN Robert 66.109.
144.173.206.240.275.282.
4--
FARLESS Climmon 282.
309.331.365.395.428.466.
FARLESS Cinthey 283.
309.331.365.395.429.
FARLESS Henry 283.308.
FARLESS Simmon 283.
309.330.364.

(15)
GREEN Celia 16.48. &

rec/t/.
GRIFFITH Alfred J. 86.
127.157.185.226.255.284.
310.331.366.396.429.467.
502.
GRIFFITH Hartwell (hire
of Negroes) 119
GATLING Mary A. 185.
225
GATLING Briggs 208.225.
256.527.531.
GATLING Catherine 209.
225.255.526.531.
GATLING Sally 209.225.
255.526.531
GRANT James 210.240.
GRANT Oliver 210.240.
GRANT Sarah 210.240.
GRANT John 210.240.
GRIFFITH Elizabeth 365.
396
GRIFFITH Julia 395.429.
467.502.
GATLING John 467.501.
GATLING Nancy 467.501.
GATLING Mary J. C. 468.
501.
GRANT John/s/. heirs 522.

(16)
HARRELL Jesse Y. 16.67.
86.128.159.186.228.256.
286.310.335.366.399.432.
HOLLOMON Jacob heirs
17.49.87.145.
HOLLOMON William 17.
66.851.129.159.187.227.
HOLLOMON Jacob 18.
67.87.129.159.187.226.257.
HARE Starkey 37.
HARRELL Starkey 88.
128.157.185.228.256.285.
310.332.366.399.432.471.
503.
HARRELL Mary 88.127.
158.
HOLLOMON Kindred
149.
HOLLOMON Abner 150.
HOLLOMON Whitmel
150.
HOLLOMON Renia &
Malichia 158.188.227.
HOLLOMON Minna E.
186.226.257.284.311.

HOLLOMON Harriott
186.226.257.285.311.335.
368.418.453.471.505.
HOLLOMON Sally 187.
226.257.285.311.335.368.
418.453.472.506.
HUTCHINGS John W.
332.333
HARRELL Cathrine A.
334.367.398.430.468.
HARRELL Jarrott. V? 334.
367.399.431.468.
HARRELL William J.
334.368.398.430.469.503.
HARRELL Marmaduke W.
334.367.398.430.469.504.
HARRELL Andrew J. 334.
367.397.431.469.504.
HARRELL John W. 396.
433.470.504.
HARRELL Alpheus 397.
432.471.505.

(17)
IRVIN Anthony 18.67.
JORDAN Mary 18
JORDAN Costen 19.
JEGITTS Barsha 19.111.
145.
JENKINS Winborne 19.50.
89.130.160.206.
JENKINS Penelope 20.49.
89.129.160.205.
JENKINS William P. 49.
88.130.
JENKINS Charles S. 49.89.
131.161.188.
JONES Wiley & King L.
161.
JENKINS Charles of Irvin
275.299.312.rec/t/.
JENKINS Emeline Eliza
275.300.356.386.
JENKINS Elizabeth E. 323.
JENKINS Milley E. 369.
419.510.
JENKINS Mary E. 369.
419.453.472.
JENKINS Sally M. 369.
419.453.473.506
JENKINS David O. 369.
419.454.473.506.
JERNIGAN Jacob D. 434.
472.506
JORDAN Mary 456.

JORDAN Robert 456.

(18)
MAGET John 21.21. [sic]
22.
KNIGHT Charles E. 90.
131.161.188.229.258.284.
311.336.370.400.421.rec/t/.

(19)
LIVERMAN Hartwell
Aidamont & Martha 50.90.
131.161.189.
LAWRENCE John J/r/.
5017.

(20)
MAGET John 21.21.22.78.
113.119.
MONTGOMERY Mary
Jane 50.109.132.162.191.
MAGET Samuel F. 76
MAGET Johannes 77.
MOORE Richard 91.179.
215.244.303.326.358.390.
MOORE A. W. 92.
MOORE A. E. 92.178.
MOORE Mary Ann 93.179
.214.
MOORE E. P. C 93.
MOORE John/s/. heirs 94.
MAGET Rebecca A. 132.
162.
MARSH Jane 189.229.259.
313.337.373
MARSH William 189.229.
258.286.313.337.371.
MARSH Levina 190.230.
259.286.312.336.373.404.
437.475.509.
MARSH Henry 190.230.
258.
MASH James 286.379.509.
MASH James Henry 287.
313.337.403.437.475.
MC GLAUGHN Mary Ann
301.324.357.389.421.
MITCHELL Briant, Wil-
liam & Celia 313.336.403.
MONTGOMERY Mary E.
337.370.400.436.475.508.
MONGTGOMERY Re-
becca C. 338.370.400.436.
474.507.
MITCHELL Nancy E. 371.

Vol: --	Years: 1823-1845	Pages: 1-531

(30) 1 Burrell **WHITLEY.**   Dr. Burrell **WHITLEY** in Account with George **WHITLEY** Guard.
1830

May C/t By am/t/ Due Ward on my last		To Cash p/d/. Tax on Land for 1828.	..25
return to May Court 1829}	5.97	" 1 pr Shoes....................	1
in/t/. from May Ct. 1829 to May C/t/ 1830	..35	" his part of renewing Guard. Bond	..27
" Am/t/ of James **WHITLEY**/s/ est.(his part)	..86	" Cash p/d/ Clk recording this act.	.20
" " his part of Rent of Land 1829	3.48	5 pc/t/ Comm..................	.30
		Balance Due orphan May Court 1830	8. 64
	Dlls 10.66	his Dlls 10.66	

E. E. George x **WHITLEY** Guard
mark

Dav_d **WHITLEY**   Dr. David **WHITLEY** in Account with George **WHITLEY** his Guard   Cr.
1830

May C/t By am/t/ Due the Ward on my last		To Cash p/d/. Tax on Land for 1828	..25
return at May Court 1829.}	5.97	" 1 pr Shoes	..75
"In/t/ from May Ct 1829 till May C/t/ 1830	..35	" his part of renewing Guard. Bond	..27
" Amt of his part of James **WHITLEY**/s/ est.	. 86	" Cash p/d/ Clk recording this act.	..820
" " " " " of Rent of Land 1829	3.48	5 pc/t/ Comm..................	.30
		Balance Due orphan May Court 1830	8. 89
	Dlls 10.66	his Dlls 10.66	

E. E. George x **WHITLEY** Guard
mark

North Carolina-Hertford County.

May Court of Pleas &c 1830.

These Accounts were returned to Court on oath by George **WHITLEY** Guard & ordered to be Recorded

Test   L. M. **COWPER** Clk

Sara1 M **WILLIAMS** Dr. Sally Maria **WILLIAMS** orphan of Benjamin **WILLIAMS** decd
In Account with Dempsy **NOWELL** Guardian.

1829	To Goods & 12 Months Board....	$55.98	1829	By return made to May Term	$168.84
	" Comms on $234.85	11.74	May	" Int thereon ...	10.02
	" Balance Due orphan 24/th/ May 1830	167.13		Hire Negroes .	58
		Dlls $234.86			Dlls $234.86
				By Balance Due 24/th/ 3 May 1830	$167.13

The above Stated account is just & true to the best of my Knowledge.   Dempsey **NOWELL** Guard

North Carolina-Hertford County _____   May Court of Pleas &c. 1830.

This account was returned to Court on oath by Dempsey **NOWELL** Guard & ordered to be Recorded.

Test   L. M. **COWPER** Clk

(30) (Cont.) Jenkins **NEWSOM** Dr. Jenkins **NEWSOM** orphan of John **NEWSOM**
In Account Current with James **NEWSOM** Guardian.

1829 To paid Sheriff Tax...	.12	By balance due at Febry Ct 1829	$ 6.33
" Comm/s/ on $7.13.	.35	" In/t/. on $6.33 up to this date	56
Balance Due Aug/t/ Ct 1830	6.42		
Dlls 6.89			$6.89
			James **NEWSOM** Guard

North Carolina-Hertford County _____ August Court of Pleas &c 1830.
This Account was returned to Court on oath of James **JENKINS** [sic] Guard & ordered to be recorded
Test   L. M. **COWPER** Clk

---

(31) 2 Martha D. **ASKEW** Dr Martha D **ASKEW** in Act with Nickolas Guardian [sic]   Cr.
1829

May Term To half of Guardian Bond pd Clark ..}	40	By Cash Rec/d/ of Elisha	
To pd Thamas **DREWRY** for Tuition}	3 34 ½	**WINBORN** Admr of Thamas	
To pd for this present Return}	40	**WINBORN** decd Will Annex/d/	$74..23 ½
To Commissions	3 35		
To Bale due The Ward Augst?}	66..74	24th 1830 E. Excepte/d/	
	74 23 ½	August 24 1830	74 23 ½
		Nickolas **ASKEW** guardian	

Emmeline A. **ASKEW**
1829   Dr Emmeline A. **ASKEW** in Act with Nickolas **ASKEW** guardian   Cr

May Term To half the Sum pd }		Guardian [sic]	
for guardian Bond}	40	By Cash Rec/d/ of Elisha	
To pd Thamas **DREWRY** for Tuition}	3 34 ½	**WINBORN** Admr of Thamas	
To pd for this present Return}	40	**WINBORN** decd Will Annex/d/	
To Commission	3 35	Just up To this day	
To Bale due the Ward August 24/th/1830	66..74	August 24/th/ 1830	74 23 ½
	74 23 ½	E Ecepted August Term 1830	

Narth carolina   }
Hertford Caunty } August Caurt of Pleas &C. 1830
These Accounts was Returned to Caurt on oaths ef by Nicko [sic] **ASKEW** guard & ardered to Recorded [sic]
Test   L. M. **COWPER**

Ann **BRITT**
1828   Dr Ann **BRITT** ophan of Etheldred **BRITT** decd in act with Elizabeth **BRITT** her guard

Decr To Cash paid for 1 pr Morocco Shoes	1..75	1827 By hire of Negro man **BRISTER** this year	$10..00
1829		1828 " hire of ditto **BRISTER** this year	15..00
Decr 24/th/ Cash paid John W **SAUTHALL** as p recpt 24..14		1829 "hire of ditto **BRISTER** this year	10 00
1830		1830	
Feby 22/nd/ Amt paid Cyprian **BRITT** admr as pr recpt 17..86		Feby 22/nd/ By Amt recd of Cyprian **BRITT** Admr of	
Augt Amt paid John W **SAUTHALL** as p recpt	8 37	Etheldred **BRITT** decd and Melisa **BRITT** with	
To Amt due the Ward	277..73	interest included up to 22/nd/ August 1830	280..35
		By hire of man **BRISTER** this year which	
		will become due the 25 Decr 1830	10
		By her proportion of land rents for year 1829	2 --
		By her proportion of land rents for 1830 due 25 decr	2..50
	$329..85		$329..85

---

(32) 3 Mary **BRITT** Dr Mary **BRITT** ophan of Etheld **BRITT** dec/d/ in act with Elizabeth **BRITT** her G [sic]

1828		1827	
June 6/th/ To Amt pd John W **SAUTHAL** acts?	4 63	Decr By hire of Negro Boy **JACOB** this year	$ 5..00
July 8/th/ " Amt paid Benja **NEWSOM** for 115		1828 " hire of ditto Boy **JACOB** this year	10. 00
days time at 5/¢/ pr day	5..75	1829 hire of ditto Boy **JACOB** this year	12. 50

(32) Mary BRITT (Cont.)

Decr To Cash pd for 5 yds Callico @ 1/6 per yd	1..25	1830	hire of Said Boy **JACOB** this year due		
" pd for pr Moroco Shaes @ 10/6	1..75	25th December 1830		15 00	
" for Leather Shaes @ 6/-	1 00	By her proportion of land rents for 1829		2 00	
" 1 Years board	25 00	/22/nd/ Agut By Amt recd of Cyprian **BRITT**}			
1829		With Interest up to this ~~ditto~~ Augt 23/rd/ 1829}		42..16	
June To 1 pr Leather Shaes @ 4/6	75	By Amt of Land rent this year 25 decr next		2 50	
" quarter tuition to Elish A **CAW** @ 9/-	1..50	hire of negro boy **JACOB** this year dec 25 day?		17 00	
Decr To board this Year	20..00			106 16	
" 1 Leather Shaes 4/6	75				
1830					
Augt 1/s./ " 1 qr tuition this Year	3 00				
" Amt Patk **BRAWN**s Act	5..87				
22/nd/ To 8 months Board up to this date	13.25				
To Amt due the Ward	21..71				
	$106..16			106..16	

Permelia BRITT Dr Permelia **BRITT** orphan of Etheld **BRITT** decd in act with Elizabeth **BRITT** her guard — **Cr**

1828		1827		
June 6/th/ To Amt pd John W. **SAUTHALL**s Act	$ 4..63	Decr By hire of Negro girl **PHILLIS**		$10.00
July 8 " Amt paid Benjn **NEWSOM** for}		1828 " hire of Said **PHILLIS**		15.00
115 days tuition a 5/¢/ pr day}	5. 75	Decr		
Decr To Cash paid for 5 yds Callico @ 1/6	1. 25	1829		
" " pd for 1 pr morocco Shaes @ 10/6	1 75	Decr " hire of Said Negro this year		8.00
" " 1 pr Leather Shaes @ 6/-	1. 00	by rent of Land this year		2.00
" " 1 years board	25 00	" Amt recd of Cyprian **BRITT** admr of		
1829		Etheldred and Melisa **BRITT**}		
June To 1 Leather Shaes @ 4/6	75	Estate with interest up to 22/nd/ August 1830}		53..56
" " 1 qr tuition to Elizath A **CAW** @ 9/-	1 50	1830		
Decr To board this year	20..00	Augt By Amt of Land rent this year due 25 Decr		2.50
" " 1 pr Leather Shaes @ 4/6	75	" hire of Negro woman **PHILLIS** and Child}		
To Amt due from paw? in division of}		due 25th decr next }		10 00
the Negraes of Etheldred **BRITT**s Estate}				
With ints up to 22/nd/ August 1830}	71..47			
1830				
Augt 22/nd/ To 1 quarter tuition @ $3	3..00			
" Amt Patk **BROWN**s act	5..87	By Amt due the guardian		54..86
" 8 months board up to this date	13..20			
	155 92			155..92

Elizabeth BRITT Dr Elizabeth **BRITT** orphan of Etheld **BRITT** in act with Elizabeth **BRITT** /her gd?/

1828		1827	
June To Amt pd John W **SAUTHALL** act	$ 3..00	Decr By hire of Negro girl **VIOLET** this year	10..00
" 4 yds Callico at 1/6	1..00	1828	
" 2 pr Shaes @ 4/6	1..50	Decr " hire of Said Negro this year	15..00
Decr To Board this year	25 00	1829	
1829 1 pr Shaes at 3/9	62 ½	Decr " hire of Said Negro this year	15..00
Decr To Board this Year	20. 00	By rent of Land this year	2..00
1830		1830	
Feby 22/nd/ To amt due in division of Negraes of		Feby 22/nd/ By Amt recd of Cyprian **BRITT** Admr of Etheld	
Etheld **BRITT**s Estate with Interest up to		and Milisa **BRITT** dec/d/ with Interest up to the=	
[End of entry.]	$51..12½	[End of entry.]	$42..00

(33) 4 Elizabeth **BRITT** Dr Elizabeth **BRITT** orphan with of Etheldred **BRITT** in act with Elizabth **BRITT** /her g/

Amt Brot forwardard [sic]	$51..12½	Amt Brot forward		42..00
22/nd/ August 1830--	71 47	22/nd/ August 1830		54..13
Augt 22/nd/ To 8 months atboard up to this date	13..20	By rent of land this year due the 25 decr next		2..50
		By hire of negro girl **VIOLET** this year due}		
		the 25 Decr next}		18..00
		By amt due the guardian 22/d/ Augt 1830}		19 16
	$135..79			$135..79

her
Elizabeth + **BRITT**
mark

North Caralina }
Hertford Caunty} August Caurt of Pleas &C. 1830
These Accaunts were returned to Caurt an oaths by Elizabeth **BRITT** Guardian
& order [sic] to be Recorded   Test L. M. **CAWPER** Clk

Martha **BRAWN** Dr Martha **BRAWN** orphan of Hardy **BROWN** decd in Act with William B **WYNNS** Guard

1830			
May 26/th/ To 1/lb/ Loaf Sugar @ 2/6 1/lb/ Cotton @ 1/3 $ 0. 37½		recd	
July 29/th/ To 5/lbs/ Loaf Sugar @ 2/6	1..25	Feby 22/nd/ By Ballance due the orphan	$209..89
To Cash pd Sheriff for Taxes for 1829	62½	Interest an the a/c to August Caurt 1830	6..26
To 5/¢/ per Cent Commissions	42	1830	216 15
To ballance due the orphan	213 48	August 23/rd/ By ballance due the orphan	213 48
	216 15	W B. **WYNNS** Guardn	

Elizabeth **PARKER** Dr Elizabeth **PARKER** for **BROWN** In Act with William B **WYNNS** guardian
Cr

1830		1830	
March To 3 lb of Catten @ 1/3 2/lb/ Sugar @ 1/2?	62½	Feby 22/nd/ By Ballance due the orphan}	
1830		at my return to Feby Caurt 1830}	204..90
May Caurt To Cash.......	35	Interest an ditto up to August Court 1830	6..14
Interest up to August 1830	52		211 04
To recording this Act	42		
To Cash paid Sheriff for Taxes for 1829	62 ½		
To 5 per cent Cammissions	2..16	1830	
To Ballance due the orphan	171..59	August 22/d/ By Ballance due the orphan	$171..59
	211..04	W. B. **WYNNS** Guardn	

North Carolina }
Hertford Caunty } August Caurt of Pleas &C. 1830
These Accaunt [sic] were returned to Caurt an oath by William B **WYNNS** Guard
& ordered to be recorded   Test L. M. **CAWPER** Clk

Julia Ann **BRITT**

1828	Dr Julia Ann **BRITT** orphan of William D **BRITT** dec/d/ Dr		
Nov/th/ 27[sic] To Cash pd Clerks ticket	$ 20	1828 By rent of land	$24..91
1829		1829 By ditto ditto	37..42
Feby 27/th/ To Act pd James **SCOTT**	16..51		62 33
1830		due the Ward	38 32
Feby 15/th/ To Cash paid John **BARRETT** for board	17..50		24..01
21/st/ To Int an 16..71 for ane year	1..00		
To Commissions an $62..33 cents	3..11		
	38..32		

---

(34) 5 Rebeckah **BRITT**

Dr Rebeckah **BRITT** orphan of Wm D **BRITT** dec/d/ Dr

1828

(34) Rebeckah BRITT (Cont.)

Nov 27th/ To Cash paid Clerks ticket	$ 20	1828 By rent of land	$24..91
1829		1829 By do do	37..42
Feby 27 To Act pd James **SCOOT**	22 89		62 33
Novr 5th/ To 1 pr Shaes......	1 12½		49 70
1830		Due the Ward	$12..63
Feby 15th/ To Cash paid John **BARRETT** for board	21..00		
25 To Int. on $23..09/¢/ for one year	1..38		
Commissions an $62..33 c	3..11		
	49..70½		

Margarett BRITT

1828	Dr Margarett **BRITT** orphan of Wm D. **BRITT** dec/d/	Dr	
Novr 27/th/ To Cash pd Clerks ticket	..20	1828	
1829		By rent of land ..	24..91
Feby 27th/ To Cash piad James **SCOTT** act	2..12	1829	
1830		By do .. do ...	37 42
Feby 21st/ To Ints an $2.12 cents for one year	..12		62..33
To Commissions an $62..33 cents	3. 11		5 55
	5..55	Due the Ward	$ 56..78

Narth carolina   }
Hertford Caunty} August Caurt of Pleas &c. 1830
This Account was returned to Caurt an oath by Davis **BYANT** [sic] Guardian
& ordered to be recarded   Test L. M. **COWPER** Clk

Davis **BRYANT** Guardian

Martha BEVERLY

1829	Dr Martha **BEVERLY** orphan of Wm **BEVERLY** dec/d/ in /act/ with James **YEATES** Guardn.		
May 14th/ To Cash pd Jas **REA & CAMP** act	$15..00	By her partion Recd from Wm **BEVERLY**s	
To Intes/t/ an do	16	Estate By **BEVERLY**s Estate Sally	
1830		**BEVERLY**s Estate & Milly **BEVERLY**s Estate	
March 1 To 1 pr Shaes ...	1..25	August 30/th/. 1828 ...	85..37
Intes/t/ an do	3	Intes/t/ an do ...	10 56
To Ballance due the orphan }		E Excepted	$96..06
August 30/th/ 1830 }	83..52	James **YEATES**	
	$ 96..06		

Narth Caralina   }
Hertforc Caunty} August Caurt of Pleas &C.1830
This Account was returned to Caurt an oath by James **YEATES** guard &
ardered o be recorded   Test L. M. **COWPER** Clk

William BEVERLY

1829	Dr William **BEVERLEY** orphan of William **BEVERLEY** dec/d/ in a/c with James **YEATES** gua/dn/		
Jany 14th/ To Cash pd Jno R **HALL** for Tuition ...	2..50	By his portion Recd of Wm **BEVERLEY** Estate	
Int/t/ an do ...	08	B **BEVERLEY** de/d/ Estate & Sally	
To pd Edw/d/ **REDDICK** for tuition}	1..95	**BEVERLEY** Estate }	85..50
Octo 18th/ To 1 pr Shaes	1..25/7½/	& Millant? **BEVERLEY** Intst from	
Intes/t/ an do	5¼	August 30/th/ 1828. up [sic]	
2 months board	5 00	August Term 1830}	10..56
Intes/t/ do	25		96 06
	11 15¼	To Ballance due the orphan	11..15
		August 30/th/ 1830	84..91
		E Excepted James **YEATS**	

---

(35) 6 William **BEVERLY** Dr William **BEVERLY** orphan of William **BEVERLY** dec/d/ in acct with James **YEATS** guard
North Carolina }   Cr
Hertford Caunty} August Caurt of Pleas & 1830
This Accaunt was returned to Caurt on oath by James **YEATS** Guard &
ardered to be recorded   Test L. M. **COWPER**

James H **BRITT**

1830	Dr James H **BRITT** in acct with E D **BRITT** his guardian			Cr
Augut 25/th/ To Cash pd Clerk for return	40	1830		
Ballance due the orphan	48..79	August 25/th/ By Ballance due the last return		$ 47..76
	49..19	6 months Intst ...		1 43
				$ 49 _9

Ballance due the orphan 25/th/ August 1830 $48..79
Narth Carolina }   E D **BRITT** Guardn.
Hertford Caunty} August Caurt of Pleas &C 1830
This Accaunt was returned to Caurt an oath by Elisha D **BRITT** Guard &
ardered to be recorded   Test L. M. **COWPER** Clk

Alexander **BRITT**

1830	Dr Alexander **BRITT** in a/c with E D **BRITT** his Guardn			Cr
Augt 25/th/ To Cash pd for return	40	1830		
Ballance due the orphan	$ 52..59	Augt 25/th/ By Bal due the last return		51..45
	$ 52..99	6 months Intes/t/ on do		1 5_
				52..99
		Ballance due the orphan 25/th/ August 1830		52..59

North Carolina }
Hertford Caunty} August Caurt of Pleas &c 1830
This Accaunty was returned to Caurt on oath by Elisha D **BRITT** Guardn
& ardered to be recorded   Test L. M. **COWPER** Clk

Martha **BRITT**

1830   Dr Martha **BRITT** orphan of James E **BRITT** decd in acot with Henry L. **WILLIAMS** her guard /Cr/
Feby 22/nd/ Cash pd Lewis M **COWPER** Ck

for half guard Bond ...	40	
Cash pd Mis Jane **CAWPER** for Board}		
from the 22 February to the 23/d/ August}	12..50	

1830
Augt 19/th/ Cash pd. John W **SAUTHALL**

for goods as pr bill ...	31..82	
Cash pd Ck for making this return	40	
Cammission an 45..12 cent at 2½ pr cent	1 02	
	46..14	
Amount due me from the ward up to this time	46..14	

    Henry L **WILLIAMS** guardn

---

(36) 7 Rebecca P **BRITT**

    Dr Rebecca P **BRITT** orphan of James E **BRITT** ded in act with Henry L **WILLIAMS** her _z_
Feby 22/nd/ Cash pd Lewis M **CAWPER** for

1830	half guardian Bond	$ 40
	Cash paid John W **SAUTHALL**}	
	for goods as pr bill }	29..38
	Cash pd Ck for moking this return	40
	Cammissions an 30 dallar/s/ 18 cents @ 2½ p cent	76

1830
Augt 23/rd/ Amount due me from the Ward up } $ 30..94

(36) Rebecca P **BRITT** (Cont.)

   up [sic] to this time . . . .}   30..94

        Henry L **WILLIAMS** guard

Narth carolina }

Hertford Caunty} August Caurt of Pleas &C 1830

This Accaunt was returned to Caurt an aath by Henry L **WILLIAMS** Guardn

&C? ardered to be recarded   Test L. M. **CAWPER** Clk

William **BOON**

1827   Dr William **BOON** orphan of Bird **BOON** Decd in act with John **BARRET** his gurd?

Jany 2/nd/ By recd fram William **FORGARSON**s}

   Estate this Amot   } $ 233..09

   To pd Clerk for guardian Bond   60

   paid Carr **DARDEN** Clerk & master for copy}

   of John **BOON**s proceedings as guardin } 2 00

   " 1 hat Bot of **MORGAN & COWPER** . . . . 2..75

   " 10 yds Catten Cloth of Do 2 00

Feby 9/t?/ ane knife 1/6 mar 31/st/ pd H **LONG** p recpt 20 25

Apl 14/t?/ 1 pair Shaes 7/6 mending Shaes 7?/6 1 50

   paid Edith **FARGARSON** for Cloth pr recpt 6..25

   Little page [sic] **ANDERSAN** for Schooling for 3 rod? 2 50

May 22/nd/ By recd from Jacob **LILES** admr of John **BOON**}

   " as pr Clerk and master report   } $2739..03

June 7/th/ To 1 doz shirt buttans 9/d/?   }

   making Clothes at home Do 44} 2 56

   pd Lydia **BRITT** for Sewing 7/6 1 25

Decr 27 To new? trunk Bot of P. **BRAWN** Bow? 20/- 3..33

1828   " Paid Benjamin **NEWSAM** for Schooling p recpt 5 00

Jany 1/st/ By recd Land rent due this day   10 00

Feby 5/t?/ To pd Richard **DARDEN** pr receipt 4 56

   " 5 yds yarn Cloth for pantalaa?ns @ 3/2yd 2..30

   " Wards Board from July 1827 till Feby 1828 50..00

   " Cammissions on $3972..12 amount recd @ 5 pr ct 148..60

      Bal due the Ward princ 2716..47

            2972 12   29732 12

   Bal Braught dawn due his Ward Feby 22/nd/ 1828 principle 2716.. 47

   By Int an $2716..47 Bal due Ward   }

   from may 22/nd/ 1827 till Feby 22/nd/ 1828} 162..98

Mr 7/th/ To paid Edword S **JEGETTS** pr recept 2..20

   " John W. **SAUTHALL** pr .. do 4 26

18   " one pr Suspender/s/ 1/6 July 8/th/ **REA & CAMP**

     pr recpt a? 98   4 20

            10..96   2879 45

---

(37) 3 William **BOON** Dr William **BOON** orphan of Bird **BOON** dec/d/ in act with John **BARRETT** his guardian Cr

1828   Amt Brot forward . . . $10..96   Amt Brot forward . . . $2879..45

   To paid **MARGAN & COWPER** pr rect $162/¢/

     1pr Shaes 9/- 3 12½

   " mending Shaes Leather & thread 45/¢/ 45

Novr 20 th/ pd James **SCOTT** pr recpt $3..72¾}

   Rebeccah **BRITT** for v?est 3/9 } 4 35¼

   " paid Rebeccah **BRITT** for Clath & make 2 shirts 1..00

Decr To pd Gillam **JOHNSON** for make Coat as pr recpt 2..50

31   " " John W **SAUTHALL** pr recpt 4..22

   " one pair Socks . . . 31¼

(37) William BOON (Cont.)

1829

Jany 1/st/ By Land rent due this day ..			10..00
Feby 16/th/ To paid Benjamin **NEWSOM** pr recept	3 00		
22/nd/ " Wards Board from Feby 22/nd/ 1828 till Feby 22/nd/ 1829	50..00		
" Commissions on $10 rec/d/ for Land rent @ 5 pr ct	.50		
Bal due the Ward ...	2809 03¾		
	2889..45		2889..45

1829

Ballance due the word Feby 22/nd/ 1829 Braught dawn ...			2809 03¾.
By Int on $2809..03¾ last Ball from } Feby 22/nd/ 1828 till Feby 22/nd/ 1829}			168_54
Feby To paid Benjamin **NEWSOM** for Schooling p rect	5 00		
" 2 & ¾ yds yarn Clath @ 3/3? pr 3 pr Socks @ 1/6	2..12½		
" make 4 pr pantaloons 6/9	1..12½		
" 1 vest 1/6 2 Shirts 3/9 make pr drors [sic]	1 06¼		
June To paid Julia **BRITT** for make 2 pr pantaloons	62½		
Sept 5 " ane pr Shaes yau Bot at Boro 11/4 pr socks 2/3	2 12½		
Octr 30/th/ paid James **SCOTT** pr recept	4.00		
23/rd/ To " John M **GURLY** for transfer of land pr recpt	..75		
" " Shff of Sauthampton yaur Land Tax pr Recpt...	07		
Nov 10/th/ To paid E S **JEGETTS** for make of Coat pr recpt..	3 00		
Decr 14/th/ To yaur Board six manths at Jas **LILES** pr recpt	16 66		
" ane pr Shaes Bot of **MORGAN & COWPER**	1 12½		
23/rd/ " paid **MORGAN & COWPER** & Co pr recpt	9 87½		

1830

Jany 11/th/ To " Jahn W **SAUTHALL** pr recpt	10 13		
29 ane pr J?acks 2/3 pd P **BACKUS** footing socks at ½?	56¼		
Feby 21/st/ To yaur Board with me from 1/st/ July 1829} till 21/st/ J Feby 1830 }	30..00		
Jany 1/st/ By Land rent due this day .			1C..00
To Commissions on $10 for land rent recd 5 p ct	50		2987 57¾
Bal due the Word ...	2898 84¼		
	2987 57¾		
Ballance due the ward Feby 22/nd/ 1830			2898 84¼
Aprl 13/th/ To Cash pd Callen W. **BARNES** pr recpt	9..37		
" To " P **BACKUS** pr do	37½		
may 20/th/ To ditto........	50		
June 5/th/ To 1 pr Shaes........$1 37½	1 37½		
	11..62		

(38) 9 William BOON

Dr William **BOON** orphan of Bird **BOON** dec/d/ In account with John **BARRETT** his guardian   Cr

Amt Brot forward $	11 62	
June 21/st/ To 1 Hat 16/6 5 yds Catten Clath @ 9/d/	3 37½	
July 10/th/ To Cash pd P. **BACKUS** for making Clathes	1 18¾	
To " pd **REA & CAMP**....	5 00	
	21..18	
Bal due the Ward	2964 63	
1830	2985 81	
Augt 25/th/ By Bal due the last return $2898.84½} Six manths Int an do 86.96½	2985..81	
Bal due the Ward 25 August 1830	2964 63	

(38) William BOON (Cont.)

         John **BARRETT** guardn

North Carolina }

Hertford County} August Caurt of Pleas &C 1830

This Account was returned to Caurt on oath by John **BARRETT** guardn

& ordered to be Recorded   Test. L. M. **CAWPER** Clk

John BARKER

Dr John **BARKER** orphan of John **BARKER** decd In act with James **RAWLS** guardian   Cr

To 6 months board and Clothing from}		By this Amt due the orphan at my return}		
Feby Caurt 1830 to August Caurt 1830}	15..00	To Feby Caurt 1830	151..40}	00 00
To recording this account...	40	Interest an ditto up August Court 1830 4..54		$155 94
To 5 pr Cent Commissions an the money}		By half of Negro hire for 1830 payl the		
expended & hause & rents say on $33..69}	1 68	4/th/ of Janyory 1831 $27..25/c/		
	17..08	duduct the Int so as to make it payl at August		
due the orphan at August Caurt 1830	168..01	Caurt 1830		26..70
	185..09	By half of Rent of land for /Half/ 1830 payl		
		the 4/th/ of Jany 1831 $2 50 deduct the Interest}		
		sa as to have it due at August Caurt 1830}		2..45
				185..09
		By Ballance due the orphn		
		at August Caurt 1830}		168..01
		E E James **RAWLS** guardian		

George BARKER

Dr George **BARKER** orphan of John **BARKER** decd In act with James **RAWLS** guardian   Cr

To 6 months board and Clothing}		By this amt due the orphan }		
fram February Caurt 1830 to August}		at my return to February Caurt 1830}	149..33$	
Court 1830 ....}	15..00	Interest an ditto up to August Caurt 1830	4..47	$153..80
To recording this Account.........	40	By half of Negro hires for 1830}		
To 5 pr cent Commissions on the money}		payl the faurth of Jany 1831 $27 25}		
expended and Lan? and rents ....}	1 68	deducts the Interest an ditto}		
	17..48	so as to make it due at August Caurt 1830}		26..70
			153..80	180..50

---

(39) 10 George BARKER

Dr George **BARKER** orphan of John **BARKER** ded In act with James **RAWLS** guardian   Cr

Amt Brot forward	$ 17..08	Amt Brot forward	153..80	1380..50
To Ballance due the orphan	165..87	By half the rents of Land for 1830 }		
		payl the 4th of Jany 1831 $2 50 deduct}		
		the Interest so as to leave it due }		
		the August Caurt 1830 }		2..45
	182..95			182..95
		By Ballance due the orphan at August Caurt 1830		$165..87

North Carolina }   E E James **RAWLS** guardian

Hertford Caunty } August Caurt of Pleas &c 1830

This Account was returned to Caurt on oath by James **RAWLS** Guar/d/ & ardered to be

Recorded   Test L M **COWPER** Clk

Dolly CLARK

Dr Dolly **CLARK** of [sic] orphan Zadock **CLARK** in act Current with B J **MONTGOMERY** guardian Dr

To guardian Bond 60/100	$ 60
Cr nathing recived	..00
due the guardian	60

(39) Dolly **CLARK** (Cont.)

B J **MONTGOMERY** guard

North Carolina }

Hertford Caunty} August Caurt of Pleas &C 1830

This Accaunt was returned to Caurt on oath by B. J. **MONTGOMERY** guardian & ardered

to be recorded   Test L. M. **CAWPER** Clk

Watson **COLSON**

Dr Watson **COLSON** orphan in a/c Current with John **PARKER** Guardian   C-

1830

Apl 3/rd/ To Cash paid **REA & CAMP** $ 4..22   /August/ 1830 Ballance due returne/d/....}

' interest 5 manths   10   August Caurt term 1830....   }   207. 21

4..32   207 21

North Carolina }

Hertford Caunty} August Caurt of Pleas &C 1830

This Accaunt was returned to Caurt on oath by John **PARKER** guard/d/ &

ordered to be Recorded   Test L. M. **COWPER** Clk

Henry **COTTON**

1830.   Dr James D. **WYNNS** Guardian of Henry **COTTON**   Supra   Cr

Novr 25/th/ To this Amt rec/d/ of Carr **DARDEN** $ 51 98½   By this Amt paid for Board }

Int on the Same 9 months up to }   up to 25/th/ Aug/t/? 1830   }   2 33

25 August 1830   }   2 33   Amt due the Ward this day   51 98½

54.31½   54 31½

Winton Aug/t/   25 1830 James D. **WYNNS**

North Carolina }

Hertford Caunty} August Caurt of Pleas &C 1830

This Accaunt was returned to Caurt an oath by James D **WYNNS** Guard &

ordered to be recorded   Test L. M. **COWPER** Clk

---

(40) 11 Peggy **CURL**

Ballance due Peggy **CURL** on a }

Settlement with the Caurt   }

Febuary term 1830 ....} $ 37 26

Jethro + **CAURL** guard

North Carolina }

Hertford Caunty} August Court   1830

This Accaunt was returned to Caurt on oath by Jethro **CURL** guard/d/ &

ordered to be recorded   Test L. M. **COWPER** Clk

Richard **DUNSTON**

1829   Dr Richard **DUNSTON** in acct Current with Hardy M. **BANKS** Guardian   Cr

Feby 23/d/ To Balance due the as [sic] p act

returned   31..25   Sr

To Interest on ditto up to Feby Caurt 1830   1..87   Amt Brot forword   60..55

24   " Cash at Winton 3/-   50   2 yds blue Clath of **MARGAN** &

do pd fr returning acct Current   40   **COWPER** $5 50/100

June 2/nd/ 2½ yds Clath for girl **MARY** at 20/¢/ 50}   Trimings of ..... ditto /11 00/ $2 34 $ 13..34

paid Edw. S. **JEGETTS** for making Coat 6..10   6 30   3 yds of Casimere Bot of ditto 62½ $1..88

Augt 22/nd/ 1 pr Shaes of **REA & CAMP**   2..25   1 Vest pattern 63/¢/ 6 yds C Clath @ 25/¢/2..13   4..01

1 pr pantalesloons & trimings of **M & COWPER** 2 00   1 Vest do of do the 10 of Octr 6/-C 1..00

1 handkf [sic].... of Do   75   1½ yds lining @ 20/¢/ buttans 3/¢ thread 10/¢/8/¢ 37   1..51

Octr 11/th/ 3 yds. Satinet of Jas **WALSCH**?/   3. 00   1 pr Shaes of **REA & CAMP** for **MARY**}

½ yds C Claths of do   06½   8. 06   the 25/th/ of Novr....................}   75

To 1 pr Shaes of Eli **CARTER** 18 Sept   2 75   1830 Jany 15/th/ Set knives & forks 9/-plates 40?/c/   1 95

(40) Richard DUNSTON (Cont.)

13	Cash to pay for Licence 6/	1 00	1 dish 50/¢/ 1 Coffee pat 56/¢/ }		1 06
	To 1 pr Socks 30/¢/ 3 yds Cambrick @ 30/¢/}		1 pr Cards 75/¢/ 6/lb/ Sugar @ 9/d/}		1..50
	Bot of **M & COWPER** }	1. 20	3/lb/ Coffee @ 20/¢/ 1 Sett Cups &		
19	1 pr fine Shaes of Jas **SCOTT** 16/6	2..75	Saucer/s/ 3/- }		90
20	Cash 1/6	..25	1 Iron pot - - - 4/6 }		75

Novr 13/th/ 2½ yds. Homespun @ 1/+ 1 Blanket 7/6}   [Written vertically between "}" & amt.: Bot of
      1¾ yds domestic @ 10/¢/ for girl **MARY** } 1 84½   **REA** /&/ **CAMP**}
[Written vertically between "}" & amt.: Bot of **CAPEHART & HARE**}

17	9 yds C Cloth @ 10/¢/ 1 Hkhf? 25/¢/}		22/nd/ paid Arthur **DARDEN** for Board .	12..00
	Bat of **M & COWPER** }	1 15	25/th/ Cash paid yau	3 00
Decr 9?/th/	Cash for repairing watch	62½	1 Tub 44/¢/ 1 piggin 20/¢/ of **REA & CAMP**	65
	ditto at Sol **SHEPHERD**s Sale	40	Feby 17/th/ 109/lb/ bacon of **MORGAN**	
		60..55	& **COWPER** @ 8/¢/	8..72

22/nd/ paid James **SCOTT** & Co for goods}[erased] _..69
pr this recept . . . . } 7..69
Commissions on hire of Negraes   [erased] 5 20
   for year 18329 Say $104..10/¢/ @ 5 pr cet)   5..20
Paid Mr/s/ **WILLS** for keeping negro Child}
MURRIER for year 1829 . . . . . . } 10..00
———————————————————— 133..58
                                        Cr
By hire of Negro **MATT** year 1829   74 10
" do of " **CHARLES**   30 00
Girl **MARY** to E **FIGUERS** . . . . . .   0..00
1830   104..10
Feby 23/rd/ By Ballance due H W **BANKS**   29 48
       133 58

===

(41) 12 Richard DUNSTON Dr Richard **DUNSTON** in acct Current with Hardy M **BANKS** guardian   Cr

Feby 23/rd/ To Ballance due . . . . $ 29 48		By Hire of Boy **CHARLES** for the year 1830} $31..00	
Ins an ditto till 23 Augt 1830 6 mo	88	due the 1 Jany next 1831 . . . . }	
paid Clerk for retg acct Current	20	By do of Man **MATT** for do	55..00
March 3/rd/ 6 yds Callico 9/- of **REA & CAMP**	1 50	By do girl **MARRY** to E **FIGURE/S/** to keep	0 00
15/lb/ flaur @ 4/¢/ molases 1/6 of W B **WISE**	..85	deduct $10 to be paid to Mr/s/ **WILLS** }	86..00
June 22/nd/ Cash to buy Bacon $4	4.00	for keeping negro Child **MURRIER** for}	
Augt 7/th/ Cash at + Roads at muster 9/-	1..50	the year 1830 palyabl [sic] 1 Jany 1831 }	10 00
7¼/lb/ twine Bot of **M & COWPER** last			76..00
fall @ 30/¢/	2..17	By Balance due the Ward . . . .}	
	40..58	August Caurt 1830 . . . . . . }	35..42
August 23/rd/ To balleance due the ward	35 42		
	76..00	H. M. **BANKS** Guardian	

North Carolina }
Hertford Caunty} August Caurt of Pleas &C 1830
This Accaunt was returned to Court on oath by Hardy M **BANKS** Guardian &
ardered to be Recorded   Test L. M. **COWPER** Clk

===

Mary DARDEN

1828   Dr Mary **DARDEN** orphan of Jaseph dec/d/ in account with Henry L **WILLIAMS** her gurd

Apl 6 To Board from the 6 of April 1828}			
to the 23 Feby 1829 . . . . . }	26 39	Decr 9/th/ Cash pd Phebee **HILL** for repairing	
may 12/th/ Cash W **SAUTHALL** for goods as per bill 1 24		Bonnet . . . . $	37½
interest fram 12 may 1828 to the 23/d/}		Cash pd for Spending money	50
Feby 1829 . . . . }	5	fbuy 24/th/ Cash pd Ck for ½ guardian Bond 40}	
July 28/th/ To Cash paid Saml **BARNES** for}		int from 24/th/ febuary 1828 to 23/d/ Feby 1829 02}	42

17

(41) Mary **DARDEN** (Cont.)

making 1 pr Shaes . . . . .}	37	
June 21/st/ Cash pd **MORGAN & COWPER** for}		
goods as pr Bill . .. .$2 . }	[blank]	
Interest fram 21 June 1828 to the 23/d/		
Feby 1829 . . . . .8¢}	2..08	
Augt 28/th/ Cash pd James S **JANES** for his fee		
in Suit the Insts for mary **DARDEN** vs		
Wm D. **BRITTs** admr.. & others . . $10 00}		
Intst from the 28 August 1828 to 23 Feby }		
1829 @ 29}	10..29	
To Cash pid L M **COWPER** Clk for his}		
fee for Stating this act in the above }		
mentioned Suit . . . . $5 }	[blank]	
Interest from 28 August 1828 to 23 Feby		
1829 /¢/ 14	5..14	
Oct 9/th/ To Cash pd Tryal **WILLIAMSON** for		
1 pr Shaes 1 12½}		
Int from 28 October 1828 to 23/rd/ Feby		
1829 03}	1..15½	
29 Cash pd John W **SOUTHALL** for goods}		
as per Bill . . . . $4 57}		
Int from 28 Octr 1828 to 23/d/ Feby 1829 09}	4 66	
Novr 25/th/ Cash pd Richard G. **COWPER** Shff}		
for Cast of Suit vs Jaseph **DARDEN** deced}		
Admist . . . . 2..79}		
int from 25 November 1828 to 23/d/ }		
Feby 1829 . . . . .03}	2..82	

Decr 19/th/ Cash paid **REA & CAMP** for }
goods as pr Bill . . . . 1..74}
int from 19/th/ december 1828 to 23/d/
Feby   02}   1..76
Jany 28/th/ Cash pd James **SCOTT** & Co. for}
goods as pr Bill . . . . 17..37   }
int from 28 Jany 1829 to 23/d/   }
February 1829 08   }   17..45
Feby 11/th/ " Cash paid John W **SAUTHALL**}
for goods as pr Bill ·. . . . . . .20..59   }
Int from 11 Feby 1829 to 23/d/ feby . 04   }   20..63
Feby 18/th/ Cash pd **SAUTHALL & PARKER**}
for goods as pr Bill . . . .}   50
Feby 23/rd/ Cash paid Ck for makeing
this return to February 1829   40

---

(42) 13 Mary **DARDEN**   Dr Mary **DARDEN** ophan of Joseph /ded/ in acct with Henry L **WILLIAMS** her guard

To Cash paid ck for makeing this return
to Fe August Caurt 1830   40
, To Commissions 2/2? per Cent on $96..63½
being the Amount paid aut   2..40   96 63½
Coms.. 2/2 p cent on $11123. 81 being
the amt recd . . . . .27..82   30..25
Ballance due the Ward up to the}   126..88½
23 Febuary 1829 . . . . . .}   985 95

1828 Octo 21/st/ By the Amount receved from
Richard G **COWPER** Shff for an Execution
in favaur of the Instes for Mary **DARDEN** agst
William D **BRITT** Adm/ist/ & other/s/ being the
—a Amount due from William D **BRITTs** decd
who was former Guard for Mary **DARDEN** the
Execution was returnable to november Caurt
1828 for . . . . $1051 29}
interest from 21 Oct 1821 to 23/r/   }
Febuary 1829 . . . . 21 37} 1072..66
1829
Jany 30/th/ By Cash rec/d/ from James **SCOTT**
Admst.. of Wil D. **BRITT** Decd for the hire of
Negro Boy **SAM** for the year 1828   [blank]
Int fram 3/th/ January 1829 to 23/d/
Febuary 1829 . . . . 15/¢/   40..15
                              1112..81

              Henry L **WILLIAMS** guard

North Carolina   }
  Hertford Caunty} August of [sic] Pleas &C 1830
This Accaunt was returned to Caurt on oath by Henry L **WILLIAMS** guard
& ordered to be recorded   Test L. M. **COWPER** Clk

(42) Mary **DARDEN** (Cont.)

Mary **DARDEN**   to Feby Court 1830

23 Feby   Dr Mary **DARDEN** orphan of Jaseph **DARDEN** Dec/d/ in act with Henry L **WILLIAMS** her guard

1829	To Board from the 23 Feby 1829 to }	
	the 22/d/ Febuary 1830 . . . . } $	30 00
1830..18/th/	To Cash pd John W. **SAUTHALL** for	
	goods as pr bill	44..12
26	To Cash paid James **SCOTT** & Co for	
	2 yds Checks	50
	int for for [sic] one year	13
27	to Cash paid for 1 pr Shaes 1 00	
	int for one year on the Same 06	1..06
March 30/th/	To Cash pd Tryal **WILLIAMS**	
	for 1 pr Shaes . . . . . 1 25}	
	int from the 3 march 1829 to the }	
	22/nd/ February 1830 . . . . .7 }	1..32
June 20/th/	To Cash pd Patrick **BROWN** for 8}	
	yds Cloth 1..00}	
	int from 20 July 1829 to Feby 23/d/	
	1830 @ 4}	1..04
July 20/th/	To Cash pd Mary **DARDEN**	
	for Spending money . . . 1. 50}	
	int from 20 July 1829 to feby 22/d/ 1830 6}	1..56
25	Cash pd Ely **CARTER** for Shaes 1..12½}	
	int from 25 July 1829 to Feby 22/d/	
	1830 4 }	1..16
July 10/th/	To Cash pd Elizabeth A **CAU** for	
	tuition 6..00}	
	interest from 10/th/ July 1829 to 22/nd/}	
	Feby 1830 . . . . : . . 22½}	6 22½
		87..61½

	Amt Brot forward .	$87..61½
Sept 8/th/	To Cash pd Portrick **BROWN**	
	as pr bill 75}	
	int from 8 Sept 1829 to 22/nd/ Febuary	
	1830 2}	77
Octr 10/th/	Cash pd Mary **DARDEN**	
	for Spending money . . . . . 66}	
	int from 10 Octo 1829 to Febuary 22/nd 1½}	67½
Decr 4/th/	Cash pd for 1 pr Shaes 1..12½}	
" 20	interest from 4 december 1829 }	
	To Febuary 22/nd/ 1830 . . . . . . 1½}1..14	
	Cash paid for Spending money 1	
Feby 19/th/	Cash pd **MORGAN & COWPER**	
	pr bill	3 62½
/1830/ 19/th/	Cash pd James **SCOTT** &	
	Co as pr Bill	5 43¼
20/th/	Cash pd doct Thomas **BAWLING**}	
	for visit to Negro **SAM** . . . .}	3..00
	Cash pd Ck for makeing this return	40
	Commisions 2½ per cent on $103..66 being	
	the amount pd out	103 66½
	Commisions on $45 dallar/s/ for negro hire	3 70½
		107 57
	Ballance due the Ward to 22/nd/ Febuary	
	1830	984 79
		1092 16

---

(43) 14 Mary **DARDEN**   to Feby Court 1830

Dr Mary **DARDEN** orphan of Jaseph **DARDEN** decd in acct with Henry L **WILLIAMS** her guard

Amt Brot forward $1092 16	amount due the ward up to the	
	23 febuary 1829	$ 986 35½
	interest from the 23/rd/ of Febuary 1829 to	
	the 22 febuary 1830 on $986.35/¢/ is	59..18
	Compl/d/ interest on $59.18/¢/ for faur	1..18
	month [sic] to Hire of Negro **SAM** to	
	Elisha **SPIRES** from 30 of december 1828	
	to the 25/th/ of december 1829 . . .	40..00
	int of 40 dallar/s/ for 2 months 40	40
	Negro **HAGER** to Samuel **CLARK**	
	for 1829 $5	
	int for 2 months on 5 dallar/s/ . . . 5/¢/	5..05
		1092..16½
	this Return was made to febuary Caurt 1830	
	Feby 22/nd/ Ballance due the ward to 22	
	febuary 1830	984..79
	Errar/s/ Excepted Febuary Caurt	
1092 16	1830	1092 16
		984..79

                                Henry L. **WILLIAMS** guardian

(43) Mary DARDEN (Cont.)

Mary **DARDEN** to Feby Court 1830

Dr Mary **DARDEN** orphan of Jaseph **DARDEN** decd in acct with Henry L **WILLIAMS** her guard

Augt 19/th/ To Amaunt of Bill pd John W **SAUTHALL** 1830	33 95	Amount due the ward to 23/rd/ Feby 1830		984..79
feby 25/th/ Cash paid for Spending maney 75}		int from the 22 feby 1830 to the 23		
int from 22 febuary 1830 to 23 Augt 1830 2½}	77½	Augt 1830 An this amount . . .		29 53
June 19/th/ Cash pd Mary **DARDEN** for Spending money $5		Compaund interest on 29 dallar/s/ &		
int from 19 June to 19 August 1830 5/¢/	5..05	53 cent for 6 months		38
July 17/th/ Cash pd for Expences going to School	1..00			1015..20
Augt 19/th/ Cash pd Trial **WILLIAMS** for Shes [sic]	1..75	To Amaunt of Negro hire for 1830		
" 19/th/ Cash pd Partrick **BROWN** as pr bill	[blank]	which will be due the 25 december		
To makeing this return	40	1830 . . .		51..00
Cash pd Ck for rifa? and renewing }				1066..20
Bond to August Caurt 1830 . . . }	1..00	This return to Augt Caurt 1830		
Commissions on $45..30 cent at 2½ pr cent		Ballance due the ward		1018. 51
Being the amount pa/i/d aut 1..13	2 40			
Also 51 dallar/s/ for Negro hire				
at 2½ pr Cent 1 27				
	47..70½			
Balance due the ward to 25 Augt 1830	1018..51			1018..51
	1066 21½	Error/s/ Excepted August		
		Caurt 1830		$ 1066..21
		Henry L **WILLIAMS** guardian		

North Carolina }

Hertford Caunty } August Caurt of Pleas &C 1830

This Accaunt was returned to Caurt on oath by Henry L **WILLIAMS** guard &

ordered to be recorded Test L M **COWPER** Clk

==

(44) 15 James DEANS

Dr James **DEANS** orphan of James **DEANS** decd In acct with Isaac **CARTER** guardian

1830			1830		
March 1/st/ T [sic] 1 pr Shaes	1..75	Jany 1/st/ By Ballance due on return}			
pd clk returing this Acct	40	to Feby Caurt 1830 . . . . . . }	233..27		
Comm/s/ on R & Exp @ 5 pr ct	55	Int from 1/st/ Jany to 23 day 1830 [sic]	8 85	$242..12	
Balance due . . . . 239..42	$242..12	By Balance Due		239 42	
		August 23/rd/ 1830			
		E E Isaac **CARTER** guard			

==

Thomas J. DEANS

Dr Thamas J **DEANS** orphan of James **DEANS** decd In Acct with Isaac **CARTER** guard

1830		1830		
Augt 23/d/ To Cash Clk [sic] this return	40	Jany 1/st/ By Balance Due on return		
Comms @ 5 pr ct	84	to Feby Caurt 1830	410 04	
Balance due 425.14	$426..38	Int from 1 Jany to 23 day 1830 16 34	426..33	
		By Balance Due	425..14	
		August 23/d/ 1830		
		E E . . . . . .Isaac **CARTER** guardian		

==

Daniel DEANS

Dr Daniel **DEANS** orphan of James **DEANS** decd In acct with Isaac **CARTER** guardian

1830		1830	
Augt 23/d/ To Cash pd clk this return	40	Jany 1/st/ By Balance due on return	
Coms on R & Exp @ 5 p ct	60	to Feby Caurt 1830 . . . . 295..25	
Balance due . . . . . .305..85	$306..85	Int from 1 Jany 1830}	

(44) Daniel DEANS (Cont.)

to 23 August 1830 . . }	11..60	306 85
By Balance due		305 85

August 23/d/ 1830

E E Isaac **CARTER** guardian

State of North Carolina}

Hertford County   } August Court of Pleas &C 1830

This Account was returned to Court on oath by Isaac **CARTER** dee/d/ & arderd [sic] to be recorded

Test L. M. **COWPER** Clk

Pennina **EVANS**   24/th/ 1830

         Dr Pennina **EVANS** In account with William **DOWNING** guardian August Court

To this Sum due the ward last

Febuary Court 1830 . . . . 46 00   dallar/s/

                William **DAWNING**

North Carolina   }

  Hertford County} August Court of Pleas &C 1830

this Account was returned to Court on oath by William **DAWNING** guard &

ordered to be recorded   Test L. M. **COWPER** Clk

Lawrence **FELLS**

         Dr Lawrence **FELLS** in account with Saml **POWEL** his Guardian   Cr

                                            1830

To Cash pd for guardian [sic]	60	Augt 24/th/ By Amt of Tho/s/ **THORN**s nate due}	
To Comissions on $16 30/¢/ @ 5 per cent	81½	1 Jany 1831 . . . . }	6...25
To this Amt paid for this return	20	Amt of James **POWEL**s nate due the	6..25
To Ints on $1.04½ Cent 7 months 5 Cent	·05	1 Jany 1831	
	1 66½	By Amt of Thomas **THON** [sic]	3..80
		To Interest on $3.80 7 months is 12 cent	.12
			16 42

---

(45) 16 Lawrence FELLS

         Dr Lawrence **FELLS** in account with Saml **PAWEL** his Guardian   Cr

Amt Brot forward	$ 1..66½	Amt Brot forward	16..42
		Balance due the orphan $14 76	14..76
	1..66½	August 23/d/ 1830 Samuel **POWEL**	

North Carolina   }   Error/s/ Excepted

  Hertford County} August Court of Pleas &C 1830

This Account was returned to Court on oath by Samuel **PAWEL** guard & ordered to be recorded

                 Test L. M. **COWPER** Clk

Cecelia **GREEN**

1830   Dr Cecelia **GREEN** orphan of Isaac **GREEN** decd in a/c Current with Watson **LEWIS** guardian /Cr/

June 3/d/ To 1 Robe $2 1 t?ucking		1830	
Comb 50/¢/	2..50	By Balance due yau on Feby Term 1830	81 34
" 1 pair Side Comb . . .	25	June 8/th/ By 1 2/3 Bbls Turpentine @ 1..40	2 33
" 1 ditto Shaes 1..62 1 pocket Hkff 1..88		19 By 1 Robe returned	2..00
" 5 yds Callico . . . . . 30/¢/	1..50	July 2/d/ By 2 Bbls Turpentine (up? 1/d/ 1..25	2..50
19 " 5 ditto Swiss muslin @ 1$	5..00	By Interest on $69..98 from 22/nd/}	
Augt 7/t?/ Cash pd M **JERNEGAN** Taxes 1 80		Feby to ye 22 August 1830 . . }	2 09
" ditto paid this return	20		
" Commissions on $101 30 @ 5/¢/ 5 06			
" Balance due	12..07		
	90..26		90..26
		By balance due the orphan	72..07
		Watson **LEWIS**	

(45) Cecelia GREEN (Cont.)

North Carolina }

Hertford Caunty} August Caurt of Pleas &C 1830

this Accaunt was returned to Caurt on oath by Watsan **LEWIS** Guard & ordered to be recorded

Test L. M. **COWPER** clk

==

Jesse y **HARRELL**

1830	Dr Jesse y **HARRELL** in account with Abner **HARRELL** Guardian			Cr
Febuary 25/th/	To Cash J? H **RICE** for tuition	1 00	1830	
26	" Cash paid for renewing guardian	60	Febuary 22/nd/ By this Sum due the Ward pr}	
May 31/st/	" 2¼ yds Stripes @ 3/9 3 yds ditto}		my return to Febuary Caurt 1830 . . . . } ͅ09..60	
	@ 1/3 1 hat Hat [sic] 25/- 1 hat 7/6}		August 24 By Interest on that Sum to	
	1 Spool Catton 1/3 Lining 2/-		this date . . . . 3..27	
	buttons 2/- 1 pr Shaes 10/ }	6..00		
June 14?/th/	To Cash pd James **SCOTT**			
	gogoraphy & a Map	1..25		
July 26	To 3 yds Catton Shirting @ 2/6 1 Spool			
	Catton 1/3	87½		
" "	To Cash pd for this return 4/-	40		
" "	To Commisions on $10..12½ cents 5 pr cent	50		
Augt 24/th/	To Balance due the ward	102 24½		
		112 87	1830	112..87
			August 24 By Ballance due the Ward	$ 102..24½
			Abner **HARRELL** guardian	

North Caralina }

Hertford Caunty} August Caurt of Pleas &C 1830

This Accaunt was returned to Caurt on oath by Abner **HARRELL** guard & ordered to be Recorded

Test L. M. **COWPER** Clk

==

(46) 17 The Heirs of Jesse **VANN**

1830		Dr The Heirs of Jesse **VANN** decd in Account with Kinsey **JORDAN** guard		Cr
May 30/th/	To recording guardian Bond	1828		
	(**COOPER** C	1..20	July 2/nd/ By Nate against Enas **STAFFORD**}	
" "	Interest an Ditto	..16	" for rent due 1/st/ January 1829 . . . . . }	10..00
Nov 25	" recording an administration Bond	..80	1830 " Interest on ditto 1 yr 8 mo	1..00
" "	Interest	..09	Jany 1/st/ By one Nate for the rent of }	
1829			" the Creep farm . . . . }	24..00
March 3/d/	To repareing fence & malling riders}		" Interest for 8 mo . . . . }	96
	" for the Creek plantation }	27 62	" " By nate for the rent of the plantation}	
	" Ints for 5 2/3 mo	78	Called the **WARREN** place for 1829 }	30..00
"	" To taxes paid for the Land }		Interest on ditto 8 mo	1..20
"	" for the year 1827 . . . .}	5..43	" " Rent of the blue water plantation	8 00
"	" Interes [sic] for 2 year/s/	64	" " Interest on ditto	..32
"	" paid taxes for 1828	7..42	" " one Nate due January 1831 }	
"	" Interest on Ditto	11	" " for rent of the **WARREN** plantation}	25..00
1830	To paid B B **BLOOM** Attaurney}		" " one ather Nate due Jany 1831 }	
March	" for Services Concerning Negros in the}		" " for rent of the Creek plantation }	20 00
25	hands of John **MOORE** Admt }	10 00	" " one ather nate due Jany 1831}	
"	" Interest on 5 mo	..25	for rent of the }	
		54..50	Blue Water plantation }	8..00
	recording the abov [sic] a/c current	90		128..48
	Commissions on the Cr Side	6..42		
	To balance due the Heir/s/	66 66	E E Kinsey **JORDAN** guardian	
		128..48		

North Carolina }

Hertford Caunty} August Caurt of Pleas &C 1830

(46) The Heirs of Jesse **VANN** (Cont.)
This Account was returned to Court on oath by Kinsey **JORDAN** guard & ordered to be Recorded
Test L. M. **COWPER** Clk

Lindy Reany and Malichia **HALLOMAN** [sic]

1830	Dr Lindy Reany and Malichia **HALLOMON** orphan of Jacob **HOLLOMON** dec/d/ In account		With Miles H **JERNIGAN** guardian [sic]	Cr
Augt 23 To recording this	20		By Ballance due the orphans at}	
" " To paid your Mather for			Febuary Caurt 1830 . . . . .}	59..06
board & Clothing	1..32		Interest on ditto up to August Caurt 1830	1 67
To 5 pr cent Commissions on $3 19	15			60..73
To Ballance due the orphans	59..06			
	60..73		By a Ballance due the orphan Augt Caurt 1830	59 06
			M H **JERNIGAN** guardian	

North Carolina }
Hertford Caunty} August Caurt of Pleas &C 1830
This Accaunt was returned to Caurt on oath by Miles H. **JERNIGAN** Guard & ordered to
be recorded
Test. L. M. **COWPER** Clk

William **HALLOMON**

1830	Dr William **HALLOMON** orphan of Saml **HALLOMON** decd In acct with James **HOLLOMON** guardon		
Apl 24/th/ To Cash pd Jasiah H **PINNER**		By this amt due the orphan at my	
for Tuition	$ 1 25	return to Febuary Caurt 1830	230..15
To Interest on ditto up to August		Interest on ditto up to Augt Caurt 1830 7 50	257..65
Caurt 1830	2¼	1830	
May 21 st/ To Cash pd Abner **HARRELL**		August 23/d/ By Ballance due orphan	251..79
for Clothing	1 43¾	James **HALLOMON**	
" Interest on ditto up to this return	02		
Augt 2 1/st/ To Cash pd Jason **HOLLOMON**			
for Bord	2 50		
	5..23		

---

(47) 18 William **HOLLOMON**

	Dr William **HOLLOMON** orphan of Samuel **HOLLOMON** decd In acct with James **HOLLOMON** guard		
Amt Brat forward	5..23	Amt Brat forward	251..79
To 5 pr Cent Commissions on $12 73	63		
To Ballance due the orphan	251..79		
	257..65		251 79

Jacob **HOLLOMON**   Cr

1830	Dr Jacob **HOLLOMON** orphan of Samuel **HALLOMON** decd In acct with James **HOLLOMON** guardian		
Apl 24/th/ To Cash paid Jas H **PINNER**		By this amaunt the [sic] orphan at my	
for Tuisheon [sic]	1 25	return to Feby Caurt 1830 $267..93	
Interest on ditto	02¼	Interest an ditto up to this return 8 03	$275..96
May 31/st/ To Cash pd Abner **HARRELL**			
for Clathing	2 68¾		
Interest on ditto	4		
To recording this accaunt	0 40		
Aug 2 /st/ To Cash paid Jason **HOLLOMON**			
for Bord	3..12		
To 5 per Cent Commissions on		1830	
$15..55/c/	77	August 23/d/ By Ballance due the orphan	$267..67
To Ballance due the orphan	267 67	James **HALLOMON**	
	275 96		

North Carolina }
Hertford Caunty} August Caurt of Pleas &C 1830
These Accaunts were returned to Caurt on oath by James **HOLLOMON** Guardian & ordered to be

(47) Jacob HOLLOMON (Cont.)
recorded   Test L. M. **COWPER** Clk

Anthany **IRVIN**

1830	Dr Anthany **IRVIN** in acct with Riddick **CROSS** Guardian			Cr
Feby Term To Cash paid for returning			By this Amt due on former return	$272 25
for mer [sic] act	40		By I [sic] interest 7 months A @ 2/3	10..46
May 20/th/ To Cash paid Tax	1 80		Say up to Augt Caurt 1830	282. 71
Augt 15/th/ To Cash paid John			deduct	5.35
A **ANDERSAN** for tbths [sic]	1. 25		Ballance due the orphan Aug Term 1830	277 36
To Cash paid for bond this acct			Error/s/ Excepted Riddick **CROSS** guard	
& Si fa	1. 90			
	5..35			

North Carolina }

Hertford Caunty} August Caurt of Pleas &C 1830

This Accaunt was returned to Caurt on oath by Riddick **CRASS** Guard & ordered to be
Recorded   Test L. M. **COWPER** Clk

Mary **JORDAN**

1830	Dr Mary **JORDAN** orphan of David **JORDAN** In A/c with Pleasant **JORDAN** her guardian			Cr
Feby paid to Mary **JORDAN** for the }			1830	
orphan Baard Last year . . . . }	40 00		Feby A ballance due on the return	
paid to Henry **CASTEN** for Bonet	12..25		of Feby 1829	474..10
paid to John W. **SAUTHALL**			Interest on the Same one year	28 44
for three lb Lace?	2..25		To the hire of Negro **TOM** the year of 1829	40 00
paid to F W S **BERY** for goods	3..00		Receved of Kinsey **JORDAN** Admtr of	
paid to Joh [sic] A **ANDERSON**			Johnthan **JORDAN** Jnr? Decd	31. 00
for 6 yds Cambrick	3 00		Intrus [sic] up to Feby Cort 1830	56
paid to ditto for Two pair Shaes	3..25		A ballance due the orphan on	
paid to Miss F **HILL** for a turbon	2. 00		the Estate of Martha **GROHAM**	25 16
paid to ditto for dressing a bonnet	2 .50		due the orphan on the division	
paid to **CAPEHART & HARE**			of Negroes	13 75
for goods	4 00			613..91
	72 25			
paid to J. A. **ADERSON** for goods	5 60		amaunts Carried over	
paid Clerk fee	40			
	78..25			

---

(48) 19 Mary **JORDAN**

	Dr Mary **JORDAN** orphan of David **JORDAN** In a/c with Pleasant **JORDAN** her guard		
Amt Brot over	78..25	Amt Brat over	613..91
Cammishions an the amount received	7..50	paid aut for the orphan	85 75
and paid aut		A Ballance due the orphan	533.16
paid aut for the orphan . . .	85..75	Pleasant **JORDAN**	

Casten **JORDAN**

1830	Dr Costen **JORDAN** orphan of David **JARDEN** In a/c with Pleasant **JORDAN** his guard		
paid Mary **JORDAN** for the orphans}		1830 A Ballance due the orphan}	
Board last year . . . . }	$25 00	on the last return . . . }	470 00
paid Mr/s/ E **GUARDNER** for tuition	3..18¾	Intrust on the Same 1 year . . .	28 19
paid Clerks fee	40	Received of Kinsy **JORDAN** Admst}	
Commitions on the amount received		of Johnathan **JORDAN** Jns? decd }	31 .00
and paid aut	3..12	Intrust on the Same up to Feby}	..56
paid aut for the orphan	31..60	Cort 1830 }	
		due the orphan on the Estate}	

(48) Costen JORDAN (Cont.)

	Martha GROHAM decd	26 16
		555..81
31 60	paid out for the orphan	31 60
	A Ballance due the orphan	524..19
	Pleasant JORDAN	

North Carolina }
Hertford Caunty} August Caurt of Pleas &C 1830
This Accaunt was returned to Caurt on oath by Pleasants **JORDAN** guard & ordered to be recorded

Test L. M. **COWPER** Clk

Barsha JEGITTS

1830   Dr Barsha **JEGITTS** In Accaunt with Edward K. **JEGITTS** her guardian

Feby C¹	To Cash pad Ck for guardian Bond	60	1830 May 21/st/ By this amt rec/d/ from Carr}	
Augt 23/d/	" Cams 2½ p Cent on $327..07	8 18	" **DARDEN** Ck & m of Hertford Caunty}	322..13
	" Cash paid Ck for returning this act	40	" " int from 21/st/ May 1830 to 23/d/ Augt 1830	4..96
		9..18		
	To Balance due this day	317 89		
		327 07	1830	327 07
			Augt 23/d/ By Bal due up to this day	347..89
			E. K. **JEGITTS** guardian	

North Carolina }
Hertford Caunty } August Caurt of Pleas &C 1830
This Accaunt was returned to Caurt on oath by Edw K. **JEGITTS** Guard & ordered to be Recorded

Test L. M. **COWPER** Clk

Winborne JENKINS

1830   Dr Winborne **JENKINS** orphan of Benj **JENKINS** decd in acct with Henry D **JENKINS** guard

Feby 22/d/	To 1 Hat 62½ 6 yds Clath @ 20/¢/	1..82	1830 Feb /23/rd/ By Ballance due Feb Ct 1829	24 50
	2 pr pantaloons & 3? Shirts $1}		12 mo int thereon	1..47
	making Coat . . . . . 75}	1..75	" Hire of Negro **NAT** 1829	35..00
	6½ yds Clath @50/¢/ 1 pr Sacks 25	3 50	" " **EVRITT** "	4..05
	making 2 pr pantaloons 50/¢/		" " **CELIA** "	4..00
	1 pr Shaes 1/25/	1 75	Rent Land **WYNNS** place	22 00
	Spelling Book 20/¢/ Tuition 6 mo $5	5 20	Neck Field	12..25
	6 mo Board $25 P **BROWN** act 2 41	27..41		103 27
		41..43	Amounts Carred forward	

---

(49) 20 Winborne JENKINS

     Dr Winborne **JENKINS** orphan of Benj **JENKINS** decd In acct with Henry D **JENKINS** guardian

	Am Brot forward	41 43	Amt Brat orward [sic]	103..27
	To keeping Woman & Children 1829 15	15	Int fram 1 Jany to 22 Feby 1830	68
	" Clk this acct	40		103 95
	" Cammson on R & E amtg to }		By Balance due }	40..15
	$136..4½ @ 5 pr ct }	6 82	int from 22 Feby to 23/d/ Augt 1830}	1 20
	Balance due	40..15	1830	41..35
		103..95	March 27 To pd Shff Taxes for 1828}	1 92
			Ballance due }	39 43
				41..35
			By Ballance due	39 43
			Augt 23/d/ 1830 H D **JENKINS** guardian	

North Carolina }
Hertford Caunty} August Caurt of Pleas &C 1830
This Accaunt was returned to Caurt on oath by H. D. **JENKINS** guard & ordered to be recorded

Test L. M. **COWPER** Clk

---

(49) (Cont.) Penelope **JENKINS**

1830   Dr Penelope **JENKINS** orphan of Benj **JENKINS** decd In acct with Henry D **JENKINS** guardian

Feby 22/nd/ To 9 yds Clath at 25/¢/ cets	2 25	1830 Feby 22/nd/ By Ballance due on return}		
" making 2 Frocks @ 20	40	to Feby Ct 1829 }	4C6..51	
" 1 pr Shaes $1 1 pr prunet		To 12 M/o/ int thereon	24 39	
Shaes $1 75	2..75		₤30 90	
" Bonnet $1..75 1 pr Shaes $1.25/100	3..00	Hire Negro **JERRY** 1829	51..34	
" 2 Spelling Books /@/'20/¢/		" **BITHA**	21 10	
1 pr Shaes $1	1..40	**TONY**	:2..21	
" 12 mo Tuition	10. 00	**LUCY**	25..25	
" 12 mo Board	40. 00	Int from 1 Jany to 22/nd/ Feby	92	
" Amt P **BROWN**s acct	10..76		541..82	
" Clk returning this Act	..40	By Ballance due	450 55	
" Coms on R & Expenditures		6 mo int up to this time	13 32	
amounting to $206..27 @ 5 pr ct	10..31		473 87	
Balance due	460..35	1830		
	541..82	March 27/th/ To Cash paid Doct}		
		BORLAND act }	10 00	
		Balance due	₤63 87	
			₤73..87	
		By Balance due	₤63..87	

North Carolina   }

Hertford Caunty} August Caurt of Pleas &C 1830   23/d/ Augt 1830 E E H. D. **JENKINS** guard

This Accaunt was returned to Caurt on oath by H. D. **JENKINS** guard & ordered to be

recorded   Test L. M. **COWPER** Clk

===

Mary Jane **MONTGOMERY**

      Dr Mary Jane **MONTMERY** [sic] orphan of John C **MONTMERY** in acct with her guardian

      Geo W **MONTGOMERY** from the year 1829 up to this day August 23/d/ 1830

1829 To keeping Negro Woman **ISSABELA**}		By her undivided Interest in one Negro	
& Children **VENUS** and **BITHA** and}		Woman **ISSABELA** and Children **VENUS**	
furnishing the Same . . . .}	10..00	and **BITHA** Supased to be too thirds	[blank]
Interest from the 1/st/ of Jany 1830 up to		By 318½ Acres of Land	[blank]
this augt 23/d/	37½	Geo W **MONTGOMERY** guardian	
Commssions on do	30		
To Cash pd Clerk for a return }			
made last Feby Caurt . . . }	40		
	11 27½		

===

(50) 21 Mary Jane **MONTGOMERY**

      Dr Mary Jane **MONTGOMERY** orphon of John C **MONTGOMERY** in acct with her guardian

      Geo W **MONTGOMERY** From the year 1829 up to this day August 23/d/ 1830

1830 Amt Brot forward	11..27½		
March 25/th/ To Cash pd Gavin **HOGG** her			
part of a fee	2..00		
Intrust on Do	05		
24th Commissions	10	[blank]	
To Cash pd Jas S **JONES** Atty in the bill in			
Equity John S **BENTHALL** for a division			
of the Negroes	20 00		
Interest	30		
Commissions	1 00		
	34 92½		

(50) Mary Jane **MONTGOMERY** (Cont.)

     To keeping & furnishing Negro Woman
     ISSABELA & h?er Children **VENUS** &
     BITHA from the 1 Jany 1830 up to this time
     August 23/rd/ at the rates of $10 pr year   6..45
          Commissions   32

North Carolina   }

  Hertford Caunty} August Caurt of Pleas &C 1830

This Accaunt was returned to Caurt on oath By George W **MONTGOMERY** guard &

ordered to be recorded   Test L. M. **COWPER** Clk

John **MAGETT**

1830   Dr John **MAGETT** orphan of John **MAGETT** dec/d/. In acct with Jacob **HARE** his guardian

July 15 To Cash pd Wm **NEAL** for tuition $6 00			By this Amt due on last return		
Inst on do up to 24 August 1830	04	6 04	to May 24/th/ 1830	1024..72	
To Cash pd Clk for this return		40	Intst up to 24 August 1830	15 37	1040 09
Coms on rects & expenditures amtg to					
$21..81/¢/ at 5 p cent}		1..09			
To Ballance due		1032 36			
		1040..09			1040..09

North Carolina   }   By Bal due the orphan Augt 24 1830   1032..56

  Hertford Caunty} August Caurt of Pleas &C 1830   Jacob **HARE**

This Accaunt was returned to Caurt on oath by Jacob **HARE** & ordered to be

Recorded   Test L. M. **COWPER** Clk

John **MAGETT**

1828   Dr John **MAGETT** orphan of John **MAGETT** dec/d/. In acct with Jacob **HARE** his guardian

May 24/th/ To this amt pd for Guardian Bond		60	1828 March 24/th/ By this Amt recd of Nichalas}		
Novr 13/th/ To Cash pd Janas **WORRELL** for Bord 16			**MAGETT** Admr of John **MAGETT** decd }	962..40	
1829 Int on do up 24/th/ May 1829		50	To 12 m/o/ Inst on do	57..74	
Jany 3/d/ To Cash pd **NEAL** for Tuition 3..25			Decr 29/th/ By this Amt recd of Nicholas}		
1829 Inst on do up 24 May 1829	7	3..32	**MAGETT** Admr for Negro Hire }	104..25	
Decr 21.st/ To Cash pd Matt **WILLIAMS** $3.75			Int on do up 24/th/ May 1829	2..52½	
1829 Inst on do up 24 May 1829	8	3 823		1126 91	
Feby 3/c/ To Cash pd Tryal **WILLIAMS**		..75	By ballance due the orphan}		
March 11/th/ To do pd Mr **NICHOLSON** for tuition 6..25			the 24 May 1829 }	1035 30½	
1828 Int on do up 24 May 1829		07	Jacob **HARE**		
Amt Carried forward		31..32			

---

(51) 22 John **MAGETT**

     Dr John **MAGETT** orphan of John **MAGETT** dec/d/. In acct with Jacob **HARE** his guardian

Amt Brot forward		31 52 [sic]	Amt Brat forward	1126..91
Nov 24 To 1 pr Shaes	1..50			
Int an do up 24 May 1829	4½	1..54½		
To Cash paid yau . . .		2 00		
1829 Coms 5 pr Cent on $1126 91		56..34		
May 24/th/ To Cash pd clk for returning th [sic] act		40		
		91..60½		
To bolance due the Ward}				
the 24th May 1829 . . }		1035 30½		
		1126 91		1126..91

North Caralina   }

  Hertford Caunty} August Caurt of Pleas &C 1830

This Accaunt was returned to Caurt on oath by Jacob **HARE** guard & ordered to be recorded

                Test L. M. **COWPER** Clk

(51) John **MAGETT** (Cont.)

John **MAGETT**

1829   Dr John **MAGETT** orphan of John **MAGETT** dec/d/. In acct with Jacob **HARE** guard

Augt 1/st/ Cash paid yau	$ 1. 00	1830	Amt Brot up		201..62
" Int to 24 May 1830	05	May 24/th/ To Cash pd clk this return			4C
13 " Cash pd Wm **NEAL** tuition	13..75		To Commissions on Recpts &}		
Int to 24 May 1830	75		expenditures amtg to $410..92}		
Septem 30/th/ To Cash pd C **DARDEN**			@ 5 pr cent}		20..9?4
clk & master Cast	8..95		Balance due		1024..72
Int to 24 May 1830	35				1247..23
Decem 24/th/ Cash pd Trial **WILLIAMSON**					
Shoes	2..63	1830			Cr
Int to 24 May 1830	07	May 24th By this amt due on last return			
28 To Cash pd Elie **CARTER** Shaes	2..25		To May Caurt 1829		1033..30
1830 Int to 24 May 1830	05		12 Months in/t/ thereon		62..12
Jayny 4 To Cash pd J. W. **SAUTHALL** act	53 65		By hire Negro **JACOB** 1829		35..0)
Int 24 May 1830	1..15		" " " **WILLS?** "		40 12
To Do pd R. G. **COWPER**			" " " **CROFFORD** "		36..0)
Shff Taxes	4 16		" " " **MIKE** "		23..0)
Int to 24 May 1830	09		" " " **EDITH** (nothing)		
16 To Do gave yau	1..00		" " " **ANNIS** Do)		
Int to 24 May 1830	..02		Rent Land to Mason **MAGETT**		11..0)
Feby 20/th/ To Do pd Mrs Nancy **YANCY**			Do " " B **BEALE**		1..66
for board	69..16		Int to 24 May 1830		3..05
" " " Wm **NEALE** for tuition	6 50				1247..28
Int to 24 May 1830	1..14		By Balance due the orphan		1024..72
" 22/nd/ To Cash pd Geo **DUNN** making			24 May 1830		
Clathes	7 50				
Int to 24 May 1830	10		Jacob **HARE**		
27/th/ To Do pd Mrs Mason **MAGETT**}					
for keeping Negro **CLARA** &					
children }	20 00				
Int /to/ 24 May 1830	..30				
March 6/th/ To Cash I? gave yau . . .	1..25				
May 18/th/ To Do pd P. **CARTER**					
(Bridle &C)	3 75				
Amt Carried up	201..62				

North Carolina   }

Hertford Caunty} [blank]

This Accaunt was returned to Caurt on oath by Jacob **HARE** guard & ordered to be Recorded

           Test L. M. **COWPER** Clk

---

(52) <u>23</u> Amon **OVERTON**

1830   Dr Amon **OVERTON** orphan of Elisha **OVERTON** decd In acct with Miles H **JERNIGAN** guard

To recording this account	40	By this Amt due the orphan at my}	
March 4/th/ To Cash pd Daniel **CLARK** & wife}		return to Febuary Caurt 1830 . }	235..75
for a difference in the division of the }		Interest on ditto up to Augt}	7..07
Negroes between yau & them}	12..50	C/t/ 1830}	
Interest on ditto up to August }			
Caurt 1830 }	35		
March 4/th/ To Cash pd Lewis M **COWPER**}			
Clerk for Cast Partition [sic] to }			
divide Negraes }	3 76½		
Interest on ditto to this return	09½		
Augt 23/d/ To Cash for R. G. **COWPER** Shff}			

(52) Amon OVERTON (Cont.)

for Taxes for 1829}	2..40	
To 3 weeks Board up to this return	3..00	
To 5 pr cet Commissions on $29..58	1..47	
To Ballance due the orphan	218..85	
	242..83	242..83

1830

Augt 23/d/ By Ballance due the orphan   218..83

M. H. **JERNIGAN** guardian

North Carolina   }

Hertford County } August Caurt of Pleas &C 1830

This Accaunt was returned to Caurt on oath By Miles H **JERNIGAN** Guard & ordered to be recorded

Test L. M. **COWPER** Clk

Dassey OUTLAW

Dr Dossey **OUTLAW** orphan of George **OUTLAW** dec/d/ in acct with David O **ASKEW** guardian Cr

By Ballance due him February}	
Term 1830 Returned that time}	358..04
Interest an ditto until this day	10..74
E E this August 24/th/ 1830	368..78

North Carolina   David O **ASKEW** guard

Hertford County } August Caurt of Pleas &C 1830

This Accaunt was returned to Caurt on oath by David O **ASKEW** guard & ordered to be

Recorded   Test L. M. **COWPER** Clk

Sarah PORTER

Dr Sarah **PORTER** in acct with Benjamin **PORTER** Present guardian

August 23/rd/ 1830 principal & interest	$ 241..11
Land 34 Acres Negroes one	

Benja **PORTER**

North Carolina   }

Hertford County } August Caurt of Pleas &C 1830

This Accaunt was returned to Caurt on oath by Benjamin **PORTER** guard & ordered to be

Recorded   Test L. M. **COWPER** Clk

Dawson William & Bryant RALEIGH

1827   Dr Dawson William & Bryant **RALEIGH** in acct with Perry **CARTER** their guard

Febuay 25/th/ Cash pd clk for Bond	..60
Cash pd Clk for deet?	..20
1828 Cash pd ditto for return	..20
Augt 24'th/ Cash pd Clerk for renewing Bond	60
	1..60

---

(53) 24 Dawson William & Bryant **RALEIGH**

Dr Dawson William Bryant **RALEIGH** in acct with Perry **CARTER** their guardian

Amt Brat forward	1 60	Augt 30/th/ Cash Recd of Kinsy **JORDAN**	$ 45..9?2
1829 Cash pd clk for return	20	1826 int on this amt from 30 Augt	
Commissions on $197..89 cent at		1826 To 23/d/ of Augt 1830 is	11..02
5 pr ct	9..89	Augt 27/th/ Recd of George **HALLOMON**	98..97
Commissions on $1 80? being the		Int from 27 of Augt 1827 to 23/d/ }	
amt pd aut	..08	Augt 1830}	17..81
Jay 1/st/ Cash pd John K **HALL** doct }		Sept 6 Cash recd of Carr **DARDEN**	53..00
for his Services Renderd William		1827 Int from Sept 6 1827 to Augt}	
RALEIGH }	25..67	23/d/ 1830 on this amaunt	9..24
Comissions on 25..67 being the amt}			236 26
paid Doct **HALL** at 5/¢/ } 1 28		this return made to Augt Caurt 1830	197 54
Ballance due the ward up to Augt}		Ballance due the wards up to Augt}	

29

(53) Dawson William & Bryant **RALEIGH** (Cont.)

23/d/ 1830 . . . . . }	197..54	23/d/ 1830 is	197..54
	236 26	E E August Caurt 1830	236..26

North Carolina }

Hertford Caunty } August Caurt of Pleas &C 1830

This Accaunt was returned to Caurt on oath by Perry **CARTER** guard & ordered to be recorded

Perry **CARTER** guard

Test L. M. **COWPER** Clk

Nancy **REA**

1829   Dr Nancy **REA** in a/c with James **SCATT** guardian   Cr

Augt 25/th/ To Cash pd Taxes for 1828	2..50	1830	
1828 " pd Clek for guardian Bond	20	May 25/th/ By Cash of F W **SEAKUMY?**}	
May 25 pd Taxes for 1827	1..76	for rent of ware Hause for 1829	10..00
July 14/th/ " " do 1829	1..46		
Augt 19/th/ "pd a/c to James **SCATT** & Co	1..50		
pd Mr **REA** a/c of Board	2..58		
	10..00		10..00

North Caralina }

Hertford Caunty } August Caurt of Pleas &C 1830

This Accaunt was returned to Caurt on oath by James **SCOTT** guard & ordered to be recorded

Augst 19-1830 James **SCATT** guard

Test L. M. **COWPER** Clk

Hannah P **REA**

1829   Dr Hannah P **REA** in a/c with James **SCOTT** guardian   Cr

Augt 25/th/ To Cash pd taxes for 1828	2..50	1830	
guardian Bond	20	May 25/th/ By Cash of F W **SEABERRY** for	
May 25/th/ paid Taxes for 1827	1 76	rent of Store for 1829	$ 25.00
Feby 14/th/ " ditto " 1829	1 56		
Augt 19/th/ Cash pd Mrs M **REA** on a/c of}			
Board . . . . . . }	18..98		
	25. 00		25 00

North Carolina }

Hertford Caunty } August Caurt of Pleas &C 1830

This Accaunt was returned to Caurt on oath by James **SCOTT** guard & ordered to be

Recorded

James **SCOTT** guardian

Test L. M. **COWPER** Clk

---

(54) 25 Mr Thomas **ROBERTS**

1830   Dr Thomas **ROBERTS** in acct with John **WHEELER** Guardian

March 1/st/ For Amt of acct Current Cash}		1830	
paid Sundry persons during the}		March 1/st/ By Ballance due yau as pr}	
year ending this day . . . .}	900..92¾	act rendered for last Feby Term 1829 }	3231 83
50 [sic] p cent Com/ms/ upon		1 year/s/ interest thereon	193..91
re [sic] by expeditures	57..65	Hire of **JIM** 1829	50..00
Clerks fee for this return	..40	Rent of Land	8..33
Sundry Nates for bal in full	2525 09¼		3483 07
	3483 07	1830	

March 14/th/ I have this day recd from

my guardian the above ballance of Two

$2525..09¾ Thausand & Five hundred & twenty

five dallar/s/ 9¾ cents in full as the bal

due to me from him.

Witness   E E   Thomas O? **ROBERTS**

William **TRADER**

(54) (Cont.)
Ether [sic] L ROBERTS

1830	Dr Esther L ROBERTS orphan on acct with John WHEELER her guardian		Cr
For Cash pd to Self & Sundry persons}		1830	
p order }	90?6 41	Bal of acct due yau 1/st/ March 1829	4087..49
5 pr cet Coms upon rents &?		1 year/s/ int to 1 March 1830	245..25
expenditures	77..95	Hire of Negraes & rent of Land	145..83
Clerks fees	40	6 Mo int upon bal due 1/st/ March last	104 81
Ballance due E ROBERTS 1/st/		1830	
Sept 1830	3598..62	Augt 23/d/ Recd from John WHEELER his nate for	
	4583..38	Thirty five hundred & ninety Eight	4583 38
		dollar/s/ & 62 Cents in full when	
		paid for the bal due from him	
		as guardian for Mr/s/ E. L. EXUM	
		Witness	
		Jno H WHEELER Jas. J EXUM	
North Carolina }		William TRADER	

Hertford Caunty} August Caurt of Pleas &C 1830

These Accaunts & Receipts Were returnded to Caurt the Receipt from Jaseph J EXUM was proved by the oath of John H WHEELER one of the Subscribing Witness [sic] thereto & ordered to be Recorded

Test. L. M. COWPER clk

Mary Ann W RAMSAY

1830		Dr Mary Ann W RAMSAY in a/c With Mat J GRIFFITH present guardian	
Feby 23/rd/ Guardion return	40		
1829 To Sundry goods Bot of John W. SAUTHALL		Amt Brot up	9..83¾
Jun 27/th/ To 1 pr leather Shaes 6/9	1 12½	Augt 24/th/ To 1 pr moroco Shaes 9/-	1..50
Decr 18/th/ To 1 pr ditto 6/-	1..00	Octr 13/th/ To 1 fine tooth Comb 1/6	25
1830		" 17 To 1 pr Leather Shaes 6/9}	
Jany 28/th/ To 6 yds Bombazett @ 3/- p yd	3..00	1 Skein Silk 4½ }	1 18¾
Sundry goods Bot of M & H D GRIFFITH		Novr 7/th/ To 1 Trunk 13/6 1 paper pins	
1829		9/d/	2..37½
Apl 6/th/ To 1 pr leather Shaes 7/6	1 25	1830	
May 21/st/ To 1 pr Side Combs 9/d/ 1		Jany 10/th/ To 1 pr Side Combs 4/6}	
Cross Combs 1/1½	31¼	1 Hantkerchief 1/6}	1..00
July 16/th/ To 1 yd Catten Clath 1/6		To board from Feby term 1829}	
1 Sits? killing pins 9/d/ }		until Feby Term 1830 }	40..00
1 Spool Catton 9/d/}	50	Amt Carried up	56..15
6 yd Callico @ 2/3 pr yd	2 25		
Amt Carried up	9..83¾		

---

(55) 26 Mary Ann W. RAMSAY

		Dr Mary Ann W RAMSAY In a/c With Mat J GRIFFITH present guardian	
Amt Brot forward	56 15	1830	
By ballance due the orphan pr contra	477 65	Feby 22/d/ By Cash	382..13
		Interest on ditto from Feby Term 1829	22..92
		By hire of Negro Man PHILLIP	55..00
		By hire of Do named TONEY	42..50
		By hire of Negro girl CLARISSA	16..00
		By hire of Negro boy EDMUND	15..20
			533..80
		By balance due the orphan p debit	56..15
	477..65		$ 477..65

North Carolina }
Hertford Caunty} August Caurt of Pleas &C 1830

(55) Mary Ann W RAMSAY (Cont.)

This Accaunt was returned to Caurt on oath by Mat J **GRIFFITH**, guard & ordered to be Recorded

Test. L. M. **COWPER** Clk

Dr Perthena Ann William H Augiad W Aragimate Assan S & Arenah S **SESSOMS** children of Elisha **SESSOMS** in an a/c Current with S Elisha **SESSOMS** there [sic] guardian

1830 Feby term By the amt due the orphans} on return made to this term . . . . }	47..8
Int on $47..81 until August term next	1..43
	49..24
Ballance due the orphans	49..25

North Carolina   }

Hertford Caunty} August Caurt of Pleas &C 1830

This Accaunt was returned to Caurt on oath by Elisha **SESSOMS** guard & ordered to be Recorded

E. S. **SESSOMS**

Test L M **COWPER** Clk

John B SHARP

Dr John B **SHARP** In a/c with Elisha H **SHARP** his guardian   Cr

1830

Augst 23/d/ By this Sum due the ward} agreeable to a return made at Feby } Caurt 1830 Say nine hundred & Seven} dallar/s/ & 12/100 with Int from 4/th/ day} of Jany 1830   }   907..12

E. H. **SHARP** guard

Jacob SHARP Dr Jacob **SHARP** In A/C with Elisha H **SHARP** his guardian   Cr

1830

Augt 23/d/ By this Sum due the ward} agreeable to a return made at Feby Caurt} 1830 Say nine hundred & ninety nine} dallar/s/ & 35/100 with Int from 4/th/ day} of Jany 1830   }   999..35

E. H. **SHARP** guard

Elizabeth SHARP

Dr Elizabeth **SHARP** In a/c with Elisha **SHARP** her guardian

North Carolina   }

Hertford Caunty} August Caurt of Pleas &C 1830 These Accaunts were returned to Caurt on oath by Elisha H **THARP** guard & ordered to be recorded   Test L M **COWPER** Clk

1830

Augst 23/d/ By this Sum due the Ward agreeable} to a return made at Feby Caurt 1830 Say} nine hundred & eighty nine dallar/s/ & ninety}   989 94 four Cents with Int from 4 day Jany 1830}

Augt 23/d/ 1830   E. H. **THARP** guard

---

(56) 27 Mr/s/ Sarah SIMONS

1830   Dr Mr/s/ Sarah **SIMONS** daughter of Watson **LEWIS** in a/c Current with Watson **LEWIS** guardian Cr

		1830	
Aprl 15/th/ To Amount paid **PHEBY** 20/¢		By Ballance due yau Feby Term 1830	18..33
1 pr Shaes 75/¢/	95	May 28/th/ By 16.666 Herrings @ 2/¢/ $	33..66
May 1/st/ To 3 yds Checks @ 20/¢/... ...	60	June 29/th/ By 9 yds Silk return @ 75/¢/	6..75?
" 3 To amount paid **PAYTON** . .	20	By Ballance due W L guardian	203..25
8 To Cash paid Mr/s/ **RAWLS** .	1..00		
" 19 To 9 yds Silk @ 75/¢/ 6 ditto			
callico @ 37½/¢/	2..00		
" " 3½ ditto Lace @ 1$ 1 Shawl $1	4..50		
" " 1¼ ditto dimoty @ 50$ . .	50		

(56) Mr.'s/ Sarah SIMONS (Cont.)

"	" 1 pr Shaes $1..75 1 do 50	
	5 hank silk @ 6¼	2..57
"	"1 Black Silk vale $3.50 Cape 25/¢/	3..75
"	" 2 yds mill net @ 10/¢/ 4 yds	
"	" Brade 6¼	..45
20	" Cash paid Miss Harriatt **HARE**	2..75
"	" ditto Mrs **RAWLS**	4 00
21	" ditto Milly **HARE**	4 00
23	" 1 Piana Fortes [sic]	205..00
1830		
"	" 3/8 yds Cover	4 69
29	To amount paid A **HARRELL**	1..87
June 1/st/	To Lace 92/¢/ Black belt 25	1..17
	1¾ yds Black Cambrick @ 20/¢/	..35
	1 ditto Ribband 12½ Catton	
	Clath 20/¢/	..32
	1 Cream Jug 12½ ½ doz neadles 6¼	19
	1 Hank Silk 6¼ 2 yds Catton @ 12½	..32
5	To 6 yds Catton @ 25/¢/	1..50
	1 Silk Hkff $1 buttons 12½	1..13
	1 pair black Catton Stockings 75	75
21	To 1 thread Cambrick Hkff	1..00
	4 yds black Lace	2..00
	1¼ ditto Gingham @ 45/¢/	..56
	½ yd Bobnett Lace @ 1..28	62
July 15/th/	To 1 pr Shaes $1..25 1 belt	
	Ribband 38/¢/	1..63
29	" 1 belt Ribband	25
"	" 2½ drillings @ 50/d/	1..25
"	" 1 Spool Catton	..13
"	" 1 paper pins 20/¢/ 1¾ yds	
	Lace @ 25	64
Augt 7/th/	To 1 yd Linen	60
	1 Bunch tape 12½ ditto Bobin 12½	..25
		261..99
To Ballance due Watson **LEWIS** guardian		203..25
up to August 22/nd/ 1830		

Watson **LEWIS**   261..99

North Carolina   }
Hertford County} August Court of Pleas &C 1830
This Account was returned to Court on oath by Watson **LEWIS** guard & ordered to be
Recorded   Test L M **COWPER** Clk

Newet VICK

1830	Dr Newet **VICK** in acct Currant with Benjamin **BRYANT** guardian		Cr	
Augt 24.th/	To 20/¢/ for returning this acct	20	By Cash	25..45¼
	To 5 p cent on 76 Cents Coms	02	By the Int of $25..45 from the 22/nd/	..76
		22	to August term	26..21¼
		26..21	Benjamin **BRYANT** guardian	
		22		
	Balance due	25..99		

---

(57) 28 Cordia **VICK** Dr Cordia **VICK** in accaunt Current with Benjamin **BRYANT** guardian   Cr
1830

(57) <u>Cordia</u> **VICK** (Cont.)

Augt 24/th/ To 20 Cents for returning this acct	$	20	By Cash	25..45
To 5 p cent on 76/¢/ cent Com/s/		02	By the Interest of 25.45 from the 22/nd/	
		22	Febuary to August term	76
		26 21		
		22		
Balance due		25..99		26..21
			Benjamin **BRYANT** guardian	

Rebecah **VICK**

1830			Dr Rebecah **VICK** in account Current with Benjamin **BRYANT** guardian	Cr
Augt 24/th/ To 20 Cents for returning this acct	$	..20	By Cash	25..45
To 5 p cent on 76/¢/ cent Com/s/		02	By the Int of $25.45 from 22/nd/	
		..22	February to August term	..76
		26 21		
		22		
Balance due		25..99		26..2?
			Benjamin **BRYANT** guardian	

Etney **VICK**

1830			Dr Etney **VICK** in account Current with Benjamin **BRYANT** guardian	Cr
Augt 24/th/ To 20 Cents for returning this acct	$	20	By Cash	25..4?
To 5 p cent on 76/¢/ cent Com/s/		02	By the Int of $25.45 from the 22/nd/	
		22	February to August term	..76
		26 21		
		22		
Balance due		25..99		26..21
			Benjamin **BRYANT** guardian	

William **VICK**

1830			Dr William **VICK** in account Current with Benjamin **BRYANT** guardian	Cr
August 24/th/ To 20 Cents for returning this acct	$	20	By Cash	$ 25 45
To 5 p cent on 76/¢/ cent Com/s/		02	By the Int of $25..45 from the	
		..22	22/nd/ February to August term	76
		26 21		
		22		
Balance due		25..99		26..21

North Carolina }   Benjamin **BRYANT** guardian
Hertford Caunty} August Caurt of Pleas &C 1830
These Accaunts were returned to Caurt on oath by Benjamin **BRYANT** guard & ordered
to Recorded [sic]   Test L M **COWPER** Clk

Elizabeth **VANN PELT** [sic]

~~Inventory of~~

North Carolina }   Inventary of the money which I recd of
Hertford Caunty} August of [sic] Pleas &c 1830   John **WINBORNE** on acct of Elizabeth
This Accaunt was Returned to Caurt on oath by   VAN PELT Cash   71..00
Henry B **VANPELT** guard & ordered to be recorded   ½ of Negraes   [blank]
        H. B **VANPELT** guardian
        Test L M **COWPER** Clk

---

(58) <u>29</u> The orphans of David **WILLIAMS**

     Dr The orphans of David **WILLIAMS** In acct with Robert **WILLIAMS** their guard

1829		1830
Augt 23/d/ To Cash paid clk for guardian Bond	60	July 1/st/ Cash recd of William **BRYANT**
Jany 1/st/ Cash paid ck for pawer of Aturnee?		Which was due from the Estate of their

(58) The orphans of David **WILLIAMS** (Cont.)

1830 to Callect money aut of the County for the Benefit of the Wards	50	uncle Jacob **LAWRENCE**	20..50
Augt 2=/d/ Cash paid ck for making this return	40	int from 1 Jany to 23 August 1830 on $20..50	..75
1830 Comisions on $31 58 ct 5 pr cent	1..63	to nate Recd from Henry L **WILLIAMS**	10 10?
Balance due the wards to 23 Augt} 1830}	27..75	for rent of Land for 1829 which was due 25 december 1829 for interest from 25 december 1829 to August 1830	..35
	30 88	this return made to August Caurt 1830	31..58
		1830	
		Augt 23/d/ Ballance due the wards to 23 August 1830	27..75

North Carolina }	$ 30..58	Robert **WILLIAMS** guard $31..58

Hertford Caunty} August Caurt of Pleas &C 1830

This Accaunt was returned to Caurt on oath by Robert **WILLIAMS** guard & ordered to be Recorded

Test. L. M. **COWPER** Clk

Margaret **WHITLEY**

Dr Margaret **WHITLEY** in act with George **WHITLEY** her guardian   Cr

To Cash paid for Land tax for 1828	25	1830 May ct	
To 1 pr Shaes	1..25	By amt due the Ward on my last return at May Caurt 1829	5..97
To her part of the Expences of } renewing guard Bond . . . }	..27	Int from may Caurt 1829 till May ct 1830	35
To Cash pd Cerk for returning this act	20	By amt of her part of James **WHITLY**s} Est . . . . }	..86
To 5 pr ct Coms on the rects and} Expenditures . . . . }	..30	By amt of ditto rent of Land for 1829	3..48
	2..27		10..66
Balance due the ward} May Caurt 1830 }	8..39		

Burrell **WHITLEY**

Dr Burrell **WHITLEY** in acct with George **WHITLY** his gurd   Cr

To Cash paid for Land tax for 1828	25	1830	
To 1 pr Shaes	1..00	May ct By amt due the Ward on my last return at May Caurt 1829	5..97
To his part of the expences in } renewing guard Bond . . .}	..27	Interes from may Caurt 1829 till May Caurt 1830	35
To 5 pr ct Com/s/ on the recets and} Expenditures . . . . }	30	By amt of his part of James **WHITLY**s} Este [sic] . . . .}	..86
To Cash paid clk for returning} This accot to May Ct }	20	By amt of his part of rent of} land for 1829 . . . . . }	3..48
	2..02		10..66
Balance due the Ward at May ct 1830	8..64		

David **WHITLEY**

Dr David **WHITLEY** in accot with George **WHITLEY** his guardian   Cr

To Cash paid for Land tax for 1829	25	1830	
1 pr Shaes	..75	May ct By amt due the ward on my} last return at May ct 1829 }	5..97
To his part of Expences in renewing guardn Bond	..27	Ints from may Caurt 1829 till may ct 1830	..35
	1..27	Amts Carried forward	6..33

---

(59) 3C David **WHITLEY**

Dr David **WHITLEY** in acct with George **WHITLEY** his guardian   Cr

Amt Brat forward	1..27	1830	
To Cash paid clk for returning} this acct to May Caurt 1830 }	..20	May ct Amt Brat forward	$ 6..32
		By amt his part of James **WHITLEY**s}	

(59) David **WHITLEY** (Cont.)

To 5 p Cent Coms on the rects & Expends	30	Estate . . . .}	..86
	1..77	By amt of his part of the rents of}	
Ballance due the ward }		land for 1829 . . . . }	3..48
At May Caurt 1830 . }	8..89		10..56

North Carolina   }

 Hertford Caunty} August Caurt of Pleas &C 1830

These Accaunts were returned to Caurt on oath by George **WHITLEY** guard & ordered to be Recorded

Test. L. M. **COWPER** Clk

William **WILSON**

1829   Dr William **WILSON** in acct Current With John G **WILSON** guardian   Cr

Feby 23/d/ To Clerks fee last return	40	1829 Feby 24/th/ By this amt due the}	
May 4/th/ To L E **CASSADY**s receipt for tuition	3..00	ward as p last return . . . . }	412..52
" Interest on Same to Feby term 1830	14	By Interest on Same to Feby Term 1830	24..55
8 To 9½ yds Catton Clath @ 25/¢/ 2 yds }		Novr 27/th/ By Sale Negro Man **HARRY** 450	
" drill @ 2d 14 buttons mol?es @ 12¼ }		deduce for Kict?ching & delivery 6	
" Silk 4 Twist 30 cets 1 doz Shirt buttons}			444 444 00
" 20/¢/ 1 Vest patron 75/¢/ buttons for }		By Interest on Same to Feby Term 1830	6..14
" Vest 6¼/¢/ }	4..21¼	1830	
22/d/ To Leather Gloves pr Shaes &		By Hire of **HARRY** Year 1829 $42	
Shae tanad? 10/¢/	1.10	1830	
24 To Gavin **HOGG**s recept for defencing Suit	10..00	Jay deduct from time of Selling him 4	
Interest on Same to Feby Term 1830	45	To Expiration of the year 38	38..00
June 5/th/ To Shae Sales & Caps	25	By Hire of Negro boy **SALOMON** 1829	26..30
July 25/th/ To Cash 25	..25		
To Jno A. **MOORE**s Act Cuting Coat	40		
Sept 21/st/ To Geo W **MOORE**s recept			
for Board &C	22..30		
" Interest on Same to Feby Term 1830	56		
Oct 15/th/ To 1 doz Suspender mates 12½			
Shae leather 12½	25		
Decr 20/th/ To L H **REVES**? Receipt for			
tuition	3 06¼		
" " Interest on Same to Feby Term 1830	0 05		
" 28 To George W **MOORE**s receipt for			
Board &C	9..45		
" " Interest on Same to Feby Term 1830	0..09		
1830			
Jay 26/th/ To Doct A **BARDWELL**s receipt			
for attendance	29 37½		
" " Interest on Same to Feby Term 1830	0..14		
16 To Sherriffs receipt for Cast in Suit of			
" **MONTGOMERY** . . . $73..87	73..87		
To Commissions on $256..74 cets being}			
Amt of Expendatures & in Come }			
For the present year @ 5 pr Cent }	12..83		
Feby 22/d/ To Ballance due the ward Feby	777..33		
Term1830 as p return made then?			
	951..71		95?..71

I believe this to a [sic] True Coppy of my return at Feby Term 1830   Jno G. **WILSON**

North Carolina   } August Caurt of Pleas &c 1830 This Accaunt was returned to Caurt on oath by

 Hertford Caunty} John G. **WILSON** guard & ordered to be recorded.   Test L. M. **COWPER** clk

				Cr
(60) 31 Wm **WARD** Dr William **WARD** in acct Curt with A **BARDWELL** guard & ords [sic]				
1830 Tc Ballance in acct Curt of last year	639..11	To Bill hire of negraes & land}		
Inst for 6 months	19..17	for 1830 due 4 Jany 1831...}		144..15
Augt Caurt To A **BARDWELL** in accot		discaunt for inst till 4 Jany 1831		3..69
for money & **A**	182..81			160..46
Comms on $160..46	8..02			949..11
North Carolina }	849..11	due the guardian		688..65

Hertford County} August Caurt of Pleas &c 1830

This Accaunt was returned to Caurt on oath by Awanah **BARDWELL** Guard & ordered to be
Recorded   Test. L. M. **COWPER** clk

Sally M **WILLIAMS**   guardian

1827	Dr Sally M **WILLIAMS** orphan of Benj B **WILLIAMS** Decd In acct Current with Dempsy **NAW___**			
To 2 yds of Catten	40	1828 By this amount Recd of Seth **NAWELL**		
" 1 yd Checks	37	former guardian on Notes		$221..26
Novr 24 th/ " 1 Bonnet & Bow . . .	3 25			10 79½?
" 1 Spelling Book	25			160 46½
" paid Mr/s/ **DAVIDSON** for				
doctoring /the/ Ward	1 75			
March 23/th/ 3 months SChooling	2..50			
" 8 yds of Clath for her Negroes	2..00			
Jany 11/th/ " goods Baught for her	3 02½			
" ½ yd Cambrick	18¾			
" 12 months Bord	36..00			
	4?1 73¾			
Commissions on $221..26	11 06			
By A ballance due the orphan	160..46	1828	By A Balance due the orphan	160..46¼?
	221..26			221..26

1829?		1829		
May 24/th/ T paid the returns made to		may 24 Returns made to may term 1828		160..46¼
may term	$ 40	Interest Calculated		9..62
1829 " paid the doctress for **FILLIS**	1..25	By hire of Negroes due 1/st/ Jany 1829	49	
Jany 7/th/ " 1 pr Shaes	75	Interest Calculated on $49 for}		
1828 " goods Bought of Abner **HARRELL**	..81¼	4 Months 23 dy }		1..17
Novr 1/st/ " 3 months Schooling	2 35			220..25¼
1828 " goods Baught of Jno. **WILSON**	2 00			56..87¼
Novr 29 th/ " 3? quarters of Schooling	1 66½			163..37½
Apl 10/th/ " goods Bought for the orphan-s-	..63			
" 12 months Bor?d	36..00			
1829 " Commishions on $22 25	11..02			
	56 87¾			
	220 25			220..25
By A Ballance due the orphan	163..37½	1829 By A Ballance due orphan		163..37½

May 24/th/ To paid the returns made to		1830		
may term	$ 40	Augt 23/d/ Return made to may term 1829		163..37½
Augt 27 " goods Baught of Edward **HARDY**	65	Interest Calculated		9..80
Oct 20 " 62 days Schooling	2 50	By hire of Negraes due 1/st/ Jany 1830		58..00
Novr 20 th/ " 1 pr leather Shaes	1..10	Interest on $58 for 7 months 23 days		2..26
Jay 27/th/ " goods Baught of Richard R				233..43½
MINTON	1 84			75..87½
	6 49	amts Carried up		157..56

(61) 32 [No heading.]

Amt Brat forward	6..49	Amt Brat forward	157 56
To goods Baught of Watson **LEWIS**	1 74		
March 20/th/ " goods Baught of Jasiah **HALLY**	1..35		
Apl 30/th/ goods Baught of John **WILSON**	2..76¼		
" " " 90 days Schooling	3..75		
May 19/th/ " doctress for **FILLIS**	1..25		
" 1 yd of muslin	40		
" ½ yd of mus?lin 1 belt Ribban	84¼		
" 3 ditto of Checks	65		
" 15 months Bord	45..00		
1830 " Commishions on $233 43½	11.67		
	75..87½		
	233..43½	1830	233..43½
By A Balance due the orphan	$157..56	August 23/d/ By A Ballance due orphan	157..56

Returns made to August term on Augt 23/d/ 1830   this a/ct is Just & true to the best of my knowlege
                                    Dempsey **NAWELL** guard

North Carolina }
Hertford Caunty} August Caurt of Pleas &C 1830
This Accaunt was returnen to Caurt on aath by Dempsey **NAWELL** guard & ordered to be Recorded
                       Test L. M. **COWPER** Clk

Jabez **WHEELER**

1830			1830		Cr
Dr Jabez **WHEELER** in acct Current with James **WORRELL** his guardian					
Augt 25/th/ To Cash paid clk for return	$	40	1830		
To Coms on receipts & Expenditures}			August 25 By bal due last return	1361..57	
Amaunting to $41..24 @ 5 pr cent }		2..06	6 mos Inst on do	40..32	
Balance due the orphan		1399..95	Balance due the orphan . . . .}	1402..41	
		1402..41	25/th/ August 1830 . . . . . }	1399..95	

North Carolina }
Hertford Caunty} August Caurt of Pleas &C 1830   James **WORRELL**
This Accaunt Was returned to Caurt on oath by James **WORRELL** guard & ordered to recorded [sic]
                       Test L. M. **COWPER** Clk

Jaseph **BENTHAL**

Dr Joseph **BENTHAL** orphan of Lewis **BENTHAL** decd. In act With

1827 Sipha **SMITH** guardian		1827		Cr
March 25/th/ To Cash paid Clerk for		March 29/th/ By yaur part of Mary **PARKER**s		
guardian Bond	60	Estate	$119..28	
" To Cash ditto David L **SWAIN** atto	5..00	compaund Int on ditto up to Novr 20/th/ 1830	28..15	
Interest on ditto up to Novr 20 1830	1 10	Sept 1/st/ By a Juagt ry [sic]		
To 1 pr Shaes	1 00	Wiaght? **NICHOLS**	47..50	
Interest on ditto	21	Interest on ditto	9 87	
July " To Cash paid for 4 yds R duck @ 3/9?}		1829		
6 yds Cattons @ 1/6	2..40	March By Cash recd of Jas **EVANS**	25	
Interest on ditto	46	By rents of Land for 1828 payl Jany 1829	6 00	
1828 To Cash pd Sheff for taxes	98	Interest on ditto	..59	
March To 3 months Bord while at School	12.00	May 26 By Cash recd of R. **CRASS** & G. M.		
Interest on ditto	1..98	**SMITH**	22..59	
	25..73	Int on ditto	2..06	
amts Carried over		By Cash recd of R **CROSS** /s/ Trustee	..75	
		" rents of Land for 1830 payl 1 Jany 1831		
			$24	
		Int off for one month	12	$ 23..28
				261..02

(62) 3? Joseph BENTHAL

Dr Jaseph BENTHAL orphan of Lewis BENTHA [sic] decd In acct with Sipha SMITH guardian

	amt Brot over	25 73	amt Brot over	261..02
March	To Cash pd A BARDWELL for tuishion	3 00		
	Int on ditto	..45		
	To 2 quires of paper	..50		
	To 1 English reader	..50		
	To 1 arithamatick	1..25		
	Int on ditto	19		
Apl	To pd for pr shaes	1..25		
	Int on ditto	19		
Augt 1.st/	To 1 english reader	..37		
	To 1 qr paper	25		
October	To paid for 36 days tuition	1..50		
	Int on ditto	..18		
	To 2 Bord while at School	8..00		
1829	Int on ditto	1..00		
March	To Cash	1..75		
	Int on ditto	..17		
	To 1 p Shaes	1..50		
	Int on ditto	15		
	To Cash paid Jethro SMITH	1..00		
	Int on ditto	..10		
June	To Sole Leather for p shaes	50		
Octr	To 6½ months Bord @ $4	26..00		
	Int on ditto	2..60		
	To Cash Lodwick RICE	6..60		
	To pd John G WILSON acct	2..77		
	To Cash pd William LINGS	2..00		
	Int on ditto	[blank]		
	To Cash 43/¢/	43		
	To Cash pd Sheff for Taxes the year 1827			
	1828-1829	4..27		
		94..20		
	To 5 p cent Commissions allawed the guardian	17..76		
	To Ballance due the orphan	149..06		
		261..02	1830	261..02
			Novr 20/th/ Ballance due the orphan	149 06

In purs?ant [sic] to the annexed order to us directed we the undersinged [sic] Commissioneres have examined the
accaunts of Sipha SMITH late guardian to Jaseph BENTHAL with Elvy LEWIS his present guardian
and find a ballance due from the former to the latter Guardian of the Sum of one hundred and
forty ni?e dallar/s/ and Six Cents which we Submit to yaur worships for approbation given under
aur han?s and Seals this 20/th/ day of November 1830   M. H. JERNIGAN (Seal)

    B. J. MONTGOMERY (Seal)

North Carolina }   David O. ASKEW (Seal)

Hertford Caunty} A November Caurt of Pleas &C 1830

This Accaunt Current with the auditors Report thereon was returned to Caurt & ordered to be
Record?d   Test L. M. COWPER Clk

---

(63) 34 Martha BOON

1830	Dr Martha BOON In acct with Wm. R. WILLIAMS Guardian			Cr
Novr 22/nd/	To this return	40	1830	
	Coms	1..50	Novr 22/d/ By this Amt due the ward this}	
	To this Sum due the Ward	28..10	day Say thirty daller/s/ . . . . .}	30..00

(63) Martha **BOON** (Cont.)

	30..00			30..00
		By this Sum due the ward this 22/d/ day		
		Novr 1830		28..10
		William R **WILLIAMS** guard		

Peterson **BOON**

1830	Dr Peterson BOON In acct with Wm R **WILLIAMS** Guardian			Cr
Novr 22/d/ To this return	..40	1830		
Coms	1..50	Novr 22/d/ By this Amt due the ward }		
To this Sum due the Ward	28..10	this day Say thirty daller/s/ . . . . . }	30..00	
	30..00		30..00	
		By this Sum due the ward }		
		this 22/d/ Novr 1830 . . . . . }	28..10	

North Carolina }
Hertford Caunty} November Caurt of Pleas &C 1830   William R **WILLIAMS** guard
These Accaunts were returned to Caurt on oath by William R **WILLIAMS** guard & ordered to be
Recorded   Test. L. M. **COWPER** clk

Wm. M. **DAUGHTERRY**s Heirs   guard

Dr The orphans of William Mills **DAUGHTERRY** in acct Current with Titus **DARDEN**

1826 To Board of Lawrence S **DAUGHTERRY**}		By this amt recd of Wm E **DAUGHTERY** }	
& Henry M **DAUGHTERRY** 1 year }		Executor of Wm Mills **DAUGHTERY** dec/d/}	157..76
ending 1 Januy 1823 . . . . }	96..00	By ballance due from Sale of }	
Int till 28 August 1826 1 year 8 mo/s/	9..80	Negraes at August Caurt 1825 & Int}	223..13
T [sic] ditto of Mary & Mariah 6 mo/s/ }		By rents recd of Henry **SMITH** for }	
ending the 1/st/ January 1825 . . . . . . }	48..00	1825?6 & Interest . . . . }	55..00
Int till 28/th/ Augt 1826 1 year 8 mo/s/	4 90	By ditto Recd of Henry **SMITH** }	
To ditto of Mary Mariah & Henry }		for 1825 & Interest up to 28 Augt 1826}	52..00
M **DAUGHTERY** from 1 Jany 1825 till }		By rent of **PORTER** place for 1824 & Int	13..20
1/st/ Jany 1826 . . . . }	144 00	By Rent of ditto for 1825 & Int	46..80
Int till August Caurt Say 8 mo/s/	5..76		547..86
To ditto of Mary Mariah & Henry }		Ballance due after deducting	
M **DAUGHTERY** from 1/st/ Jany 1826 till}		Commissions . . . . $41..63	
AugustCaurt Say 8 mo/s/ . . . . }	96 00	An Inventory of the lands & negraes belonging	
To pd Patrick **BRAWN**s acct as pr rect	23..09?	to the Estate of Wm Mills **DAUGHTER** [sic] decd	
Int up to Augt Caurt Say 7 mo/s/ 8 days	..83	**JIM JACOB VINEY MINERVA RACHAEL CRECY**	
To pd **O BRYAN & PIPKIN**s a/c as pr recet	23 25	& child **VILET** & child **CHERRY** & two children	
Int up to Augt Caurt Say 3½ mo/s/	40	**CLARRISA** & two children - The manor	
To pd **MARGAN & CAWPER** for		plantation & **PORTER** plantation all	
Arithmetic	45	of which are rented & hired for	
To pd Richd G **COWPER** for taxes	4 73	the present year Augt 28/th/ 1826	
Int till August Caurt 1826 Say 6 Mo/s/	13	North Carolina } Titus **DARDEN**	
To pd Wm B **WISE** acct	2 87½	Hertford Caunty} November Caurt of Pleas &c 1830	
To pd Mr/s/ **MONTGOMERY** acct for bonnets	8..30	This Accaunt was returned to Caurt on oath by Titus	
To 4 p Shaes $4.75 2 p do $2 to pd midwife		**DARDEN** guardd & ordered to be Recorded	
fee /1.50/	8 25	Test. L. M. **COWPER** clk	
To furnishing gallon brandy at Sale Decr 1825	1..00		
	478..84		

---

(64) <u>35</u> Wm. M. **DAUGHTERRY**s Heirs Dr The orphans of William Mills **DAUGHERRY** [sic] in acct Current with
Titus **DARDEN** guard

1826		1827		Cr
Augt To paid Lewis M **COWPER**	2..00	Feby 25/th/ By this amt due as pr last		
1827 " pd James S **JONES**	20..60	return to August term 1826		$ 43..63

(64) Wm. M. **DAUGHTERRY**s Heirs (Cont.)

Feby 25/th/ " 6 months Bord of Mary Mariah &}		Int up to Feby Term 1829	[blank]
Mills **DAUGHTERY** @ $40 pr months ead}	72..00	By amt of rents & hires due	
5 pr cent Commissions on $102	5..00	25 december 1826	102..00
Balance due the heirs	46..18	Int up to Feby 1827	1..00
	$145..88		$145..88

North Carolina }

Hertford County} November Court of Pleas &C 1830

This Account was returned to Court on oath by Titus **DARDEN** guard & ordered to be

Recorded

Titus **DARDEN**

Test. L. M. **COWPER** Clk

Wm. M. **DAUGHTEREY** [sic] Heirs   guard

1827	Dr The orphans of William Mills **DAUGHTERRY** in acct current with Titus **DARDEN**		
To pd for keeping Negro **VILET** & 2}		1827 By ballance due the orphans as pr}	Cr
children for the year 1827 . . . . . . }	20..00	a/c returned to Feby 1827 . . . . }	46..18
" Int from 1/st/ Jany 1828 to 25 Feby 1828	..19	Int on the Same for 12 mo/s/	2..76
" amt paid for keeping Woman **CHERRY**}		By Hire of Negro **JIM**	42..25
& 3 children for do . . . . }	33..00	Int from 1/st/ Jany 1828 till 25 Feby 1828	..42
" Int on the Same from 1/st/ Jany 1828}		By Hire Negro **JACOB**	20..00
to 25/th/ of Feby 1828 . . . . }	30	Int from 1/st/ Jany 1828 till 25 Feby 1828	..20
" amt paid for keeping **CLARRISSY**}		By Hire of Negro **VINEY**	15..00
& 3 children for ditto . . . . }	35..00	Int from 1/st/ Jany 1828 till 25 Feby 1828	..12
" Int on Same from 1 Jany 1828 to }		By Hire of **CECY** [sic] & child	12..00
Feby 1828 . . . . }	32	Int from 1/st/ Jany 1828 till 25/th/ Feby 1828	..10
1828		By Hire of Negro **RACHEL**	5..00
Feby 16/th/ To this amt for Samuel **NIKALSON**}		Int from 1/st/ Jany 1828 till 25/th/ Feby 1828	..04
for tuition for the year 1827 . . . .}	30..00	By Hire of Nergro **MANEVA**	2..00
" Int from 16/th/ Feby 1828 to 25 Feby 1828	..08	By rent of Land	60..00
7 this amt pd **SAUTHALL & PARKER** for a/c	14..96	Int from 1/st/ Jany 1828 till 25 Feby 1828	58
Int for 7 Feby 1828 to 25 Feby 1828	..04	By Rent of Land	50..00
1827		Int from 1/st/ Jany 1828 till 25 Feby 1828	48
Decr 4 " amt pd Doct Thomas **OLD?** for		By Rent of Land	10 00
medical a/c	1..00	Int from 1/st/ Jany 1828 till 25/th/ Feby 1828	09
Int from 14th Decr 1827 to 25 Feby 1828	..03	By Ballance due the guardian	31..68
1828			
Feby 25/th/ To Board of Mary Marriah & Mills}			
DAUGHTERRY for one year ending 25/th/}			
Feby 1828 @ $48 . . . . }	144..00		
" amt pd R. G. **CAWPER** Sheff for}			
the taxes on Land for the year 1826}	6..63		
Commissions on $267..23	13..32		
	298..91		298..91

North Carolina }

Hertford County} November Court of Pleas &C 1830

This Account was returned to Court on oath by Titus **DARDEN** guard & ordered to be

Recorded

Titus **DARDEN**

Test. L. M. **COWPER** Clk

Wm M **LAUGHTERY** Heirs

1828	Dr The orphans of William Mills **DAUGHETERRY** in acct current		
	with Titus **DARDEN** guardian		
To amt pad for keeping Negro **VILET**		1829	
& 2 children	10..00	By Hire of Negro **JIM**	36..00
		amts -A- carried up	

(65) <u>36</u> Wm M. **DAUGHTERY** Heirs Dr The orphans of William Mills **DAUGHTERRY** in acct current with
Titus **DARDEN** guardian

amt Brot up	10 00	amt Brot up	36..00
Int from 1/st/ Jany 1829 to 23 Feby 1828 [sic]	87½	Int on the Same from 1/st/ Jany 1829 to }	
" amt pd for keeping Negro **CLARRISY** &		23 Feby 1829 . . . . }	31½
three children	20..00	By Hire of Negro **JACOB**	30_00
" Int on the Same from 1/st/ Jany 1829 to		Int on the Same from 1/st/ Jany 1829}	
23 Feby 1829	17½	to 23/d/ Feby 1829 . . . . }	26½
" amt for furnishing negro **CHERRY** & 3		By Hire of Negro **VINEY**	10 .00
Children left on my hands By Henry}		Int on the Same from 1/st/ Jany 1829}	
G **CUTTER** [or **CUTLER**] . . . }	21..75	to 23/d/ Feby 1829 }	08¾
Int on the Same from 1/st/ Jany 1829 to 23		By Hire of Negro **CRÉCY** & Chil/d/	10 .00
Feby 1829	..19	Int on the Same from 1/st/ Jany 1829 to 23/d/}	
" This amt pd Trial **WILLIAMS** for a/c	2..50	Feby 1829 . . . . }	08¾
Int on the Same from 13 decr 1828}		By Hire of Negro **RACHEL**	∠_00
to 23/d/ Feby 1829 . . . . . . }	02¾	Int on the Same from 1/st/ Jany to 23/d/ of}	
" amt paid Carr **DARDEN** for a/c	11..32	Feby 1829 . . . . }	03½
Int on the Same from 23/d/ Sept 1828 to		By Hire of Negro **MANERVA**	1 00
23/d/ Feby 1829	28¼	Int on the Same from 1/st/ Jany 1829 to}	
this amt paid Thomas P **LITTLE** for}		23/d/ Feby 1829 . . . .}	00¾
medical acct . . . . }	33..50	By rent of Land	70_00
Int on the Same from 19/th/ July 1828}		Int on the Same from 1/st/ Jany 1829 to}	
to 23/d/ Feby 1829 . . . . }	1..17	23/d/ Feby 1829 . . . .}	62
" Boarding Mariah **DAUGHTERRY** from}		By rent of Land	50..00
25 Feby 1828 to 23 Feby 1829 . . . . }	48..00	Int on the Same from 1/st/ Jany 1829 to	
" Boarding Mariah [sic] **DAUGHTERRY** from 25/th/}		23/d/ Feby 1829	44
Feby 1828 to 23 Feby 1829 . . . . . }	48..00		
" Boarding Henry Mills **DAUGHTERRY**}			
from 25/th/ Feby 1828 to 23/d/ Feby 1829}	48..00		
amt pd Patrick **BRAWN** for a/c	17 58		
int on the Same from 2/d/ April 1828}			
to 23/d/ Feby 1829 . . . . }	76		
This amt pd **MORGAN & COWPER** for a/c	30..13		
	293..47¼		
	212 85¾		212 85¾
	80..61½	Titus **DARDEN**	

North Carolina }
Hertford County} November Court of Pleas &c 1830
This Account was returned to Court on oath By Titus **DARDEN** guard & ordered to be recorded
Test L. M. **COWPER** clk

Wm. M. **DAUGHTERY** heir/s/
Dr The orphans of William Mills **DAUGHTERRY** in acct current with Titus **DARDEN**

1830 To amt pd John **GATLING**	7..50	1830 By Hire of Negro **JIM**	46..00
Int from July 14/th/ 1829 to Feby 22}		" Int on the Same from January }	
1830 . . . . }	27	1/st/ 1830 to Feby 22/d/ 1830 . . . }	40¼
amt pd Patrick **BROWN**	8 57	" Hire of Negro bay **JACOB**	3₺.50
Int from September 24/th/ 1829		Int on Same from January 1/st/ To	
to February 22/d/ 1830	21¼	Feby 22/nd/ 1830	33¼
	16..55¼	Amts Carried over	85. 23½

(66) <u>37</u> Wm M **DAUGHTERY** heirs Dr The orphans of William Mills **DAUGHTERRY** in acct current with Titus **DARDEN**

1830 amt Brot over	16..55¼	amt Brotover	85..23½
To amt pd Thomas **SHAW**	13..05	To Hire of Negro [sic] & Two children	25
Int from Janry 18/th/ to Feby 22/d/ 1830	06½	" Hire of Negro **VINEY** & one chid	12 .00

(66) Wm M DAUGHTERY heirs (Cont.)

" amt pd Jeptha FAWLKS	10..25	Int on the Same from Jany 1/st/ 1830}	
Int from January 14/th/ to Feby 22/d/ 1830	06	to Feby 22/d/ 1830 . . . . }	10½
" amt pd Thos P. LITTLE	5..00	" Hire of Negro RACHEL	8..00
" amt pd Richd M. JOHNSON	3..38	Int on the Same from Jany 1/st/ to}	
" amt pc Eley CARTER	1..50	Feby 22/d/ 1830 . . . .}	07
" amt pc ditto ditto	1..50	" Hire of Negro CREECY & one child	12..00
" amt pc DAUGHTERRY & WEBB	3..66 2/3	Int on the Same from Jany 1/st/ }	
" amt pc ditto ditto	9 38	to Feby 22/d/ 1830 . . . . }	10½
" amt pc ditto ditto	2..75	" Hire of g Negro girl MANERVA	5..00
" amt pc ditto ditto	..88	Int on Same from Jany 1/st/ }	
" amt pc Robert S PARKER	1..08	to Feby 22/d/ 1830 . . . . }	04½?
" amt pc MORGAN & COWPER & Co	30..18	" Hire of Bay ABRAHAM	3..00
" amt pc Jeptha FAWLKS	3..75	Int on Same from Jany 1/st/ to Feby 22/d/ 1830	02½
" Boarding Marry DAUGHTERY from}		Rent of PORTER plantation	65..00
the 23/d Feby 1829 to Feby 22/d/ 1830 }	48..00	Int on Same from Jany 1/st/ to Feby 22/d/ 1830	56¾?
" Boarding Mariah DAWGHTERRY from}		Rent of manor plantation	50..00
23/d/ Feby 1829 to Feby 4/th/ 1830 }	45..33½	Int on Same from Jany 1/st/ to Feby 22/d/ 1830	43¾
" Boarding William Mills DAUGHTERY			
from 23.d/ of Feby 1829 to 23/d/ March 1829}	4..00		
" Keeping Negro Woman CLARRISA}			
& thre [sic] children for the year 1829 }	25..00		
Int on the Same from Janry}			
1/st/ to Feby 22/d/ 1830 }	21¾		
" amt pc the clerk Feby 23/d/ 1829	60		
Int on the Same to Feby 22/d/ 1830	03½		
By Balance due according			
to return made rendered Feby}			
23/d/ 1829/d/ . . . . }	80..61½		241..83½
To Int on the Same from Feby 23/d/}			Titus DARDEN
1829 to Feby 22/d/ 1830 }	4..83		
To 5 pr ct Commissions on $241..83½ cts	12..09		
	323 76¼		

North Carolonia [sic]}

Hertford County }   November Court of Pleas &c 1830

This Account was returned to Court on oath by Titus DARDEN guard & ordered to be recorded

Test. L. M. COWPER clk

Starkey S HARE

1823   Dr Starkey S HARE orphan In acct current with Thomas HARE his gua__

Feby 2/d. To 1 pr Shaes 1..50	1..50	1824	
March 2/H/ " 1 pr do do	1 50	Jay 1/st/ By hire of Negro man BEN	46..20
" 28 " 1 Trunk $1 & 2 pr socks @ 50/100	2 00	By do do bay JACK	28..25
Apl 1/st/ " pd William TRADERs acct	50	By do . .do man ARTHUR	20..00
" 11 " Cash pd John WHEELER for tuition	6..00	By do . do woman MARY	6..00
	$11..50	By Cash recd for Starky }	
amts Carried forward		SHARP former guardian . . .}	164..36
			264 81

---

(67) 38 Starkey s HARE Dr Starkey /s/ HARE orphan In acct current with Thomas HARE his guardian   Cr

amt Brat forward	$11.50	1824 amt Brot forward	264..81
May 9/th' To Cash p ncy?	..50	Jany 1/st/ By Cash recd from the Exect of}	
July 8/th " do pd J & E. WHEELER acct	2 06	George GORDAN his former guardian}	442..90
" " " do pd W B WISE & Co acct	4 38		
" " " do pd Mases CLEMENTS do	2..00		

(67) Starkey S **HARE** (Cont.)

Decr 22/d/ " do pd Charles **FREEMAN** for}
  keeping Negro waman **RACHALE** & 4}
children 2 years ending 1/st/ day of Jany 1824} 46..20

1824

Jany 1/st/ To Bord from 6th July to
      1/st/ of Octr   11..33
" Cash pd Wm J **RHODES** for keeping}
  Negro woman **PRISS** & 4 children}
  2 year/s/ ending 1/st/ day of Jany 1824} 50 00
Feby 18/th/ To Cash pd Mases **CLEMENTS**
    act   52..67
" To do pd William H **CLARY?** do   10..00
" To do pd P **BROWN**s act   23..00
" To do pd Benj/a/ M **EVANS** do   4..50
" To do pd T **O GRADY** for tuition   19..00
" To 5 pr cet commissions on $707..71   35..38
" To ballance due the ward   435..19
        707..71

By Ballance due the ward   707..71

Thos **HARE** $455..19

1824

July 1/st/ To Cash pd Peter **BUTT**s ac? for
    tuition   3 00
    Int on do do to Feby caurt   12
Novr 1/st/ To Cash pd Tuition   6 62½
    Int on do do do   12
" 8   To Cash pd E **MURPHY** acct   6..25
    Int on do do do   10
1825
Feby 5/th/ To Cash pd J. W. **SAUTHALL** act   1..00
"   To do gove him   4 00
" 7 To do pd Richd G **CAWPER**   5..61
" 9 To do pd for 1 quarters Tuition   6 62
" 25 To do pd Doct **O BRYAN** &
          PIPKIN acct   6..50
    To do pd **MORGAN & COWPER** do   3..25
    To do pd Benj/a/ m **EVANS** . . . do   7..25
    To do pd Elizabeth **GORDAN**s   do   18..57
    To do pd J. & E **WHEELER**s . . do   8..34
    To do pd Mases **CLEMENTS**   do   21..25
    To 6 months board from 1/st. April to   24..00
" to [sic] 1/st/ October . . . . . $4 }   [blank]
" 5 p cet commissions on $234..86   }   11 74
    To Ballance due the ward   439..20
        573..55

1824

Feby By Ballance due the ward up to Feby ct   435..19
  Int on ditto 12 months   26 11
By hire of Negro man **BEN**   48..75
By do . do boy **JACK**   37..50
By do . do man **ARTHUR**   18..00
By do . do Girl **MARY**   8..00

    573..55

By Ballance due the ward   439..20

Thos. **HARE**

---

(68) 39 Starkey S **HARE** Dr Starkey S **HARE** orphan In acct curent with Thomas **HARE** his guard

1825

Apl 17/th/ To Cash p ncy? 1..50 do
    pd tuition 5..50   7..00
    Int from 17/th/ April to Feby caurt 1826   ..35

1825

Sept 20/th/ By Ball ance [sic] due the ward}
up to Feby Caurt 1825 . . . . }   439..20
By Cash recd for the Sale of the}

(68) Starkey S **HARE** (Cont.)

Aug: 11/th/ To do $2 to do 30/¢/	2..30	5/th/ of the Roneoak Land . . }	1000..00
Int on do . do	..06	Int on the from [sic] 11/th/ Augt 1823 to The}	
Sept 20'th/ To Cash pd Wm J **RHODES** for}		Feby Caurt 1826	152..50
keeping Negro woman **PRISS** & 5 Children}	35 00	By Hire of Negro man **BEN**	40 00
Int on do	..93	By Hire of do boy **JACK**	40..00
To Cash pd Cast & Charges}		By do do man **ARTHUR**	18..00
in division of the Roan?eoak Lands}	32..90	By do do girl **MARY**	11..00
Int on do up to Feby Caurt	83		
Int on the above Sum from 15/th/}			
August 1824 until 20 of Sept 1825}	3..03		
28 To Cash pd **MARGAN & CAWPER** act	5..51		
To do pd John **WHEELERs** do	2..13		
Int on do	19		
Oct 1/st/ To Cash pd Benj/a/. M. **EVANS** acct	15 88		
" To do Edward **MURPHY** do	10..75		
To do for 1 Trunk	3..00		
To do pd Martha J. **DARDEN** act	3..50		
Int on the above act	..83		
6 To Cash pd Warrenton & Hillsborough	19..58		
To do pd Doct J **ROGER/S/** for 3? months			
board	30 00		
To do pd da for Tuition	6..00		
To do pd yau	5..00		
1826 Int on the above accts	1..27		
Feby 17/th/ To Cash pd **MORGAN &**			
COWPER act	72..10		
To do pd P **BROWNs** acct	54..94		
To do pd Board & Tuition &}			
Hills borrugh [sic] }	80..00		
To 5 pr ct commissions on $1654..58	82..72		
due the ward	1224..90		
	1700..70		1700..70

By ballance due the ward up to}
Feby Caurt 1826 . . . . }   1224..90

Thos **HARE**

1826		By ballance due the Ward up to}	
march 27 To Cash pd Charles **FREEMAN**		Feby Caurt 1826 . . . . }	1224..90
for keeping Negro Woman		12 months Int on do	73..49
RACHEL & Children for 1824 85$	55 00	1827	
Int on do up to Feby caurt 1827	3 03	Feby 25/th/ By Hire of Negro Man **ARTHUR**	18..00
May 10.th/ To Cash Sent yau to Hillsborough	10..00	By do do **BEN**	45..00
To Int on do ---------	48	By Do do **JACK**	42..50
June 17.th/ To do pd yau	41 00	By do do girl **MARY**	16..00
Int on do ----------	1..70		1419..89
July 3/d/ Cash pd yau	51..50		
Int on do ----------	2..00		
8 To Cash pd Mr/s/ **YANCY**	48 50		
Int on do ----------	1 79		
	215..00	amts Carred forward	

---

(69) 40 Starkey S **HARE** Dr Starkey S **HARE** orphan In acct current with Thomas **HARE** his guardian

amt Brot forward	$215..00	amt Brot forwd	$1419..89
Nov 12/th/ To Cash Sent to oxford	20..00		

(69) Starkey S **HARE** (Cont.)

Int on do -------	35	
To for [sic] Exepences & /going/ coming from oxford	5..00	
Int on do ---------	..09	
Decr 12/th/ To Cash pd Edward **MURPHY** acct	14 75	
1827 Int on do	..18	
Jany 7/th/ To Cash pd do do	..88	
Feby 24/th/ " Cash pd P **BROWN**s do	14..67	
" Commissions at 5 pr ct on $392..42	19..62	
" Ballance due the ward	1129 89	
	1419..89	

	1419 39
By Ballance due the ward up to}	
Feby Caurt 1827 ------------- }	1129 .35
Thos **HARE**	

1827

Feby 26/th/ To Cash pd David **MITCHELL**s act	28..50	
" Int on do 12 months	1..71	
April 2/d/ " Cash----- -----	75	
May 12/th/ " do ---- do	1..00	
Sept 28/th/ " Cash pd bill clerk & master	32..50	
" Int on do -----------	81	
Deçr 6/th/ " Cash pd Nancy **YANCY** acct	4..25	
" Int on do ----------	06	
9 " Cash pd Midwifes fee	2..00	
" do pd for keeping **PRISS** & children	25..00	
Int on do -------------	37½	
1828		
Jay 12/th/ To Cash pd Edward **MURPHY** act	14 62½	
Int on do -----------	..20	
" Cash ------------	39½	
Feby 1/st/ " do	..75	
25 " Cash pd Smith **FREEMAN** for keeping Negro **RACHAL** & 5 Children	30..00	
27 To cash pd Jacob **HOREP**s? acct	2..85	
5 p cet Commission on $336..02	16..80	
To ballance due the ward	1156..05	
	1319..61	

By Ballance due the ward up to}	
Feby Caurt 1827 ------------- }	$1129..35
By Int on do 12 months	67..76
By Hire Negro Man **ARTHUR**	17 00
By do do **BEN**	45 00
By do do **JACK**	42..50
By do do girl **MARY**	18..00

	1319. 61
By ballance due the Ward up to}	
February Caurt 1828 }	1156. 05
Thas. **HARE**	

1828 March 22/d/ To Cash pd Benja **EVANS** dec/d/ act	21..06	
Int on do to Feby Caurt 1829	1..25	
May 16/th/ To do pd John **WHEELER**s act	..30	
" To do pd P. **BROWN**s do	89..92	
int on do ---------------	4..50	
22 To Cash pd **MORGAN** & **COWPER** do	94..18	
Int on do -----------------	4..75	
	215..96	

By ballance due the ward up}		
to February Caurt 1828 . . }		1156..05
By Int on do 12 months		69..56
By Hire of Negro Man **ARTHUR**		15..00
By do ----- do **JACK**	42..50	
By do ----- do **BEN**		37..50
By Hire of Negro girl **MARY** 6 By Hire of do $16		22..00
amts carried f over [sic]		1348 41

(70) 41 Starkey S. HARE Dr Starkey S. HARE orphan in act current with Thomas HARE his gu___

	amt Brot over	215 96	amt Brot over	1348..41
July 3/c/	To Cash --------------	1 00		
" 26	To do pd Doct BORLAND act	6..50		
	Int on do -------	..22		
Novr 15/th/	To Cash p ncy?	50		
24	To do pd Richd G COWPER Shff	87 84		
	Int on do -------	1 31		
	To Cash pd H W LONG	4..00		
	Int on do -------	06		
Decr 15	To Cash -----------	4..00		
23	" do pd Elizabeth CALESON act	3..00		
	Int on do --------	10		

1829
Jany 4/th/ To Cash pd Mr P BROWN for}
keeping RASHAL & children for 1828 }   30..00
Int on do -------   ..30
Feby 3/1/ To Cash pd MURPHY &
CARTERs act   13..00
To do pd Z? BERRYs acct   2..50
20 To pd Mases CLEMENTS do   3..00
To do pd O BRYANs & PIPKINs do   3..25
To george DUNN act   12..00
To keeping PRISS & children   25..00
To 12 months Board   60..00
  5 pr ct commissions on $665..90   33..29
  To Ballance due the Ward   841..58
      1348..41   1348..41

By ballance due the Ward up to}
February Caurt 1829 . . . }   841..58
      Thas HARE

North Carolina }
Hertford Caunty} November Caurt of Pleas &c 1830
These Accaunts were returned to Caurt on oath by Thamas HARE guardd? &
ordered to Recorded [sic]   Test L M COWPSOR [sic] clk

Inventory of the amt Recd of John WINBORNE as an admr of Jaseph PERRY decd due
heirs of Said decd

	Peston PERRY ---------	$ 57..56
	Mary PERRY -----	57 56
Names of the Negraes	Patterick PERRY	57..56
TRECY STEPHEN	Jaseph PERRY	57..56
PETER NANCY	Elizabeth PERRY	57..56
DAN TILDY	John D. PERRY	57..56
NAT JANE	her	345..36

North Carolina }
Hertford Caunty} November Caurt of Pleas &c 1830}
This return was made to Caurt on oath by Agatha PERRY guard & order [sic] to be recorded
return made by Agatha X PERRY guardian
to Novr Term 1830   mark
      Test L. M. COWPER clk

1829 Charles SKINNER
      Dr Charles SKINNER minor In acct With John WADDILL guardian
April 23/d/ To Cash advanced yau   5..00
      Int to Feby ct 1830 ------   25
      amt carred forward $5..25

(71) 42 Charles SKINNER Dr Charles SKINNER minor In acct With Jno WADDILL guardian

amt Brot forward	5..25	By this amt due my Ward }	
Augt 9/th/ To pd Edward S JEGITTS for}		at Feby Ct 1829 --------- }	1465 .23
taylaring [sic] & Int to Feby Caurt 1830 }	1..31	Int on Said amt to Feby ct 1830	87 91
15/th/ To pd Miss Sidney THOMPSONs}		By hires & rents for 1829	348 25
act & Int to Feby Caurt }	2 08		
30 To Cash advanced yau $5 Int up}			
To Feby Caurt 1830 }	5 22		
June 15/th/ To pd Mr KINGs fee for }			
services as dancing master and Int up }			
to Feby Caurt 1830 . . . . . }	10..40		
Augt To pd part of Mr HILs? act for }			
tuition & Int to Feby Caurt 1830 . }	21..15		
Sept 22/d/ To Cash advanced yau to defray			
yaur expences at Prineton $2..50 }			
Int on Same to Feby ct 1830 6 25}	256..25		
Oct 6/th/ To pd James CAMBELLs act}			
for Sham?aking & Int }	1..80		
To pd Eli CARTERs act for}			
Shaemaking & Int }	6..30		
To pd part of George SPIRES act}			
for board & Int to Feby ct }	51..20		
Sept 20/th/ To pd Geo DUNNs ditto for}			
taylaring & Int to Feby caurt }	5..15		
Novr 14/th/ To pd Edward S JEGITTS }			
act for Tal?yloring & Int . . . . . }	4..30		
To pd Jno BEAMAN act for}			
old Books Coffin & Int }	4..04		
1830			
Jany 1/st/ To pd Jno W. SAUTHALLs act}			
25..85 & Int to Feby Ct 1830 . . . . }	26..11		
" 1/st/ pd Jeremiah BEALE for keeping}			
expensive Negraes in 1829 & Int to Feby}			
ct 1830 . . . . }	30..15		
To 5 p cet commission $866..31) }			
eight hundred & Sixty Six dallar/s/}			
& thirty one cts being the amt of }			
recpts & expenditures for the }			
last year including the Int on the }			
amt due my Ward at Feby ct 1829 }	43..31		
	474..03	due my Ward at Feby ct 1830	1427..?6

North Carolina }
Hertford Caunty} November Caurt of Pleas &c 1830
This Accaunt was returned to Caurt on oath by John WADDILL guard
& order [sic] to be recorded

Jn/o/ WADDILL

Test L. M. COWPER clk

(72) 43 Levina ASKEW

Dr Levima ASKEW orphan of D. ASKEW decd In act with Aaron ASKEW Jun guar

1831

Jany 1/st/ To Cash pd Abner HARRELL			
p'act	5 06¼	By Ballance due the orphan at my return	
Interest on ditto up to Feby ca?t 1831	04¾	to Feby Caurt 1830	209_16
Feby 13/th/ To Cash pd Mary ASKEW for		Interest on ditto up to ditto	12_54
12 months Board	36..00	By yaur half of Negro hire}	
Interest an ditto up to ditto	..15	for payl 1831 . . . . }	94_62¼?

(72) Levina ASKEW (Cont.)

1830		Int on ditto up to this return	94
Decr 4/th/ To p? the Taxes pd Sheff		By yaur half rents of Lands	
of Hertford for 1829}	2..08	for 1830	10..00
Int on ditto	..11	Interest on ditto from 1/st/ Jany}	
1831		1830 To Feby Court 1831 . . }	09
Feby 2£/th/ To Cash pd Alexander O			
ASKEW Schooling ------------	9..00		
1830			
Augr 1£/th/ To Cash pd Shff of Bertie			
for Taxes	1 22½		
Int on ditto	03½		
To recording this account	..40		
To 5 pr cet commissions on the money}			
expended and recd as pr Negro hire}			
& Int Say on $171..90 }	8..59		
To Ballance due the orphan	264..66		
	327..36	1831	327..36
		Feby 28/th/ By Ballance due the orphan	264..66
		Aaron O ASKEW guardian	

Emily ASKEW

1831   Dr Emily ASKEW orphan of David ASKEW decd In acct with Aaron ASKEW Junr gua_d

Jany 1/st/ To Cash pd Abner HARRELL		By Ballance due the orphan at my	
pr act	4..85	return to February Court 1830 . ..205..10	
Interest on ditto up to the return	[blank]	Interest on ditto up to Feby ct 1831 12..30?	
1830		By yaur half of Negro hire for 1830	
Augr 1£/th/ To Cash pd Shff of Bertie for		payl 1/st/ Jany 1831	94 62½
Taxes	1 22½	Int on ditto	94
Int on ditto	03½	By yaur half of rents of Land for 1830	
Decr 4/th/ To Cash pd Shff of Hertford for		payl . . . . ditto	10..00
Taxes	2..08	Int on ditto	09½
Int on ditto	..11		
1831			
Feby 1£/th/ To Cash pd Mary ASKEW			
for board	36..00		
" Int on ditto	..15		
28 To Cash pd Alexander O }			
ASKEW for Schooling . .}	9..00		
To recording this account	..40		
To 5 p ct commissions on the}			
money Expended & recd for}			
the? Negro hire Int & [sic]}	8..59		
	62..44		
To Ballance due the orphan	260..52		
	322..96	1831	322 96
		Feby 28/th/ By Ballance due the orphan	260..52
		Aaron O ASKEW guardian	

North Carolina }
Hertford Caunty} Febyary Caurt of Pleas &c 1830 [sic]
These Accaunts were returned to Caurt on oath by Aaron ASKEW guard & ordered
to be Recorded   Test. L. M. COWPER

Rebeckah BRITT   guardian

1830   Dr Rebeckah BRITT orphan of Wm D BRITT ded in act with Davis BRYANT
March 11/th/ To Cash pd J. SAUTHALL acct $ 9..87½

(72) Rebeckah BRITT (Cont.)

To Int on 9 87½ for 11 mo & 2 days	57½
amt Carried forward	10..45

---

(73) <u>44</u> **Rebeckah BRITT**

Dr Rebeckah **BRITT** orphan of Wm D **BRITT** decd in act with Davis **BRYANT** guardian   Cr

Amt Brat forward	$ 10..45	By amt due the ward Feby 21/st/ 1830	12..63
To Cash pd J **SCOTT** acct	4..02¾	By Int on $12..63 for one year	95¾
To Interest on $4..02¾ pr 11 mo & 20 days	24	By her part of rent of Land	35..25
Augt 29/th/ To Cash pd clerks ticket & ferriage ..50			
1831			
Feby 28/th/ To Cash pd R W **JOHNSON**s a/c 10..93			
To Cash pd Board Last year	20..00		
To Commissons on $35..25	1..76		
To Cash pd for Taxes of Land	3..57		
	51..47¼		48..63¾
	48 63¾	Davis **BRYANT** guardian	
Due the guardian	2 83½		

Margaret BRITT

1830   Dr Margaret **BRITT** orphan of Wm D **BRITT** decd in acct with Davis **BRYANT** guardian

March 11th/ To Cash pd J. **SAUTHALL**s act 4..17		By amt due the ward Feby 21/st/ 1830	56..90
1831		By Int on $56.90 for one year . . .	3..41
Feby 28/th/ To Cash Int on $4 17 for 11 m/o/		By her part of rent of Land	35..25
& 21 days	..23		
To Cash pd clerks ticket & ferriage	..50		
To do pd R. W. **JOHNSON**s a/c	1..50		
To Cash pd Board for last year	20..00		
To Commissions on $35..25	1..76		
To Cash pd for Tax of Land	3 57		95 56
	31..73		31..73

North Carolina }
Hertford Caunty} February Caurt of Pleas &c 18301   Due the ward   63..83
This Accaunt was returned to Caurt on oath by Davis **BRYANT** guard & ordered to be recorded   Davis **BRYANT** guardian
                                        Test. L. M. **COWPER** clk

---

Alexander BRITT

1830   Dr Alexander **BRITT** orphan of Wm D **BRITT** decd in acct with E D **BRITT** guardian   Cr

Augt 25/th/ To Cash pd clk for return &}		1830	
renewing guardian Bond }	1..15	Augt 25/th/ By Bal due last return	52..59
1831		6 mo Int on do . . .	1..57
Jany 1/st/ To Cash pd for Hat & Shaes	2..00	1831	
" 25/th/ To 1 pr Shaes -------	1..25	Feby 28/th/ By his proportional part}	
Feby 18 To Cash pd C **ROCHELL** for		for rent of Land 1830 }	35..25
tuition	7..29		89 41
" 22 To pd Elizabeth **BRITT** for 7 mo			
board	15 68		
25 To Cash pd J **SCOTT** & Co act	2..66		
To pd Taxes on Land . . .	3..55		
To 5 pr ct Commissions on recepts &}			
Expenditures . . . . }	3..50		
To Ballance due the orphan	52..32		
	89..41		89..41

North Carolina }

Ballance due the orphan 28/th/
February 1831 E. D. **BRITT** Guardian

(73) Alexander **BRITT** (Cont.)
Hertford County} February Court of Pleas &c 18301
This Account was returned to Court on oath by Elisha D **BRITT** guardd & ordered to be
Recorded   Test L M **COWPER** clk

---

(74) 45 James H **BRITT** Dr James H **BRITT** orphan of Wm D **BRITT** decd in act with

1830	E D **BRITT** Guardian		1830		
Augt 25/th/ To Cash pd clk for return &}			Augt 25/th/ By Balance due Last return	$	48..79
renuing Guardian Bond }		1..15	1830 6 m/os/ Int on ditto		1..46
Sept To 3 mo/s/ board @ $4		12..00	Feby 28/th/ By 1/5 part for rent of Land 1830		35..25
1831					85..50
Feby 28/th/ To Cash pd Tax on Land		3..55			
To Commissions on rects &					
Expenditures		2..45			
		19..15			
To Bal due the orphan		66..35			
		85..50			

Balance due the orphan

North Carolina }   28 Feby 1831   66..35
Hertford County} February Court of Pleas &c 1831   E. D. **BRITT** Guardian
This Account was returned to Court on oath by Elisha D **BRITT** guard & ordered to be
Recorded   Test. L. M. **COWPER** clk

George **BARKER** Dr George **BARKER** orphan of John **BARKER** decd in acct with James **RAWLS** guard   Cr

1830 To recording this acct . .•. .	40	By Balance due the orphan at }	
Decr 2/d/ To Cash pd James L **GRIMES**	2..50	my return to August Court last including}	
Int on ditto up to this return	03	Negro hire & rents of Lands . . . . }	165..87
To Board & clothing from augt ct		Int on ditto from August Court last}	
last up to this return 28 Feby 1831	20..00	up to this return . . . . }	4..97
To 5 p ct commissions on the mony			
Expended and recd as Int &c	1 39		
	24 32		
To Ballance due the orphan	146..52		
	170..84	1831	170..84
		Feby 28/th/ Ballance due the orphan	146..52
		James **RAWLS** guardian	

John **BARKER** Dr John **BARKER** orphan of John **BARKER** decd in acct with James **RAWLS** guardian

To recording this acct	40	By Ballance due the orphan at my }	
To Board & clothing from august court		return to august Court 1830 including}	
1830 up to Feby Court 1831	20..00	Negro hire rents of Land &c . . . }	168..01
To 5 p ct commissions on the many}		Int on ditto up to Feby Court 1831	5..04
Expended & recd as pr Int & [sic]	1.27		
	21..67		
By Ballance due the orphan	151..38		
	173..05		173..05
		1831	
		Feby 28/th/ By Ballance due the orphan	151..38
		James **RAWLS** guardian	

North Carolina }
Hertford County} February Court of Pleas &c 1831
This Account was returned to Court on oath by James **RAWLS** guard & ordered
to be Recorded   Test L M **COWPER** clk

---

(75) 46 Watson **COLESON** Dr Watson **COLESON** orphan in acct current with John **PARKER** guardian   Cr

(75) Watson COLESON (Cont.)

1830			1830	
Augt term To natice	90		Augt By Ballance due return}	
Bond	60		August Term 1830 . . . }	207..21
Return	..40		Interest on ditto Six months	6..21
Int on ditto	05			213..42
	1..95			1..95
	211..47		Ballance due Feby Term 1831 . . .	211..47
	213..42		John **PARKER**	

North Carolina }
Hertford Caunty} Febyary Caurt of Pleas &c 1831
This Accaunt was returned to Caurt on oath by John **PARKER** guard & ordered to be
Recorded   Test. L. M. **COWPER** clk

═══

Wm Mills **DAUGHTERRY**s heirs

Dr The orphans of William Mills **DAUGHTERRY** in acct current
With Titus **DARDEN**   Cr

1831 T [sic]			1831	
To amount Francis **MURPHY** for tuition	2 35		By Hire of Negro man **JIM**	45..00
Int on Same from 3 Jany 1829}			Interest on Same from 1/st/ Jany 1831}	
to 28 Feby 1831 . . . . . }	24¼		28 Feby 1831 . . . . }	45
To amt pd R G **CAWPER** Shff}	7 05		By Hire of boy **JACOB**	35..00
as p rect . . . . }			Int on Same from 1/st/ Jany 1831 to 28	
Int on Same from 24 March 1830}			Feby 1831	..35
to 28 Feby 1831 . . . . . . }	38½		By Hire of Negro girl **RACHEL**	10..25
To amt pd Miss Lauisa **JAMES**}			Int on Same from 1/st/ Jany 1831 to 28	
as p rects . . . . }	32..30		Feby 1831	..10¼
Int on Same from 18 Decr 1830}			By Hire of Negro woman **GREACY**	13..27
to 28 February 1831 . . . .}	37		Interest on Same from 1/st/ Jany 1831 to}	
To amt pd Washington **SMITH** as p rects	29 00		28 Feby 1831 . . . . . . }	13½
Int on Same from 14/th/ Decr 1830 to}			By Hire of Negro girl **MANERVA**	11 00
28 February 1831 . . . . . . }	..36		Interest on Same from 1/st/ Jany 1831 to}	
To amt pd Washington **SMITH** as pr rect	25..00		Feby 1831 ----------- }	11¾
Int on Same from 14 Decr 1830}			By Hire of Negro girl **ELIZA**	1..50
To 28 Feby 1831 . . . . }	..31¼		Interest on Same from 1/st/ Jany 1831}	
To amt pd Robert **SMITH** as pr rects	7..38		to 28 Feby 1831 . . . . . . }	01½
Int on Same from 3/d/ April 1830}			By Hire of Bay **ABRAM**	2..00
to 28/th/ Feby 1831 . . . . }	..40		Interest on Same from 1/st/ Jany 1831 to}	
To amt pd R G **COWPER** as pr recet	5 18		28 Feby 1831 . . . . }	02
Int on Same from 12 Jany 1829}			By rent of **PORTER** Plantation	70..00
to 28 Feby 1831 ---------------- }	21		Interest on Same from 1/st/ Jany 1831 to}	
To amt pd Lewis M **COWPER** as pr rects	2..50		28 Feby 1831 . . . . . . }	70
Int on Same from 4 Nov 1830 to 28 Feby 1831	03½		By rent of Manor plantation	49..99
To amt pd John W. **SOUTHALL**	50		Interest on Same from 1/st/ Jany 1831}	
Int on Same from 4 Octr 1830			to 28 February 1831 . . . . }	..50
to 28 Feby 1831 . . .	01			240..39½
To amt pd Matthias **WILLIAMS**	15..00			
Int on Same from 3/d/ Jany 1831 to}				
28 Feby 1831 }	15			
To amt pd Dr James C **HARRISSON**	2 50			
Int on Same from 3/d/ Jany 1831 to 28/th/}				
Feby 1831 }	02¼		amts Carried over	240..39½
	131..45¾			

(76) 47 William M **DAUGHTERY**s heirs Dr The orphans of William Mills **DAUGHTERY** in acct Current
with Titus **DARDEN**   Cr

amt Brot over	131 45¾	amt Brot over	240 39½
To amt pd Lewis M **COWPER**	20 77		
Int on Same from 25/th/ Feby 1831} to 28 Feby 1831 . . . . }	[blank]		
To amt pd John W **SAUTHALL**	26..72		
Int on Same from 25 Feby 1831} to 28 Feby 1831 . . . . . . }	[blank]		
To amt pd R G **COWPER** as pr rect	12..22		
Int on Same from 25 Feby 1831} to 28 Feby 1831 . . . . . . }	[blank]		
To amt pd James **SCOTT**	1..25		
Int on Same from 5 Nov 1830 to 28} Feby 1831 . . . . }	[blank]		
To keeping Negro woman **CLARRISA** & 3 children for the year 1830	25..00		
Int on Same from 1/st/ Jany 1831 to} 28 February 1831 . . . . . . }	..25		
To Boarding Mary **DAUGHTERY** 6 mo up to this 28/th/ Feby 1831	24..00		
To Boarding Mariah **DAUGHTERY**} 5 mo/s/ up to 28 Feby 1831 . . . }	20..00		
	261..67		
Ballance due according to return} rendered Feby 22/d/ 1830 . . }	71..93½		
Interest on Same from from [sic] 22 Feby} 1830 to 28 Feby 1831 . . . . }	4..37½		
5 pr ct Commissions on $240..39¼ cts	12 00		
	349..92		240..39½

North Carolina }   Titus **DARDEN**
Hertford County} February Court of Pleas &c 1831
This Account was returned to Court on oath by Titus **DARDEN** guard & ordered to be
Recorded   Test. L. M. **COWPER** clk

Thomas J. **DEANS**

1831   Dr Thomas J **DEANS** orphan of James **DEANS** decd in acct with Isaac **CARTER** guardian

Feby 24/th/ To Cash pd George **SPIRES** for board	16 14	1830	
		Augt 23/d/ By Ballance due augt 23/d/ 1830	425..14
To Interest on ditto	25	Interest up to Feby 23/d/ 1831	12..75
To Cash pd Mr Wm **NIEL** for tuition	8 00		437..89
To Intest on do	..12		27 19
To pd David **CROSS** for Taxes	1..00	Ballance due Feby 23/d/ 1831	$410..70
To pd for this present return	40	E E Isaac **CARTER** guard	
To Commissions 5 p cet	1.29		
	27..19		

Daniel **DEANS**   guardian

Dr Daniel **DEANS** orphan of James **DEANS** decd in act with Isaac **CARTER**

To Cas [sic] pd David **CROSS** for taxes	1..00
Commissions	..05
amt carred forward	$1..05

(77) 48 Daniel **DEANS**

Dr Daniel **DEANS** orphon of James **DEANS** decd in act with Isaac **CARTER** guardian Cr

amt Brot forward	1..05	By Ballance due augt 23/d/ 1830	305..35
To Cash pd for this present	40	Interest up to Feby 23/d/ 1831	9..17
		By Cash recd for rent of Land	
		Jany 1831	[blank]
		Interest up to Feby 23/d/ 1831	7..75
			6
			322..33
	$ 1..45		1 45
		Ballance due Feby 23/d/ 1831	321..38

North Carolina }   E E Isaac **CARTER** guard

Hertford Caunty} February Caurt of Pleas &c 1831

These Accounts were returned to Caurt on oath by Isaac **CARTER** guardian & ordered to be Recorded

Test. L. M. **COWPER** clk

===

Celia **GREEN**

1830   Dr Celia **GREEN** orphan of Isaac **GREEN** dec/d/ in a/c Current with Watson **LEWIS** guard

Augt 24/th/ To Cash pd for Bond natice		1830		
& return	1..70	Augt 24/th/ By Ballance due the orphan	72..07	
" 31 To 2 yds Catton Cambrick @ 25	..50	By Lumber	1..25	
Nov 6 To 1 Leghorn Hat	6..00			
" " " " Band Box	75			
" " " 3 yds Ribband @ 40/¢/	1..20			
" 1½ do do @ 25¢	..38			
Wire & Tasle [sic]	25			
1 belt Ribband	..25			
1 Hkff $1 1 Cape 50	1..50			
1 p gloves 50/¢/ 1 Hkff 25/¢/	75			
	11 08			
1831				
Feby 9/th/ To 9 yds Brase @ 80/¢/	7 20			
To 1½ do Bro Halland @ 31½				
2 yds brade 12½}	82			
1 do Catton 20/¢/ 3 hanks Silk 20/¢/	40			
1 p prume [or prunel] Shaes	1..63			
2 yds Ribband @ 30/¢/ 2 do @ 25/¢/	1..10			
2 doz buttons @ 25 1¼ do hooks				
& ys [sic] @ 25/¢/	75			
Commissions on $98..50 @ 5 pr ct	4..92			
To Ballance due the orphan	43..22			
	73..32		73..32	
		By Ballance due the orphan	43..22	

Rect of Watson **LEWIS** guardian of Celia **GREEN** now my wife forty three dallar/s/ & twenty two cents in full of the above accaunt   Evret **PILAND**

Witness   Watson **LEWIS**

M. H. **JERNIGAN**

North Carolina }

Hertford Caunty} February Caurt of Pleas &c 1831

This Accaunt was returned to Caurt on oath by Watson **LEWIS** Guard & at the Same time the Receipt from Evrett **PILAND** to Watson **LEWIS** was proveed in open Caurt by the oath of Miles H. **JERNIGAN** Subscribing Witness thereto & ordered to be Recorded

Test. L. M. **COWPER** Clk

===

(78) 43 Sindy R & M HOLLOMON

Dr Sindy Renea & Mallchoa [sic] HOLLOMON orphan of Jacob HOLLOMON dec/d/ In
1830   acct with Miles H. JERNIGAN guardian

Novr 9/th/ To Cash pd clerk to return			By Ballance due the orphans at }	
guardian bond	..60		my return to Augt Caurt 1830 . }	59 06
To Recording this account	..60		Int on ditto up to Feby caurt 1831	1..77
To Cash pd Alexander O. ASKEW}				
for Schooling Renea . . . . }	1..40			
Commissions on $4..37 @ 5 pr ct	..21			
To Ballance due the orphan	58..02			
	60..83			60..83
			By Ballance due the orphans	58..02

North Carolina }
Hertford Caunty} February Caurt of Pleas &c 1831
This Accaunt was returned to Caurt on oath by Miles H JERNIGAN guardian & ordered to be
Recorded   Test. L. M. COWPER clk

          M. H. JERNIGAN guardian

Wm P. JENKINS

1830   Dr William P JENKINS orphon of Charles JENKINS dd [sic] in acct with Michael DEANS his guard

Novr Term To Cash pd the clerk pr		1831	Cr
Guardian Bond	30	Feby 28/th/ By this amt recd of Silas }	
To Cash pd the clerk pr Return to}		PARKER Executor of Thamas DEANS}	
Feby Caurt 1831 . . . . . . }	..60	decd who was the former Guardian . . }	152..22
	90		
	152..22		
	151..32	By Ballance due the orphan Feby ct 1831	151..32

          Michael DEANES

Charles S JENKINS

1830   Dr Charles S JENKINS orphan of Charles JENKINS dd in acct with Michael DEANS his guard

Novr c To Cash pd clerk pr guardian Bond	30	1831	Cr
To " " " p return to Feby}		Feby 28/th/ By this amt re/d/ of Silas }	
Caurt 1831 . . . . }	60	PARKER Executor of Thomas DEANS}	
	90	ded who was the former Guardian . . }	176..05
	176..05		
	175..15	Ballance due the orphan Feby ct 1831	175..15

North Carolina }
Hertford Caunty} February Caurt of Pleas &c 1831
This Accaunt was returned to Caurt on oath by Michael DEANES guard & ordered to be
Recorded   Test. L. M. COWPER clk

          Michael DEANES

Penelope JENKINS

                                                           guardian
1830   Dr Penelope JENKINS orphan of Benjamin JENKINS dec/d/ In acct with Henry D JENKINS

Decr 25/th/ To Cash pd Robt COBB Tuition	8 70	1831	
1831		Feby 24/th/ By Ballance due on return}	
Jany 1st/ To 12 months Board 1830	48..00	to augt Caurt 1830 . . . .}	463..87
" 8 yds Striped Clath for frocks		" Int thereon 6 mo up to this time	13..93
@ 25/¢/	2..00	" Hire of JIM 1830	40..00
" making dress	38	" " BETHA "	18 00
Feby 24/th/ " Cash pd Jas SCOTT & co		" " LUCY "	28 00
fo [sic] Books	5..02	" " TONY "	18..00
" do pd clk for returning this act	40	Int from 1/st/ Jany up to 23 Feby 1831	..90
" " " " notice to return	90		582..71
Commissions on R & expenditures			
amtg to 5 p ct}	9 21		

(78) Penelope JENKINS (Cont.)

Ballance due	508..10	
	582..71	amts carried forward

---

(79) 50 Penelope JENKINS

Dr Penelope JENKINS orphan of Benjamin JENKINS decd In acct with Henry D JENKINS guardian

			Cr
amt Brat forward	582..71	Amt Brat forward	582. 71
		By Balance due ward this 24/th/ Feby 1831	$508. 10

North Carolina }

E E H. D. JENKINS guardian

Hertford Caunty} February Caurt of Pleas &c 1831

This Accaunt was returned to Caurt on oath by Henry D JENKINS guardian & ordered to be recorded

Test. L. M. **COWPER** Clk

1830 Winborne JENKINS   guardian

Decr 25/th/ [sic]   Dr Winborn JENKINS orphan of Benjamin JENKINS decd In acct with Henry D JENKINS

To Cash pd Robt **COBB** Tuition	8..00	1831 Feby 24/th/ By Balance due on return}		
1831		to augt Ct 1830 . . . . }	39..43	
Jany 1/st/ To 12 mo Board 1830	48..00	int thereon to Feby Caurt 1831 6 mo	1..20	
" " 2½ yds ct? @ 50/¢/ 2½ yds		By Hire of **NAT** 1830	45..75	
do @ 31¼	1..95	**EDITH** & Child	8..00	
" " 4¼ yds @ 20/¢/ 2 yds Wesced?		**EVRITT**	6..00	
Do @ 30	1..45	Rent Land **WYNNS** place	21..10	
" " 2¼ " @ 20/¢/ 2 pr Socks @ 25/¢/	95	" Neck field	12 00	
making 2 vest @ 20/¢/ Do 2 Jackets		" hire **CELIA**	5..00	
@ 25/¢/	90	Int from 1/st/ Jany up to 24/th/ Feby 1831	.88	
Do 5 pr pantaloons @ 25/¢/	1..25			
Do 2 Shirts @ 25/¢/ 1 p Shaes 1.00	1..50			
Feby 24/th/ To Cash pd J. **SCOTT** & Co for				
Books	1..75			
Do " Clerk this return	40			
" " Natice to return				
this acct	..90			
Coms on R & expend amtg . .}				
to $167.04 @ 5 pr ct . . . .}	8..35			
Ballance due	63..92			
	139..37		139..37	

By Balance due the Ward this 24/th/ Feby 1831   63..92

E E H. D. **JENKINS** guardn

North Carolina }

Hertford Cuunty} February Caurt of Pleas &c 1831

This Accaunt was returned to Caurt on oath by Henry D. JENKINS guard & order [sic] to be recorded

Test. L. M. **COWPER** clk

H & A & M LIVERMAN

1830   Dr Hartwell Aidement & Martha **LIVERMON** In a/c with Mat J **GRIFFITH** Jr Gn

Novr 27/th/ To Guardian Bond	..60		Cr
Hartwell **LIVERMON** To 1		By Cash	$186..15
Hat 16/6	2..75	" Interest on ditto from 26 day of augt}	
Aidement **LIVERMAN** To 1		1830 until Feby Term 1831 . . . . }	5..58
Hat 16/6	2..75	By Ballance due the orphans & debt?	191..73
Martha **LIVERMAN** To 1			
Bonnet 15/-	2..50		
" do do To 1 p Shaes 7/6	1..25		
	9 85		

(79) H & A & M **LIVERMAN** (Cont.)

By Ballance due the
orphans @ Contra   191..75
                          181..90

By Ballance due the orphans Feby Term 1831   181..90
                                Mat. J. **GRIFFITH** guardian

North Carolina }
Hertford County} February Court of Pleas &c 1831
This Account was returned to Court on oath by Mat J. **GRIFFITH** guard & ordered to be Recorded
                                Test. L. M. **COWPER** clk

---

(80) 51 Mary Jane **MONTGOMERY**

1831   Dr Mary Jane **MONTGOMERY** in a/c current with her guardn George W. **MONTGO** [sic]

Feby 25 To the ballance of Keeping Negro woman}
  ISABEL and Two Children **VENUS** &}
  BITHA and furnishing the Same from}
  August Court last up to the 1/st/ day Jany 1831}
    at Ten dallar/s/ p year . . . . .   3..33 1/3
  To Cash pd Clk for return made last augt}
  Court omited . . . .}   1..90
  To Cashpd Clk for this Return 40
  To Interest up 1/st/ Jany 1831 10
                                          5..73 1/3

1831
Feby 28/th/ By her undivided Interest
in three negroes one Woman **ISABED** and
2 Chldren **VENUS** & **BITHA** Supased
to be 2/3. By three hundred &
Eighteen Acres of Land

1831
Feby 28/th/ George W **MONTGOMERY** guardian

North Carolina }
Hertford County} February Court of Pleas &c 1831
This Account was Returned to Court on oath by George W **MONTGOMERY** guard & ordered
to be Recorded   Test. L. M. **COWPER** clk

Dossey **OUTLOW**

1830   Dr Dossey **OUTLOW** orphan of George **OUTLOW** decd. In acct with David O **ASKEW** guardn   Cr

May 6 To Cash pd Doct Geo **ASKEW**   8..65
  Interest on ditto up to this return   ..40
  27 To Cash pd William **NIELL** for Tuition 20..00
    Int on ditto 90
Augt 29"th/ To Cash pd Mr/s/ **YANCY**
    for Board   66..40
  "   "   Int on ditto 2 00
  "   "   To Cash let you have when went}
    on to North . . . .}   150..00
    Int on ditto . . . . . .   4..50
May 1/s/ To Cash let you have for
    packet money   10..00
    Int on ditto   45
Sept 8/th/ To Cash ditto ditto . . . .   2..00
    Int on ditto 05
Nov 20/th/ To Cash Sent you to Prinston}
    New Jersey for mail . . . .}   50 00
    Int on ditto   78
1831
Feby 5/th/ To a draft on Henry Marria **YONS**?}
    sent you to prinston New jersey p mail} 100..00
    Int on ditto 33
1830
Augt 27 To Cash pd William **NIAL**   11..31
    Int on ditto . . . . . .}   ..33
1831
Jany 16 To Cash pd Penelope **VANPELT**

Amt Brot up . . . .   226..72
Int on ditto 0 03
28 Cash pd Benj/a/ **WHITE** to keep
  Blind **PETER** . . . .   27..00
    Int on ditto 13¼
Feby 19/th/ To Cash pd Doct
    A **BOARDWELL**   3..00
  " 28 To Cash pd James **SCOTT**   2..75
  "   " To Cash pd Richard **JOHNSON**s   5..37½
  "   " To Cash pd **REA & CAMP**   3..00
1831 Feby Cash pd Patrick **BROWN**   4..51
1830 augt 25 To Cash pd Clerk for Bond
    Sa? fodl?   1..90
    To recording this acct pd clerk   40
1831 Jany 16/th/ To Cash pd B J **MONT-**}
  GOMERY to keep **MINY** & children } 22..50
  Intererest on ditto up to this return   14
  To keeping **SEAR** & children 1830   4..00
    Int on ditto ufrom 16 Jany 1831   ..02
                                        567..02
To 5 p ct Commissions on the money}
Expended and hire of Negraes Int   ]&c   45..16
To Ballance due the orphan   92..80
                                        704 98

Amt Carried forward

(80) Dossey OUTLOW (Cont.)

to keep negraes	23..75	
Int on ditto	16	

1830

Augt 26 To Cash pd Mases

CLEMENTS	2..00
Interest on ditto . . .	..06

1830

June 1/st/ To Cash pd John **SCOTT**

for making claths	5..00
Int on ditto	20

1831

Jany 1/st/ To Cash pd Abner

HARRELL	25..58
Int on ditto	..25
To Cash pd Watson	
LEWIS	6..97
	226..72

amt Carried up

---

(81) 52 Dossy OUTLOW

Dr D̲assy **OUTLOW** orphan of George **OUTLOW** decd In acct with David O **ASKEW** guard

Amt Brot forward	704..98	By Ballance due the orphan at February Caurt 1830 }	
		which was returned to August Caurt 1830 on accaunt}	
		of the records being distroyed and Interest Calculated }	
		up to August court 1830 . . . . }	368..78
		Interest on ditto from augt Caurt up to	
		to [sic] this return Feby Caurt 1831	11..16
		By hire of Negroes the year 1830 payl	
		the 16 of Jany 1831 -----------------------	323..00
		Int on ditto up to this return	2 14
	704 98		704..98
		1831	
		Feby 28/th/ By Ballance due the orphan	92..80

North Caralina }

Hertford Caunty} February Caurt of Pleas &c 1831

This Accaunt was returned to Caurt on oath by David O **ASKEW** guardian & ordered to be Recorded

David O **ASKEW** guardi̲n

Test. L. M. **COWPER** clk

Amon OVERTON   guarc

1830   Dr Amon **OVERTON** orphan of Elisha **OVERTON** decd In acct with Miles H **JERNIGAN**

Sept 10/th/ To 9 days board	1..20		Cr
Nov 9 To Cash pd Alexander O}		By Ballance due the orphan at my }	
ASKEW for Schooling}	3 00	return to AugustCaurt 1830 . . }	218..85
Int on ditto up to this return [blank]		Int on ditto up to Feby Caurt 1831	6..55
1830		by hire of Negro man **MEREDITH** for 1830	35..00
Augt 23/d/ To Cash pd Clerk to		Int on ditto from 1/st/ of Jany 1831 up to}	
renew guardian bond	60	this return . . . . }	..35
To recording this acct	40		
To 5 p cet Commissions			
on $47..11	2..35		
To Ballance due the orphan	253..21		
	260..76	1831	260..76
		Feby 28/th/ By Ballance due the orphan	253..21

North Caralina }

M. H. **JERNIGAN** Guardian

(81) Amon OVERTON (Cont.)
Hertford County} February Court of Pleas &c 1831
This Account was was [sic] returned to Court on oath by Miles H JERNIGAN Guard & ordered to be
Recorded   Test. L. M. COWPER clk

==

Aron CUTLOW

1830   Dr Aron OUTLOW orphan of Aron OUTLAW dec'd/ In act current with John DAWNING guard

		1831	Cr
Augt To Clerk fee returning Bond	1..80	Jany 4 By this Sum due the from [sic] Feby}	
To Commissions	09	Term 1830 }	115..08
1831		By up [sic] to Jany 4/th/ 1831	6..90
Jany 4 To Ballance due the orphan	140 909	By Negro hire 1830	20..00
	141..98		141..98
		By a ballance due the orphan	140..09

North Carolina }
Hertford County} February Court of Pleas &c 1831   John DAWNING guardian
This Account was returned to Court on oath by John DAWNING Guardian & ordered to be
Recorded   Test. L. M. COWPER clk

==

(82) 53 Mary Jane PERRY

Dr Mary Jane PERRY orphan of John W PERRY dec'd/ In acct with William SLAUGHTER gu___

			Cr
To Balance due the guardian on my} return to Feby Court 1830 . . . }	69..03	By yaur half of Negro hire for 1830}	
Interest on ditto up to this Return	4..14	payable the 4/th/ of January 1831 . }	42..50
1830		Interest on ditto up to this return	..35
Nov 22/d/ To yaur half of Taxes pd		By Yaur half rents of Land for 1830	2..50
Shff for 1829	1..74	Int on ditto	..02
Int on ditto	02	1831	
1831		Feby 28 To A Ballance due the Guardian	90..59
Jany 4/th/ To Yaur half of keeping			
RACHAL & 2 children for 1830}	12..50		
Int on ditto	..12		
To half of keeping PEGGY & 4			
children do	15..00		
Int on ditto	15		
Feby 25 To Cash pd J S GRIMES for			
Schooling	2..50		
To recording this Account	..40		
To Board & clothing for 1830 up to			
this return	25 00		
To 5 p cet commissions on the money			
Expended & Negro hire Int &c Say			
on $107..15	5..35		
	135..96	1831	135..96
		Feby 28 By a? Ballance due the Guardian	90..59
		William SLAUGHTER guardian	

North Carolina }
Hertford County} February Court of Pleas &c 1831
This Account was return [sic] to Court on oath by William SLAUGHTER Guardian & ordered to be
Recorded   Test. L. M. COWPER clk

==

William PERRY

Dr William PERRY orphan of John W. PERRY decd In acct with William SLAUGHTER guardian Cr

To a Ballance due the Guardian }		By your half of Negro hire for 1830}	
on my return to Feby court 1830}	52..35	payable the 4 of Jany 1831 . . . }	42..50
1830 Int on that Sum up to this return	3..15	Int on ditto up to this return	..35

(82) William PERRY (Cont.)

April 10 To Cash pd Jasiah H **PINNER**		
for tuition	2..00	
Int on ditto	..10	
Novr 22/d/ To yaur half Taxes pd Shff		
for 1829	1..74	
1831 Int on ditto	02	
Jany 4 To Yaur half of keeping **RACHAL &**		
3 Children	12 050	
Int on ditto up to this return	12	
To Yaur half of keeping **PEGGY & 4**		
Children	15 00	
Int on ditto	..15	
Feby 26 To Cash pd J S **GRIMES** for		
Schooling	2..50	
To recording this Accaunt	..40	
To Boord & clothing for 1830 up to		
this return	25..00	
To 5 p ct Commissions on the money}		
Expended & negro hires Say on		
$108 05/¢/	5..40	
	120..43	

By yaur half of rents of Land for 1830	2..50
Int on ditto	..02
	45..37
To a Ballance due the Guardian	75..05
	120..43

1831
Feby 28 by a Ballance due the Guardian   75..05

North Carolina }
                               William **SLAUGHTER** guardiar.

Hertford Caunty} February Caurt of Pleas &c 1831
This Accaunt was returned to Caurt on oath by William **SLAUGHTER** guard & ordered to be Recorded
                                     Test L M **COWPER** clk

---

(83) 54 William PERRY

        Dr William **PERRY** orphan of Freeman **PERRY** decd In acct Current with John **WINBORNE** guard Cr

1830		
Jany 1/st/ To the Sum due the guardian		
in Settlemnt	4 08	
Int on ditto up to Jany 1/st/ 1831	29	
March 5 To James **WARD** aacct yaur part	83¼	
" 1 p Shaes WH [sic] Store	87½	
_n 3/d/ " 2½ yds Rusha Sheeting @ 40/¢/}		
" 5 do Stripeed Clath @ 20/¢/ } **WH**	2..09	
thread 9 }		
8 " 1 pr Shaes J **HALLY**	1 00	
18 " making 2 p Trawsers 1 over Jacket		
& finding thread	..80	
30 " 1¾ yds Lining @ 60/¢/ **WH** 1..05 }		
" ½ Spool Catton ½ doz Shirt		
buttons 12½}		
" ½ yard Rusha Scheeting . . 20 }		
" ½ grass Horn buttons **WH** . . . }	1..50	
making 1 p Trawsers 25/¢/ do 1 Shirt		
Lining 37½	62½	
Augt 6 " 5 yds Catten Shirting @ 20/¢/ 1		
Spool Catton 12½}	1..12½	
12 " making 2 Shirts @ 25/¢/	..50	
23 " pd Clerk for natice Sent /out/ to		
renew guard bond	50	

1830	
Nov 25 By Sum recd of Carr **DARDEN** it}	
being yaur part Sales Liberty Hill fisherry }	
Sold by a decree of the Caurt }	57..73¾
By Int from 25/th/ of Novr 1830 up to}	
Jany 1/st/ 1831 . . . . }	43?
1831	
Jay 4/th/ By yaur part 1000 hoop pales 3 pense}	
Tole? brandy & Some old plank Sold Jas **WHITE**}	43¼
By yaur part Tole brandy Negro hire}	
rent Corn Land rent Pine Baxes? }	
& Tole Tar 1830 . . . . }	94..03¼

(83) William PERRY (Cont.)

27 " Cloth homespun & making 1 vest		
& Trimms &c	..40	
Sept 4 " 1 pocket Hdhf **WH**	26	
7 " Cash pd John P **MITCHEL** for		
Tuition	3..50	
Oct 12 " 2 pr wooling Socks @ [blank]	50	
Nov 4 " 2½ yds Casinett @ 90/¢/ 2 ditto		
ditto 87½	4..00	
" " 2 Skains Silk @ 6¼ **WH**	12½	
6 2 yds wooling clath & making		
1 p Trawser/s/ }	1..50	
& finding Trimings &c for the Same}		
8 " 1½ yds Catton clath 12½ 1 doz		
buttons 37½ /**WH**/	56¼	
Decr 3 " 1 pr Shaes made at home . .	1 12½	
8 " pd John P **MITCHEL** for Tuition	2..35	
9 " pd Sarah **PERRY** making 1 Caat	50	
16 " making 1 pr Trawsers finding lining		
& thread	25	
17 " 1 vest patron 75/¢/ ¾ yds }		
bombazett 27½}	93½}	
" " 1 Skain Silk 6¼ ½ yds Catton		
cloth 6¼	12½}	
" " ½ doz buttons . . . **WH** 12½}	1..18¾	
" " making 1 vest	..20	
24 " pd Jacob **PERRY** making 1 Hat	2..00	
" " pd clerk for coppy bill Sale		
Freeman **PERRY**}		
1831 " Jasiah **PERRY** at Windsor Office}		
yaur part }	16½	
Jany " pd Jemima **VANPELT** yaur part		
Support old **YORK** 1830}	8..33½	
" pd Jas **WHITE** for Support Negro}		
gir **ANIST** d? 1830 Yaur part . }	4..12½	
" " John **WINBORNE** Board of the orphans}		
" from the 2/d/ Jany 1830 until 2/d/ Jany 1831}50..00		
" yaur part 2 blankets given **HESTOR** & }		
ANIST at Smith **FREEMAN**s this present}		
year }	75	
" yaur part Doct **SESOMS** bill	66¾	
" 1 pr wooling Socks 30 1 p Shaes 1 12½	1 42½	
" yaur part blanket given **AZETT** this		
present year	37½	
" Commissions on $99..79¼	4 98	
" A Balance due the orphan	48 44	
	152..84	

1831

Jany 5/th/ By Ballance due the orphan   48..44

John **WINBORNE** Guardian

152 84¾

North Carolina }

Hertford Caunty} February Caurt of Pleas &c 1831
This Accaunt was retuned to Caurt on oath by John
WINBORNE Guard & ordered to be Recorded

Test. L. M. **COWPER** clk

---

(84) 55 James PERRY

1830   Dr James **PERRY** orphan of Freeman **PERRY** decd In act current with John **WINBO___**

March 5th/ To yaur part James **WARD**s acct   83½

June 30/th/ To 2¾ yds Linning /@/ 60 @ 7 Spool}
Catton To ½ doz Shirt buttons @ 12½ **WH**} 1 77½

July 3/d/ To 1 black Silk vest pattron **WH**   1 75

1831 " To Clerks fee giving Natie renew?

1831   Cr

Jany 1/st/ By a Balance due from return

Feby term 1830}   61..12

By 12 mo Int on Sam [sic]   3..66

By this Sum Recd of Carr **DARDEN** it}

(84) James PERRY (Cont.)

guardian bond	..50	being yaur part Sale Liberty Hill }	57 72
Jany " To 1 fine Hat 30/ 2½ yds Casinett		Fisherry Sold by a decree of the Caurt}	
@ 120/¢/	6..00	Int from Nov 25/th/ 1830 up to Jany 1/st/ 1831	43
" To pd Jas WHITE Support ANIST 1830	4..12½	By yaur part 1000 hoop pales 3 pints	
" To pd Cash at windsor for Examine the}		Tole Brandy & Some old plank Sold Jas WHITE	63
office for a bill Sale Freeman PERRY to}		By Tole brandy Sold W LEWIS by negro}	
Jasiah PERRY . . . .}	16½	Hire rent corn Land rent pine baxes Tale Tar}	94 53
" To 1 vest patron 75 Cash 40/¢/	1..15		
" To this Sum pd Jemima VANPELT yaur part			
" Support old man YARK 1830	8..33 1/3		
" " yaur part 3 blankets by the guardian			
to OZETT HESTOR & ANIST this}			
present year }	1..12½		
" " yaur part Doctor SESOMS bill	66 2/3		
" " Commissions on $26..42 1/3	1..32		
To a ballance due the orphan	189 68 2/3		
	217 62 2/3	1831	217..62¾

Jany 1/st/ By a Ballance due the orphan   189 68 1/3

North Carolina }
John WINBORN guardian

Hertford Caunty} Febuary Caurt Pleas [sic] 1831.

This Accaunt was returned to Caurt on oath by John WINBORNE guardian & ordered to be Recorded

Test. L. M. COWPER clk

Joseph PERRY

1830   Dr Joseph PERRY orphan of Freeman [sic] decd In act current with John WINBORNE guardian

Jany 5 To this Sum due the Guardian in }			
Settlement return to Feby Term 1830}	28..22	Amt Brot up	38..33
Int up to Jany 5/th/ 1831	1 69	June 30/th/ To ½ yd Rusha	
March 5/th/ To yaur part Jas WARD on act	83 1/3	Sheeting WH	20
" 1 p Shaes . . . . . . WH	87½	Augt 6 T 5 " Catton Shirting @ 20}	
May 11/th/ To 1 Quire paper	25	" 1 Spool Catton . . . . 12½}WH	1..12½
June 3/d/ To 2½ yds Rusha Sheeting 40/¢/}	1..00	" 12/th/ making 2 Shirts @ 25/¢/	..50
T 5 ditto Striped Cloth @ 20/¢/ }	1..00	" 23/d/ To pd Clerk for Sunding}	
To 1 ditto Catton ditto }	12½	aut natice to renew Guardian }	..50
" Thread 9/d/ 1 p Shaes 10/ }	1 09	Sept 7 To pd John P MITCHELL	
" 1 p Suspender/s/ J. H.	12½	for tuition 95 days	3..96
" making 1 p Trawser/s/ & thread	..25	Octr 27 To 1 pr? Wooling Socks	..30
" 1¾ yds Linning @ 62½ A HARRELL	1..09½	Novr 4/th/ To 2½ yds Casinett @ 90/¢/	
" pd Harrell B VANPELT making 1 Linning}		2 do @ 87½	4..12½
" Shirt &? thread }	..30	" 6 " 2 Junes? Wooling cloth & }	
18 " making 1 p Trawsers 25 do 1 over}		" " making 1 pr Trawsers . }	1..50
" Jacket 50/¢/ . . . .}	55	" " 1½ do Catton Cloth @ 12½/¢/	
" making 1 Stripeed p Trawsers	..25	1 doz buttons 37½ WH	56½
" ½ gross battans horn WH	12½	15/th/ To 1 p Shaes made at home	1 12½
" 1 Spelling Book H B V	25	24 To 1 English reader WH	50
Amt Carried up	38..23	Decr 8/th/ To pd John P MITCHEL for tuition	2 37½
		" 9 To pd Sarah PERRY making 1 Coat	50
		" 11 To 1 pr Shaes made at home	1..12½
		" 16 To making 1 pr Trawsers finding}	..25
		Lining & Thread }	56..87¾
		amt Carried forward	

(85) 56 Joseph PERRY

Dr Joseph PERRY orphan of Freeman PERRY decd In act current with John WINBORNE guad

Amt Brot forward	$ 56..87¾	1830
Decr 17/th/ To 1 vest patron 75/¢/ ¾ yds		Novr 25/th/ By this Sum Recd of Carr DARDEN}
bombazett @ 30	95½	" it being Yaur part Sale Liborty Hill}
To 1 Skain Silk 6¼ ½ yd Catton @		" Fisherry Sold by a decree of the Court} 57 72¾
6½/¢/ WH	12½	1831 " Interest up to Jany 5/th/ 1831 ..43
½ doz buttons	12½	Jany 4/th/ This Sum recd of James WHITE}
24 Making 1 vest	20	for " yaur part 1000 hoopples }
pd Jacob PERRY 1 Hat	2..00	" 3 pints Tale brandy on hand and Some }
31 To Cash pd Clerek for Coppy Freeman}		old plank . . . . } 63 1/3
PERRY bill Sales to Jasiah PERRY }		" yaur part Negro Hire Corn Land}
Windsor office	16½	" rent Tole Brandy Sold W LEWIS}
To pc James WHITE yaur part for Support}		" & the amt Tole Tar recd of Jas WARD}
Negro ANIST the year 1830 & Carting }		" & Pine Boxes 1830 . . . . } 94 05¾
HANDY? }	4..12½	
" pc Jenimia VANPELT for Support old}		
" man YARK yaur part 1830 }	8..33 1/3	
" John WINBORNE for Board of the orphan}		
from the 2 day of Jany 1830 until 2/d/ Jay 1831}	30..00	
" Yaur part blankets given to ANIST}		
" HESTOR at Smith FREEMAN 1 do AZETT}	1..12½	
" pd Doctor SESSOMS yaur [sic] his Act	66 2/3	
" Commissions on $124..29¾	6 21	
5 " a Ballance due the orphan	21..97¾	
	152..84	152 84¾
		1831

North Carolina }
Hertford County} February Caurt of Pleas &c 1831   Jany 5/th/ By a Balance due the orphan 21 97¾

John WINBORNE guardian

This Account was returned to Caurt on oath by John WINBORNE guardian & ordered to be Recorded [End of entry.]

John B. SHORP [sic]

1830		Dr John B SHORP orphan of Jacob SHARP decd In acct with E H SHARP guard	
March 1/st/ To pd Mr/s/ PIERCE making		1830	
2 shirts	..75	Jany 4 By Sum due the Ward . .}	
" 30 To 1 Silk Vest	3 00	as pr Last return . . . . }	907..12
July 24 To pd Jas C JENKINS act yr pt	1..25	1831	
Sept 16 To pd Doctor HALLS a/c	1..81¼	Jay 4/th/ By Int on the above Sum}	
Decr 29.th/ To pd John A ANDERSONs acct	46 74	12 mo/s/ up to this day Jany 4/th/ 1831}	54..42
1831		By yaur part Negro hire for	
Jay 4 To pd E B NORFLEET CHERRY &		the year 1830 on demand 4th Jany 1831}	48 22
chldren	2..50		
To pd Wm NIEL tuition a/c	11..25		
To pd Mr/s/ Nancy YANCY act board	18..00		
" pd Eli CARTER act Shaes	2..00		
" pd James SCOTTs & Co act books	1 25		
" pd Abner HARRELLs act	1 37¾		
" pd Eryant ASKEW mid wife fee &}			
Doc: TAMOR? yr pt . . . . }	50		
This return	40		
1831 Commissions on $193..48 @ 5 pct	9..69		
Jany 4/th/ To sum due the ward	909..25		
	1009 76	1831	1009..76

North Carolina }
Hertford Caunty} February Caurt of Pleas &c 1831   Jany 4/th/ By this Sum due the ward this day 909..25

E. H. SHARP guardian

(85) John B **SHARP** (Cont.)
This Account was returned to Court on oath by Elisha H **SHARP** guard & ordered to be Recorded

Test. L. M. **COWPER** clk

---

(86) 57 Miss Elizabeth **SHARP** Dr Miss Elizabeth **SHARP** orphan of Jacob **SHARP** decd in a/c with E. H. [sic]

1830			1830	
March 4 To pd Miss Pheby **HILL** a/c	$ 3..00		Jany 4/th/ By Sum due the ward}	
July 24 To " Jas C **JENKINS** act yr pt	1..25		as pr Last Return }	989..94
Sept 16 To pd Doct **HALL**s act " "	1 81¼		1831	
" 29 To pd Jno A **ANDERSON** a/c	6..04		Jany 4/th/ By Int on the above Sum 12 mo/s/}	
Oct 4 " Cash gave you to pay Miss **BROWN**	1 25		up to this day . . . . }	59..41
" " 1 Thimble	37½		By your part Negro hire 1830}	
" 13 " 1 Torter Shell Comb	3..50		on demand Jany 4 th 1831 }	48..22
Decr 20 " pd Patrick **BROWN** act	21..24			
1831				
Jany 4 " pd E B **NARFLEET** Supt **CHERRY**				
& Child	2..50			
" pd Mr/s/ H. W. J. **BANKS** a/c Board &				
tuition	147..50			
" pd Mr/s/ Nancy **YANCY** 1 mo board	6 00			
" pd Jas **SCOTT** & co act Books	3..50			
" pd Eli **CARTER**s act Shaes	6..43			
" pd Abner **HARRELL**s a/c	9..30			
" pd Bryant **ASKEW** mid wife fees}				
and Doct **TAMER** yr pt }	50			
" This return	40			
" Commissions on $322..22 a 5 p ct	16..10			
1831	230..70			
Jany 4 To This amt due the ward	866..86			
	1097..56		1831	1097 56

Jany 4/th/ By this Sum due the ward this day}
eighh hundred and Sixty Six dallars & 86/100} 866..36

North Carolina }
Hertford County} February Court of Pleas &c 1831
This Account was Returned to Court on oath by Elisha H **SHARP** Gurdian & ordered to be Recorded

E H **SHARP** Guardian

Test. L. M. **COWPER** g? clk

Jacob **SHARP**

1830	Dr Jacob **SHARP** orphan of Jacob **SHARP** dec In act with E. H. **SHARP** Guardian			Cr
March 1/st/ To pd Mr/s/ **PIERCE** making			1830	
3 Shirts	1..00		Jany 4/th/ By this Sum due this day as}	
July 24 To pd Jas. C. **JENKINS** a/c yr pt	1..25		p last Return . . . . }	999..35
Aug 27 To pd Wm **NIEL** Tuition & Books act	31..25		1831	
Sept 16 To Doct **HALL**s act Doctr **SAWP?**	1..81¼		Jany 4/th/ By Int on the above Sum 12 mo up}	
Decr 20 To Patrick **BRAWN**s act	45..40		to this day . . . . }	59..96
1831			By yr part Negro Hire for 1830}	
Jany 4 To E B **NORFLET** Supt **CHERRY**}			on demand this Jany 4/th/ 1831}	48..22
" & Child last year Yor pt . . . . . . }	2..50		1831	1107..53
" To Mr/s/ Nancy **YANCY** act Board	61..00		Jany 4/th/ By this Amt due the ward this}	
" " To E S **JEGGITTS** a/c	10..25		day Say nine hund & twelve dallar/s/ & 10/100}	912..10
" " To James **SCOTT** & co act	7..25		E. H. **SHARP** Guardian	
" " To Eli **CARTER**/s/ act	16..38			
" " To Abner **HARRELL**s a/c	2..17¾			
" " To Bryant **ASKEW**s a/c midwife for}				
" " &c **TAMER** Yor pt . . . . }	50			

(86) Jacob SHARP (Cont.)

" " To this Return	40	North Carolina }	
" " To Coms on $289..35 @ 5 p cet	[blank]	Hertford County} February Court of Pleas &c 1831	
" " To this Sum due the ward this day	912..10	This Account was Returned to Court on oath by	
	1107..53	By [sic] Elisha H. **SHARP** guard and ordered to be	
		Recorded Test. L. M. **COWPER**. Clk	

---

(87) 38 Dr Porthena Ann **SESSOMS** William H. **SESSOMS** Amgrad W **SESSOMS** Aragonmut **SESSOMS** Assaad S. **SESSOMS** Aronah? L **SESSOMS** Children of Elisha **SESSOMS** in an a/c current with Elisha **SESSOMS** their Guardian

1830		1831	Cr
Augt term To this amt paid for guardian Bond}		Augt term By this Amt returned to augt term 1830 $ 49..00	
at August Term 1830 . . . . . }	..60	Int on the above Sum until the present date 1..47	
To this Amt pd for return made Janu term	..20		50..47
To this Amt pd for Sumons to the above term	..90	Ballance due the wards up to this time}	
Interest on the above Sum from augt}		August 1831 . . . . }	47..72
term 1830 to Feby Term 1831 }	..05	E E Elisha **SESSOMS** Guardian	
$	1..75		

North Carolina }

Hertford County} February Court of Pleas &c 1831

This Account was was [sic] Returned to Court on oath by Elisha **SESSOMS** Guardian and ordered to be Recorded

Test. L. M. **COWPER** clk

Lovinia **SIMONS**

1829   Dr Lovinia **SIMONS** orphan of John **SIMONS** decd In a/c Current with John **WINBORNE** Guardian   Cr

Nov 23/d/ To your part Guardian bond	..12	1829	
1830 " pd Harry **HALLER** Colouring		Decr 16/th/ By your part Sales of Beds &}	
1 frock	25	furniture agreeable to Will . . }	24..43
Augt 25th/ " do John **MOORE** 1 p shaes	1 25	By Interest from 16/th/ June 1830 up to}	
Sept " " do Clerk renewing Guardian bond	25	Jany 5/th/ 1831 }	..85
" " do Taxes in Bertie County	20	1830	
" " this amt property you baught at your}		Novr 23/d/ your part Sales Liberty Hill fisherry}	
farhers Sale decr 16/th/ 1829 . . . . . }	29 84	Sold by a decree of the Court }11..54	
an demand June 16/th/ 1830 Int 1 a/c to}		Interest up to Jany 5/th/ 1831	..08
January 5th 1831 . . . . }	1..09	1831	
" " your part Lock & Hinges & nails for the}		Jany 5/th/ your part 1/5 Negro hire & rent	
use Crib at **BLANCHARD** place . . . }	40	Pine baxes near **WALTON** Mill 1830	45..07
" pd Marry **RAWLS** Mid wife fee to		" ditto 1/6 Negro hire rent Pine baxes & Sale	
PHILLIS	33 1/3	fish Liberty Hill 1830	47..46
" 5 yds Callico @ 40/¢/ E **HARDY**	2..00	" your part Sale Fodder Sald W **LEWIS**}	
" 1 " black Cambick Jno **WINBORNE**	..25	" & Wm **PERRY** . . . . }	4..24
1831		" A ballance due the Guardian	30..94
Jany 1 " pd Loderick H **RICE** Judgmt	16..93		164..61
" spirits use negro hire your part	30	John **WINBORNE** Guardian	
" pd Jemima **VANPELT** your part	3..00		
Suport **ANIST** 1830			
" p Jemima **VANPELT** on Judgmet	50..00		
" your part 4 Blankets **LUCY** & 6 Children}			
at H B **VANPELT**s this present Year }	..87½		
" 1 Bandanno Hkf	62½		
" pd William **LASSITOR** old **DEND** mid}			
wife fee to **CELIA LUCY** & **SABRA** . . }	62½		
" To 1? Abner **HARRELL** Acct	9 15½		
" " Watson **LEWIS** ditto	29..25		
" pd Joseph **HARE** your Support **LUCY** /&/}			
6 Children 1830 . . . . }	6..66¾		

(87) Lovinia SIMONS (Cont.)

" yaur part 2 Blankets given **ANIST** }	
& Children at H B **VANPELT**s 1831}	45½
" John **WINBORNE** & Henry B **VANPELT**	
act yaur/s/ Hausing Tole Carn & Fensing	
Stacks	2..91½
Commissions on $156..78	7..83
	164..61

164..61

---

(88) 59 Mary SIMONS Dr Mary SIMONS orphan of John SIMONS decd in a/c with John **WINBORNE** Guard

1829			1829	
Novr 23 To Yaur part Guardian Bond	..12		Decr 16 By Sale Beds & furniture Yaur part	24..43?
Decr 5 To 1 pr Shaes	62½		interest from 16/th/ June 1830 up to	
June 8 To 1 " " Ame? J H	1..00		Jany 5th 1831	..83?
Augt 23/d/ To Yaur part renewing Guardian bond	..25		1830	
" Taxes in Bertie Caunty 1829	..20		Nov 25/th/ By this Sum Recd of Carr **DARDEN**	
" property Baught at yaur farthers			it being for yaur part of Sale Liberty Hill fisherry }	
Sale	1..27		Sald by a decree of Caurt }	11..54?
" yaur part Lack Hinges & nails }			Interest up to Jany 5/th 1831	..03
use hause at **BLANCHARD** place}	40		1831	
" pd Mary **RAWLS** mid wife to **PHILLIS**	33 1/3		Jany 5/th/ By 1/5 Negro hire rent Pine baxes	
" 6 mo Interest on 4 20	..12		**WALTON** Mill 1830	45..07
" pd Seth **DEANS** 1 p Shaes	75		By 1/6 Negro hire Rent Pine baxes}	
1831			& Sale of Fish at Liberty Hill }	
Jany " " Loderick H **RICE** in Judgmt	12..45		fisherry 1830 . . . . }	47 ..6
" yaur part Spirits use negro hire	..30		By yaur part Tale fodder Sold Watson **LEWIS** &}	
" pd Jemimia **VANPELT** Support **ANIST**			Wm **PERRY** }	4..24
& Children 1830	3..00			
" pd ditto ditto in Judgmet	52..60			
" Yaur part 4 Blankets use **LUCY** & 6				
Children at H B **VANPELT**s	87½			
" pd Wm **LASSITOR** old **DEND** mid wife				
fee to **CELIA LUCY** & **SABRA** 1830	62½			
" pd Abner **HARRELL** on act	5..35½			
" pd Watson **LEWIS** ditto	10..99			
" pd Jaseph **HARE** yaur part Support}				
LUCY & Children 1830 . . . . . . }	6..66¾			
" Yaur part 2 Blankets given **ANIST**				
" Children at H B **VANPELT**s	[blank]			
" John **WINBORNE** & Henry B **VANPELT**s}				
hausing Tole Corn & fenseing Stacks}	2..91½			
" Commissions on $107..29	5..16			
5 A Ballance due the orphan	27..32			
	$ 133..67			133..67

By A Ballance due the orphan	27..32

John **WINBORNE** Guardian

Elizabeth SIMONS

1829		Dr Elizabeth SIMONS orphan of John SIMONS decd In acct Current With John WINBORNE Guardian	
Nov 23/d/ To Yaur part Guardian Bond	12	Mary **RAWLS** mid wife fee to **PHILLIS**	33 1/3
Decr 8 To pr Shaes	62½	1830 Interest 6 months on $5 7 [sic]	..15
March 13 To 1 pr ditto . . J. H.	1 82½	To 1 p Shaes . . . . E **HARDY**	1
June 8 " 1 pr ditto . . . . . Do	[blank]	Jany 1/st/ 1 pr Coarse dito made at home	1
" Taxes in Bertie Caunty	20	1831 To pd Loderick H **RICE** on Judgmet	12..17
Articles Baught at Yaur farthers Sale}		" Spirits use negro hire	..30

(88) Elizabeth SIMONS (Cont.)

for the use of yau acct? Trunks &c . }	[blank]	" Jemimia VANPELT Support ANIST}	
Augt 23/d/ Clerk fee renewing		& Children 1830	3..00
Guardian bond	25	" Jemimia VANPELT Judgmet	51..62¾
" yaur part Lock Hinges & nails for use			69..57¾
Crib at BLANCHARD place built by			
H B VANPELT 1831	40		
	$ 3..99		

---

(89) 6C Elizabeth SIMONS

D Elizabeth SIMONS orphan of John SIMONS decd In a/c current with John WINBORNE guard

Amt Brot forward	69 57¾	1829	
To Yaur part 4 Blankets use LUCY & 6}		Decr By yaur part Sales beds & furniture	24..43
" Children at H B VANPELTs . . . }	87½	given by Will	
" pd William LASSITER old DINOA for		Int from 16 June 1830 up	
mid wife fee	62½	to Jany 5/th/ 1831	85
" pd Abner HARRELL on acct	5 33 1/3	1830	
" pd Watson LEWIS ditto	11..00	Novr 25/th/ By yaur part Sales Liberty Hill}	
" pd Joseph HARE yaur part LUCY}		fisherry Sold by a decree of the Caurt & }	
& 6 Children 1830 . . . . }	6 66 2/3	recd of Carr DARDEN . . . . . . }	11..54
" yaur part 2 blankets given ANIST}		1831	
& Children at H B VANPELTs }	45	Jany 5/th/ By yaur part negro hire & rent}	
" John WINBORNE & Henry B VANPELT}		pine baxes near WALTON Mills 1/5 part}	45..07
act Hausing Tole Corn & fensing }		" By 1/6 Negro hire Rent Pine baxes}	
Stacks 1830 . . . . }	2 91½	& Sale fish at Liberty Hill fisherry 1830}	
" Watson LEWIS acct	1 37½	With Int . . . . }	47..44
" Commissions on $103 80/¢/	5..19	By your Tale fodder Sole Watsan LEWIS}	
5 " A Ballance due the orphan	24..68	& William PERRY }	4..24
	133..67		133..67
		By A Ballance due the orphan	24..68
		John WINBORNE Guardian	

John SIMONS

1829			Dr John SIMONS orphan of John SIMONS decd In a/c current with John WINBORNE gud/an/ [sic]		
Nov 23/d/ To Yaur part Guardian Bond	12½	1829			Cr
1830		Decr 16/th/ By your part Sale beds & furniture			24..43
Feby 20/th/ To 1 Hat J P	1..25	By Joseph PERRY Will			
Augt 23/d/ To 1 p Shase J H	75	Int from 16 June 1830 up to Jany 5/th/ 1831			..85
" Clerk fee renewing Guardian Bond	25	By yaur part Sale Liberty Hill}			
" Taxes Bertie 1829	20	Fishery }			11..54
" yaur part Desk Trunks at Sale	1 27	1830			
" ditto Lock Hinges & nails use}		Nov 25 By 1/5 Negro hire rent Pine }			
Crib at BLANCHARD place }	40	baxes near WALTON Mill 1830 . . . }			45..07
" pd Mary RAWLS mid wife fee to		1831			
PHILLIS	33 1/3	Jay By 1/6 Negro hire rent pine baxes}			
" pd John G WILSAN on act . . .	35½	& Sale Fish at Liberty Fishery }			47..46½
" pd Edward HARDY 1 Hk Dk	..50	By yaur part Tale fodder Sold }			
" pd Sarah PERY making 1 Coat	..30	Watson LEWIS & Wm PERRY . . }			4..24
" finding Leather making 1 p shaes	62½				133..67
" pd Seth DEANS making 1 p Shaes	75				
" yaur part Spirits Negro hire . .	30				
1831 Jay Jemimia VANPELT Support}					
ANIST & Children 1830 . . . . }	3 00				
pd ditto ditto on Judgmet	53..75				
" yaur part 4 Blankets given LUCY					

(89) John SIMONS (Cont.)

& Children 1831 at H. B. VANPELTs	87½	
" Wm **LASSITER** old **DINA** mid Wife fee		
to **LUCY CELIA & SABRA** 1830	62½	
" pd Abner **HARRELL** on acct	6..69	
" pd Watson **LEWIS** ditto	4 87½	
	77..31½	Amt Carried over . . . 133..€7

---

(90) 61 John SIMONS

1829   Dr John **SIMONS** orphan of John **SIMONS** ded In a/c current with John **WINBOR__**

Amt Brot over	77 31½	Amt Brot over	133..67
To pd Jaseph **HARE** for Support}			
LUCY & 6 Children 1830 }	6 66¾		
To Yaur part of 2 Blankets given}			
ANIST & Children at H B **VANPELT**}	..45		
To 1 p Shaes made at home	62½ .		
To Yaur part Expence houseing}			
Tole Corn & fensing Stacks }	2 91½		
To Forting 2 pr Stockings @ 12½	25		
To Commissions on $89..12 . .	4.. 45		
Jay 5 To A Balance due the orphan	40.. 10		
	133..67		133..57
		5 By A Ballance due the orphan	$ 40..10

John **WINBORNE** Guardia_

Edward **SIMONS**

1829   Dr Edward **SIMONS** orphan of John **SIMONS** decd In a/c current with John **WINBORNE** gu_____

Novr 23 To Yaur part Guardian Bond	$ 12	1829	
1830 " do renewing ditto	25	Decr 16 By yaur part Sales beds & furniture}	24 43
Augt. To Taxes Bertie Caunty	20	given by Jaseth [sic] **PERRY** Will }	
To property Baught at Yaur farther/s/}		1830	
Sale for use orphan . . . . . }	1..27	Novr 25/th/ Int from 10/th/ June 1830 up to}	25
To 1 p Shaes made at home	..50	Janry 5th 1831 . . . . }	
" Yaur part Lack & Hinges & nails}		By yaur part Sale Liberty Hill }	
use crib at **BLANCHARD** Place }	40	Fisherry Sold by a decree of Court}	11 56
" pd Mary **RAWLS** Mid Wife fee **PHILLIS**	33 1/3	" Int up to Jany 5th 1831	..)8
" " Edward **HARDY** act 2	2 62½	1831	
1831		Jay 5 By yaur part Negro hire rent Pine}	
Jany 5/th/ To Yaur part Spirits use negro hire	30 .	Baxes near **WALTON** Mill 1/5 part }	45..)7
To Jemimia **VANPELT** Support}		By 1/6 part Negro hire rent Pine }	
ANIST & children 1830 }	3 00	Baxes & Sale fish Liberty Hill Fisherry}	47_46½
ditto ditto on Judgmet	52 37½	By your part Tole Fodder Sold }	
Yaur part 4 Blankets given **LUCY**}		Watson **LEWIS** & Wm **PERRY**}	4 24
& 6 Children at H B **VANPELT**} 1831	87½		
" pd Wm **LASSITER** old **DINIA** mid wife}			
fee to **LUCY CELIA & SABRA** 1830}	62½		
" pd Abner **HARRELL** on act	3..29		
" " Watson **LEWIS** do	5..14		
" pd Jaseph **HARE** Support **LUCY**}			
& 6 Children 1830 . . . . . }	6 66¾		
" yaur part 2 Blankets given **ANIST**}			
& Children at Henry B **VANPELT**s}	45½		
" yaur part Expences Hauseing}			
Corn Tole & fensing Stacks }	2 91½		
Commissions on $81..34	4 06		

(90) Edward SIMONS (Cont.)

To A Ballance due the orphan	48..27		
	133..67		133..67
		By A Ballance due the orphan . .	48..27
		John **WINBORNE** Guardi__	

---

(91) 62 Sarah SIMONS

Dr Sarah **SIMONS** orphan of John **SIMONS** dec In act current with John **WINBORNE** Guardian Cr

1830			1831		
Augt? 23 To yaur part Guardian bond	25		Jany 5/th/ By 1/6 Negro hire rent Pine baxes}		
" yaur part Lock Hinges nails use Crib}			& Sale Tole Fish }	47	46½
at **BLANCHARD** place . . . . }	40		By 1/6 Tole Fodder Sold Watson **LEWIS**}		
1831 " pd Mary **RAWLS** mid wife fee to			& William **PERRY** . . . . }	4..	24
Jany? 5 **PHILLIS**	33 1/3				
" yaur part Spirits use Negro hire . . .	20				
" do 4 Blankets given **LUCY** & }					
Children at H. B. **VANPELTs** }	87½				
" pd Wm **LASSITER DINEA** mid wife}					
fee to **LUCY CELIA** 1830 }	41½				
" S [sic] Joseph **HARE** Support **LUCY** &}					
6 Children 1830 . . . . }	6	66¾			
" yaur part Expences huseing }					
Tole Corn & fensing Stacks }	2	91½			
To A Ballance due the orphan	39..66				
	51..70			51..70	

North Carolina }

Hertford County} February Caurt of Pleas &c 1831   By this Balance due the orphan $ 39..66

These Accaunts were returned to Caurt on oath by John **WINBORNE** Guard & ordered to be Recordeded

John **WINBORNE** Guardian

Test. L. M. **COWPER** clk

Sarah **SIMONS**

1830		Dr Sarah **SIMONS** daughter of Watson **LEWIS** In a/c current with Watson **LEWIS** Guardian		
Augt 24 To Ballance due the W. L. Guardian	203..25	Amt Brot up	233..77	
" " " Bond Notice & Return	1 90	Nov 8 To Cloth Polece	26..50	
31 " 6 yds Callico	1 50	" 9 1 Silk Hkff 50 ¾ yds Silk @	1..25	
" 2½ ditto Mull Muslin @ 60	1 ..50	" " 1/8 yds ditto	12	
" ½ ditto goronap @ 75/¢/	..38	" " 4 " Piping Cord @ 25$ [sic]	1..00	
" ½ ditto black Silk @ [sic]	84	16 " Amt pd Mr/s/ **RAWLS**	4..00	
" 2 ditto Catton Cloth @ 12½	25	22/d/ " 1 pr Shaes @ 1..25 1 ditto 75/¢/	2..00	
" 1½ ditto Ribband @ 12½	19	" " 1 Belt 25/¢/ 1 Bunch Brade 50/¢/	..75	
Sept 10 " 10 ditto Catton cloth @ 20	2 ..00	" " 1 Battle Colgne	63	
16 " 1 Stran beads 10/¢ 1 p Shaes 1..63	1 ..73	" " 1 Cape	50	
21 " 1½ yds Checks @ 20/¢/	..30	" " 2 yds flannel 50/¢/ 3 ditto Cattons @ 20	1 60	
29 " ½ ditto	10	29 " 2 bunches thread Lace @ 9/d/	25	
Oct 11 " ½ oz Indigo	13	" " 1 yds Ribband @ 20/¢/	20	
30 " 1 Worked Cap	3 ..00	" " 3 ditto ditto @	19	
" 1 ditto Cape	..50	Der 8/th/ To 1 Shawl	2 00	
" 1 Black belt	25	" " " 1 Crape dress	7..50	
Nov 2 " 1 p Side Combs	75	" " " 1½ yds Checks @ 25/¢/	38	
" " " 1½ yds Second mouring retd @ 50	..75	" " " 1½ ditto black Janes @ 25/¢/	38	
" " " 1½ ditto ditto 30	45	" " " 1 doz Silk Buttons	37	
" " " 1 Shawl	75	13 " " 2 Bunches Brade @ 12½/¢/	25	
" " " 7 yds Blk L?ushing Silk @ $1	7 00	16 " Amt for Isane?	25	
" " " 1 p over Shaes @	1 ..00	24 " 1 p Shaes	1..25	
" " " 1¼ yds blk Cambrick @ 20/¢/	25	28 " 3 hkff @ .60 1 Viol oil 60/¢/	2..40	

(91) Sarah SIMONS (Cont.)

3 " 1 Buench? hare 2$ 1 p Gloves 50/¢/	2 ..50		" " 2¼ yds Cattons @ 12½		28
6 " 2 yds Fig/d/ Muslin @ 1..25	2..50		" " 1? Bonnett		2 00
Amt Carried up	233 77		Amt Carrie [sic] over		289 82

(92) 63 Sarah SIMONS

Dr Sarah SIMONS daughter of Watson LEWIS In a/c current with Watson LEWIS Gu__

			1830	
Amt Brot over	$289..82		Novr 3/d/ By Shaes & Curls Returned	2..50
Decr 29 To 2¾ yds diaper @ 40/¢/	1..10		29 By 2566 /b/ Fodder @ 50/¢/	12..83
" " " Amt pd A. **HARRELL**	6..75		Decr 3/d/ By 84 1/3 Bbls Sound Corn @ 2..25	189..75
" ditto Doct **BARDWELL**	7..63		" " " 10 ditto Rotten ditto @ 18	10..80
			" 31/st/ " hire of Negro Bay **PAYTON**	25..00
			" " " By Ballance	65..12
1831	305..30			305..30
Feby 28 To Ballance due the Guardian	65..12		Watson **LEWIS** Guar___

North Carolina }
Hertford Caunty } February Caurt of Pleas &c 1831
This Accaunt was returned to Caurt on oath by Watson **LEWIS** Guardian & ordered to be Recorded

Test. L. M. **COWPER** cl_

Hillery SOWEL

1830   Dr Hillery **SOWEL** orphan of Christian **SOWEL** decd In act current with John **DAWNING** gu___
May 18/th/ To pd John P. **MITCHEL** act

Tuition	2..50	1831	
To Int up to Feby 1831	11	Feby By this Sum due the arphan from}	
To 3 months Board	9..00	the Estate of his mother Christiain **SOWEL**}	
Octo 5 To p Shaes	1..12½	decd as the audited acct will Sho the}	
Nov 8 To 1 Hat	2 50	Ballance due from the Settlement}	
" 2 yds Shirting @ 25 7? yds cloth @	1 50	of the Said Estate return to Novr}	
" A Balance making return Feby}		term 1830 . . . . }	197..00
Term 1830	20	Interest up to Feby 1831	2..55
1831 To this Sum pd Guardian band	60	By rent hause & Corn Land 1830	4..00
Jany 1/st/ To 1 Slate 25/¢/ 1 pencil 6¼	31¼		
" pd John P **MITCHEL** Tuition Decr			
4/th/ 1830	2..50		
" Board 3 months @ 3 of?	9..00		
Feby 23/d/ " pd John P **MITCHEL** for Tuition	2..50		
" 3 Months Board @	9..00		
24 " pd Rul **FLOWED** for reparing fense	8..00		
" " " Jas **TOAD**? for Repairing fense	8..68		
" " Commissions on $57..52	2..87		
To A Ballance due the orphan	143..56		203..95
	203..95	By A Balance due the orphan	143..56
		John **DAWNING** Guardian	

North Carolina }
Hertford County} February Caurt of Pleas &c 1831
This Accaunt was Returnd to Caurt on oath by John **DAWNING** guardian & ordered to be Recorded

Test. L. M. **COWPER** Cl_

William WARD

1831   Dr William **WARD** in act Current With A **BARDWELL** Guardian   Cr

Feby 28 To Ballance due on act Currt of}		1831	
August 1830 returned to Caurt }	688..65	Jany 4/th/ To Bill of Sale of Corn Fodder}	
To Int for 6 months on $688..65	21..65	& Peas from **JOHNSON** D [sic] }	36..36
To Taxes for 1829 A [sic]	10..40	Interest to 28 Feby	..25

(92) W lliam **WARD** (Cont.)

To In on 10..40 6 months	31		
To Cash pd by A **HARRELL** B [sic]	78..75		
	798..76	Amt Carried forward	36..61

---

(93) 64 William **WARD**

Dr William **WARD** in acct Current With A **BARDWELL** Guardian — Cr

Amt Brot forward	798..76		36..61
Interest on $48..75 4 months	1 57		
To A **BARDWELL** act	C 86 90		887..23
	887..23	Due Guardn	850..62
			A BARDWELL

North Carolina }
Hertford County } February Court of Pleas &c 1831
This Account was Returned to Court on oath by Arranah **BARDWELL** Guardian & ordered to be recorded
Test. L. M. **COWPER** clk

Sally M. **WILLIAMS**

1830   Dr Sally M. **WILLIAMS** orphan of Benj B **WILLIAMS** In a/c current with Dempsey **NOWELL**

Augt 24 Cash of the Returnable at		1830	
Augst Term	1..90	August 24/th/ Returns made to Augt term	157..92
To tu tion	3..70	1831	
1830		Jany 5 By hire of Negro	57 00
March 5/th/ To pare of Shaes 1 quire of Paper	75	Interest on $57 dallar/s/	..85
1831		Interest on $157..92 for 6 months	4..73
Jany? 21 To pair of Shaes	1..25		220..50
1830 To keeping **FILLIS** & faur children	20..00		67..97
To 4 yds of Clath	1..25		155..53
" 8 " of Cloth	3..00		
To 6 Months board	21..00		
Commissions on $220..50/¢/	11..12		157..92
	64..97	1831	
Due the orphan	155..53	February 24/th/ Returns made to February Term	$155..53
			Dempsey **NOWELL** Guardian

North Carolina }
Hertford County} February Court of Pleas &c 1831
This Account was Returned to Court on oath by Dempsey **NAWELL** Guard & ordered to be Recorded
Test. L. M. **COWPER** clk

William **WILSON**

1830   Dr William **WILSON** in account Current With John G **WILSON** Guardian — Cr

Feby 22/d/ To Clerk fee Last return	..40		
March 11 To Watson **LEWIS** Recept	..75	1831 Amt Brot forward	35..21
Interest on Same to Feby term 1831	04	Feby 28 To Commissions on $7?11..84 cts}	
To Abner **HARRELL** Recept	13..31¼	being Amt of Income and expenditures for }	
To Interest on the Same to Feby term 1831	..79	the Last year @ 5 p cet . . . . }	5 59
Apl 22/d/ To Mis Molly P. **FLEETWOOD**s		To Ballance due the Ward	813..16
recept	4..00		853 96
22/d/ To Interest an the Same to Feby term 1831	20	1830 Cr	
Augt 22/d/ To Clerks fees & Sheriffs		Feby 22/d/ By Ballance due the Ward the}	
nate on bond	1..30	Last Return . . . . }	777..33
To Clerks return to Augt term 1830	40	By Interest on the Same to Feby term 1831	46..63
Octr 16 To Ballance of Sundries Bot p? me	75	By hire of Negro **SOLOMON** Year 1830	30..00
Nov 6 To John **HARRELL**s recpt	2..00		853..96
Interest on the Same to Feby Term 1831	04		Jno. G. **WILSON** Guardian
Feby 4 To Watson **LEWIS**/s/ Recpt	10..99		

(93) William **WILSON** (Cont.)
To Interest on the Same to Feby Term 1831   04
                                          35..21

North Carolina }
Hertford Caunty} Febuary Caurt of Pleas &c 1831
This Accaunt was Returned to Caurt on oath By John G **WILSON** Guard & ordered to be Recorded
                                     Test. L. M. **COWPER** clk

---

(94) 65 Elva **BEST**   Dr Elva **BEST** In account with Warren **WILLIAMS** his Guardian   Cr

1825 To Boarding Elva BEST from may}		1831	
1825 till July or August 1826 . . }	5..00	..May ct By amount recd from the Sales }	
Int for five year/s/	1..60	of the Lands of their farther/s/ after paying}	
To pd Clerk for bond	20	the Executor [sic]which was levied on the}	
To 5 p ct Coms	1..95	Land his part . . . . }	28..00
To Ballance due the Ward may caurt 1831	30..95	Int for Six year/s/ at Compound Int	11..70
		there is no other property belonging to the	
		Ward Except the amount of this act	
	$39..70	his	39..70
		Warren x WILLIAMS	
		mark	

Timothy **BEST**

      Dr Timothy **BEST** In account With Warren **WILLIAMS** his Guardian   Cr

1825 To Schooling one quarter	2 00	1831	
To Boarding Timothy from the year}		May cet By amount recd from the Sales}	
1825 till may 1831 at $5 pr year . }	30..00	of the Land of their fathers int after paying}	
To 5 pr cet Coms	1..40	the execution which the Land was Sold }	
		under }	28..17
		Int on $20 for one year 1826	1..21
		Int on $15..75 for the year 1827	9 90?
		Int on $10..75 for the year 1828	64
		Int on $5..75 for the year 1829	..31
		By Ballance due the Guardian	..32
		there is no other property belonging to the Ward	
	33..40	his	31..41

North Carolina }
Hertford Caunty} May Caurt of Pleas &c 1831   Warren x **WILLIAMS**
These Accaunt was returned to Caurt on ooth by Warren **WILLIAMS** Guard & ordered to be   mark
Recorded
                                    Test. L. M. **COWPER** C__

Martha **BROWN**

1830   Dr Martha **BROWN** orphan of Hardy **BROWN** decd In act with William B **WYNNS** gu___

& 1831 To Sundries of necessares		By Ballance due the orphan at my}	Cr
furnished yau	16..27	return to August Caurt 1830 }	215..48
Apr 4 To Sundres pd yaur mather	2..50	Int on ditto	7..60
To recording this Accaunt & Receipt	..70		
To 5 p ct Commissions	1 35½		
To Ballance due the orphan	204..46		
	223..08		223..08

North Carolina }
Hertford Caunty} May 24/th/ 1831 Know all men by these present that I William H **LAND** doth for and in consideration of the
Sum of Two hundred & faur dallar/s/ & forty Six cents to me in hand paid By William B. **WYNNS** Guardian to Wife Martha
formerly Marthar **BROWN** have devised released and for ever quit Claim unto him the Said William B **WYNNS** Guardian
afore Said all manner of action or actions Suit or Suits that I have or Cauld have either my Self or any person for me on Law or
Equity against the Said William B. **WYNNS** Guardian and his heir/s/ executors or administrator/s/ from the beginning of the

(94) Martha **BROWN** (Cont.)

Warld up to the day & date aforesaid In testimony Where of I the Said William H **LAND** have hereunto
Set my hand and Seals in presents of   William H. **LAND** (Seal)
Test
M. H. **JERNIGAN**

---

(95) 66 Martha **BROWN**

Dr Martha **BROWN** orphan of Hardy **BROWN** decd In act with William B **WYNNS** Guardian Cr

Amt Brat forward	223..08		223..08

North Carolina }
Hertford County} May Caurt of Pleas &c 1831
This Account was returned to Caurt on oath by Wm B **WYNNS** Guardian at the Same time the recept was duly proved in open Caurt by the of [sic] Miles H **JERNIGAN** the Subscribing Witness thereto & ordered
to be Recorded   Test. L. M. **COWPER** clk

Peggy **CURL**

Dr Peggy **CURL** orphan In act With Jethro **CURL** Guardian   Cr

1831 To 1 p Shaes	1..50	By this amt due February Caurt 1830	29..26
To 1 bed & furniture	12..00	Interes [sic]	2..23
To Cash	01 50		39..49
To Cash pd for the Return	..20		14 20
	$14..20	Ballance due the orphan Feby court 1831	25..29

his
E E Jethro x **CURL** Guardian
mark

North Carolina }
Hertford County} May Caurt of Pleas &c 1831
This Account Was Returned to Caurt on oath by Jethro **CURL** Guard & ardered to be Recorded
Test. L. M. **COWPER**. Clk

Robert **FLYNN** [Portions of remainder of left side of page are obscured.]

Dr Robert **FLYNN** In A/c Current With Saml **MOORE** Guardian   Cr

_830		1830	
_ay 25 To Cash pd Clerk for Bond	..60	augt 1/st/ By Cash received of Carr }	
__h? 14 To ditto J **SCOTT** & Co amt Act	5..63	**DARDEN** Admr of Robert **FLYNN**}	
__ly 28 " ditto James S **JANES** his fee in Suit}		decd . . . .}	429..44
of Martha **FLYNN** as Robert **FLYNN** }	4 00	Int on ditto the Above Amt up to the	
" 5 p ct Coms on the above amts $10..93	..50	23/d/ May 1831	18 81
5 " Coms on $429..44 being the Amt of}			
_831 money received into my hands }	21..67		
1831			
_ay? Cash paid R. G. **COWPER** as Shffs}			
Ans? Execution in favar of Martha **FLYNN**}40..11			
5 p cet coms on the above Execution			
of 40..11	2 00		448..25
Cash paid Clerk for this return	..40		74..72
	74..72		373..513

North Carolina }   Ballance due the Ward   373..53
Hertford County} May Caurt of Pleas &c 1831   S. **MOORE** Guardian
This Account Was returned to Caurt on oath by Samuel **MOORE** Guard & ordered to be Recorded
Test. L. M. **COWPER** Clk

William **HOLLOMON**

Dr William **HOLLOMON** orphan of Samuel decd In acct with James **HOLLOMON** guard

_30		1830	Cr
Augt 23/d/ To Cash pd clerk	45	Augt 25/th/ By Ballance due the orphan}	
Nov 28 To Cash pd Abner **HOLLOMON**	4..16	at my return to August Caurt 1830 . }	251 79
Interest on ditto up to Feby Caurt 1831	06		

(95) William HOLLOMON (Cont.)

Der? To Cash pd Abner **HORRELL**	12½	Interest on ditto up to Feby Ct 1831	7 55

1831

Jay 1/st/ To Cash paid A. O. **ASKEW** for			
Schooling	2..00		
Interest on ditto up to Feby Cot? 1831	..02		
To rercording this account	..30		259..34
To 5 p ct Coms 74/¢/ To Ballance due		By Ballance due the orphan Feby caurt 1831	251..29
the orphan $251..29	252..03	James **HOLLOMON** Guardian
	259 34		

---

(96) 67 Jacob HOLLOMON Dr Jacob **HOLLOMON** orphan of Saml decd In a/c With James **HOLLOMON** Guar_

1830 / **1830**

Augt 23/d/ To Cash pd Clerk	45	Augt 25/th/ By this Amt due the orphan at}	
Novr 26 To Cash pd Abner **HARRELL**	4..70	my return to August Caurt 1830 }	267. 6_
Interest on ditto up to Feby Court 1831	06	By Interest on ditto up to Feby ct 1831	8. 0_
Der 20 To Cash pd Ab. **HARRELL**	..12		
1831			
Jany 5/th/ To Cash paid Alexander O **ASKEW**			
for Schooling	2..25		
Interest on ditto up to Feby ct 1831	02		
To Recording this Account	5?0		
To 5 p cet Commisions	76		
To Ballance due the orphan	267..44		275..70
	275..70		

1831

Feby 22/d/ By Ballance due the orphan	267..44
	James **HOLLOMON** Guard

North Carolina   }
Hertford Caunty} May Caurt of Pleas &c 1831
These Accaunts were returned to Caurt on oath by James **HOLLOMON** Guardd & ordered to be Recorded
Test. L. M. **COWPER** cl_

Jesse HARRELL

1830   Dr Jesse **HARRELL** orphan of Jaseph **HARRELL** decd In acct with Abner **HARRELL** Guard

August 25 To Cash pd for Sire fia &		**1830**	Cr
returns of Guardian acct	1..90	August 25 By Ballance due the Ward this}	
Novr 20 To 1 p Shaes 10/-	1..00	day by my Return to this Caurt . . . .}	102..25
30 To **MURRY** Grammer 3/9	37½	**1831**	
Decr 2 To 4½ yds Satinett @ 8/9 thread &}		Interest on ditto up to Feby Caurt 1831	3?..06
Silk 1/00½ 2½ " C cloth @ 1/3 . }	4..43¾	Feby 1/st/ By Cash 2/6 for Knife	25
9 To Cash pd Doct J R **HALL** for tuition	2..25	28 By 2/3 of hire of Negroes for 1830	
1831		payable 1/st/ Jany 1831	29 50
Jany 25 To 1 quire paper 2/6 1 Knife 2/6	50	Interest on ditto up to Feby Caurt 1831	..25
Feby 20 To Cash pd E **WILLIAMSTON** for			135..34
tuition	13..50		
" To Cash pd Leviana **BEVERLY** for			
board	36..00		
22/d/ To 1 Slate	37½		
" Cash pd clerk for this return	..40		
28 To 5 p cet Commissions on the many	4..68		
Expended & recd			
To Ballance due the orphan	69 92¼		135 .34
	135..34		

1831

(96) Jesse HARRELL (Cont.)

North Carolina }

Hertford County} May Court of Pleas &c 1831

This Account was returned to Court on oath by Abner HARRELL guard & ordered to be

Recorded

Feby 28 Ballance due the orphan   69..92¼

Abner **HARRELL** Guardian

Test L. M. **COWPER** clk

Anthony IRVIN

1831	Dr Anthony IRVIN orphan In act with Riddick CROSS Guardian		Cr
Feby To Cash pd for band & Si fa	90	1830	
To Cash paid for former return	[blank]	By this Amt due on former return	277..96
To Cash paid John A ANDERSON	6..00	Interest on $277..96 up to Feby court	
To Cash paid for board & tuition up to	10 00	1831 Say Six months from August to	
Feby Court To Cash pd B USHER fo Hat	4 00	Feby ct Are? $8..34	8..34
To Cash paid for making cloths	6..00	By rent of Land due	8 12½
	26..90		294..42

---

(97) 68 Anthony IRVIN

	Dr Anthany IRVIN In acct with Riddick CROSS Guardian		Cr
Amt Brot forward	26..90		294..42
To Cash pd for Linen for Shirt	2..44	Deduct	40 32
To Cash pd for Cloth for coat	3 75		254..10
To Cash pd for p Shaes	1..25		
To Cash pd Tax due for 1829	3..12		
To Commissions on $45 26½ cets	2 06		
To Cash pd for this return	40	Ballance due the orphan Feby Court 1831	254..10
	40..32	E E Riddick **CROSS** Guardn	

North Carolina }

Hertford County} May Court of Pleas &c 1831

This Account was returned to Court on oath by Riddick CROSS Guardian & ordered to be Recorded

Test. L. M. **COWPER** clk

Peston PERRY [Portions of remainder of left side of page are obscured.]

29	Dr Peston PERRY orphan of Joseph PERRY decd In a/c current With Agatha PERRY guard			
vr To your part Guardian bond	20	1829		Cr
To your part Devision of Negraes part}		Decr 1/st/ By this Sum received of John		}
30 Henry B VANPELT & Wife . . }	3 12½	WINBORNE admr of Joseph PERRY decd}	57 56	
Interest on ditto up to Jany 1/st/ 1831	18	Int up to Jany 1/st/ 1831	3..73	
Do Taxes 1829	50	1831		
To Clerk for renewing Guardian bond	16	Jany By your part Negro hire 1830 . . .	8..29	
To Agatha PERRY for 12 months boarding}		" " do do rent Land &c do	5..28	
Clothing the orphan Schooling &c }	12..93	" 1/st	74..86	
" your part division in Land	2 58			
1831 Commissions	20			
May? To A Ballance due orphan	54..99	Jany 1/st/ By this Ballance due the Ward	54..99	
	74 86		her	

Agatha x **PERRY** Guardian
                      mark

Mary PERRY

1829	Dr Mary PERRY orphan of Joseph PERRY decd In acct current With Agatha PERRY guard		Cr
Novr To your part Guardian bond	20	1829	
" do do Henry B VANPELT &}		Decr 1/st/ By this Sum Recd of John	}
" wife in division of Negroes . . . . }	3 12½	WINBORNE admr of Joseph PERRY decd}	57 56
Int	18	Int	3..73
" Taxes 1829	50	1831	

(97) Mary PERRY (Cont.)

" Clerk for renewing Guardian bond	16	Jay 1/st/ By yaur part Negro hire 1830	8..29
" pd Miles H **JERNIGAN** division}		" do do rent Land	5..28
on Negroes Cast . . . .}	2..58		
" board Clothing & Schooling}			
the orphan 12 months . . .}	12..93		
1831 Commisions	20		
Jany 1/st/ A Ballance due the Ward	54..99		
	74 86		74..86
		By this Sum due the Ward	54..99

her
Agatha x **PERRY** Guardian
mark

---

(98) 69 Paterick PERRY Dr Paterick **PERRY** orphan of Jaseph **PERRY** decd In a/c current with Agatha P____

1829		1829	
Novr To yaur part Guardian bond	20	Decr 1/st/ By this Sum Recd of John }	
To do do H B **VANPELT** & wife}		**WINBORNE** admr of Jaseph **PERRY** }	
in division of Negraes . . . }	3 12½	decd . . . }	57..5_
Int on ditto	18	Int up to January 1/st/ 1831	3..7_
To yaur part Taxes for 1829	50	1831	
Clerk fee renewing Guardn bond	16	Jany 1/st/ yaur part Negro hire 1830	8..29
To M H **JERNGAN** Cast }		ditto ditto rent Land &.	5..2_
division Land 1830 }	2 58		
" board Clothing Schooling	12..93		
" Commisions	20		
1831			
Jay 1/st/ To A ballance due the Ward	54..99		
	74..6886		74..8_
		By A Ballance due the Ward	54..99

this is to Certify that the above accts is
Just & true return to Feby Term 1831   her
Agatha x **PERRY**
mark

Joseph **PERRY**

1829   Dr Joseph **PERRY** orphan of Jaseph **PERRY** decd In a/c current with Agatha **PERRY** g____

Novr To yaur part Guardian Bond	..20	1829	Cr
" do do H B **VANPELT** In division}		Decr 1/st/ By this Sum recd of John }	
of Negroes . . . .}	3 12½	**WINBORNE** admr of Jaseph **PERRY**}	
" Int up to Januy 1/st/ 1831	18	decd }	57..5_
" Tax 1829	50	Int up to January 1/st/ 1831	3..7_
" Clerk fee renewing Guardian bond	16	1831	
" yaur part division on? Lands	2 58	Jany 1/st/ By yaur part negro hire 1830	8..29
" Board clothing & Schooling 1830	12..93	" do do Rent Lands 1830	5..2_
" Commissions	20		
1831			
Jany 1/st/ To A Ballance due the Ward	54..99		
	74..86		74..8_
		To A Ballance due the Ward her	54..99

Agatha x **PERRY** Guardian
mark

Elizabeth **PERRY**   gu___

1829   Dr Elizabeth **PERRY** orphan of Jaseph **PERRY** dec In a/c current with Agatha **PERRY**

(98) Elzabeth PERRY (Cont.)

Novr To your part Guardian bond	..20	
" this Sum paid H B **VANPELT** &}		
wife on division of Negroes . . }	3..12½	
" Int on ditto up January 1/st/ 1830	18	
" Taxes 1829	50	
" Clerk fee Guardian Bond	16	
" yaur part division Land	2 58	
" board Clothing & Schooling 1830	12..93	
" Commissions on [sic] . . .	20	
" A Ballance due the Ward	54..99	
	74..86	

1829		
Decr 1/st/ By this Sum Recd of John }		
WINBORNE admr of Jaseph }		
PERRY decd . . . . }	57 56?	
Int on ditto up to Janry 1/st/ 1831	3..73	
1831		
Jay 1/st/ By yaur part Negro hire 1830	8..29	
ditto ditto rent Land ditto	5..28?	
	74..86	
By this ballance due the Ward her	54..99	

               Agatha x **PERRY** Guard
                    mark

---

(99) 7C John D PERRY

1829   Dr John D **PERRY** orphan of Joseph **PERRY** decd In a/c current with Agatha **PERRY** Guardian

Novr To yaur part Guardian bond	20	
To this Sum paid H B **VANPELT** &}		
wife In division Negroes . . }	3..12½	
" Int up to Jany 1/st/ 1830	..18	
" Taxes 1829	50	
" Clerk fee renewing Guardian Bond	..16	
" yaur part division Land	2 58	
" Board Clothing & Schooling 1830	12..93	
" Commissions . . .	20	
" A Ballance due the Ward	54..99	
	74..86	

1829		
Decr 1/st/ By this Sum recd of John }		
WINBORNE admr of Jaseph }		
PERRY decd . . . . }	57 56	
Int on ditto up to Janry 1/st/ 1831	3..73	
1831		
Jay 1/st/ By yaur part Negro hire 1830	8..29	
" ditto ditto rent Land ditto	5..28	
	74..86	
By A Ballance due the Ward	54..99	

This is to Certify that the above Stated
accaunts is just & True   her
              Agatha x **PERRY** Guardian
                  mark

North Carolina }
Hertford Caunty} May Caurt of Pleas &c 1831
These Accaunts were returned to Caurt on oath By Agatha **PERRY** Guardian & orderered [sic] to be Recorded
               Test. L. M. **COWPER** clk

Hannah P REA

1830   Dr Hannah P **REA** to James **SCOTT** Guardian   Cr

__gt Cc? To pd Guardn Bond	40	
__y 1/s: To pd Mr/s/ **REA** for Board	19..60	
	20..00	

1831		
Jay 1/st/ By G **SEARBERRY**s Note for		
rent of Store Feby Co 1831 }	20..00	
	20..00	

              James **SCOTT** Guard

Nancy REA

1830   Dr Nancy **REA** to James **SCOTT** Guardian   Cr

__gt Co pd Gudn [sic] Bond	40	
1831		
Jay 1/st/ pd Mr/s/ **REA** for Board	9..60	
	10..00	

1831		
Jany 1/st/ By amt of Capt **SEARBERRY** for		
rent of Ware hause	10..00	
	10 00	

Feby Co 1831   James **SCOTT** Guard

North Carolina }
Hertford Caunty} May Caurt of Pleas &c 1831
These Accaunts were Returned to Caurt on oath by James **SCOTT** Guard & ordered to be
Recorded   Test. L. M. **COWPER** clk

(99) (Cont.)

William H SMITH

1831	Dr William H SMITH orphan In act With Riddick CROSS		Cr
To Cash paid for Guardian Bond	60	By hire of Negros due the 1/st/ January 1832	158..75
To Commissions on $158..75 @ 5 p ct	7..93	By Ballance due the orpan the	8..93
To Cash pd for this return	..40	1/st/ of January 1832	149 82
	8..93	E E Riddick CROSS Guardian	

North Carolina }

Hertford Caunty} May Caurt of Pleas &c 1831

This Account was Returned to Caurt on oath by Riddick CROSS Guard & ordered to be
Recorded   Test. L. M. COWPER clk

---

(100) 71 Elizabeth VANPELT Dr Elizabeth VANPELT in A/c current with Henry B VANPELT

1829		1829		Cr
Novr Term To Cash pd Lewis M COWPER}		Decr 2/d/ By Cash recd of John WINBORNE		7..3_
for Guardian Bond }	60	By Int on do up to Jany 5/th/ 1831		4..7_
1830 To Interest on do up to Jany 5/th/ 1831	04	By her part of Negro hire for up to}		
Sept 1/st/ To Cash pd Abner HARRELL	3 26	Jany 5/th/ 1831		∠0..8_
To 1 pr Shaes	1..75			
To Int on $5..01 from Sept 1/st/ till Jany 5/th	10			
Nov 16 To Cash pd J G WILSON	3 57½			
1830				
Novr Term To Cash pd Lewis M COWPER	1..90			
Der. 20 To Cash pd for Negro Blanket	62½			
To returning this Guardian acct	20			
To Commissions allawed the Guardian	6..45			
To Ballance due the orphan	98..60			
	117..10			117..1_
		1831		
		Jany 5/th/ By Ballance due the orphan		98..60

North Carolina }

Hertford Cauntey} May Caurt of Pleas &c 1831   Henry B VANPELT Gua__

This Accaunt was returned to Caurt on oath by Henry B VANPELT Guardian & ordered
To be Recorded   Test. L. M. COWPER c__

Joseph YEATES

Dr Joseph YEATES orphan of William YEATES in act with James B YEATES Gu___			
To Cash pd Clerk for Bond Sci fa	1..60	1831	
&? for this Return	20	May 23/d/ By Cash from the Estate of Jesse YEATES}	
To 5 p cet Commisson	3..07½	decd yaur former Guardian }	6..50
To Ballance due the orphan	67..12	By rent of Land for 1829 due the	
		8 of Jay 1831	2..00
		Int on ditto up to this return	1..41?
		By rent of Land for 1830 and hire	
		of Negroes	44..37
		Int on ditto from 8/th/ Jany up to this}	
		return Jany Feby Caurt 1831 }	..37
	72 64	Feby Caurt 1831	72 64
		Balance due the orphan	67..12

North Carolina }   James YEATES Guardian

Hertford Caunty} May Caurt of Pleas &c 1831

This Accaunt was returned to Caurt on oath by James YEATES Guard & ordered to be Recorded
Test. L. M. COWPER clk

(100) (Cont.)

Martha WIGGINS   guar_

1831   Dr Martha WIGGINS orphan of Joshua WIGGINS decd in a/c with Susannah WIGG___

To Cash pd Sheff for Taxes due for 1829	85	**1831**	**Cr**
do paid do? pr Returns	20	By this Sum due pr Last return} made to Feby Ct 1830 }	17..74
		By Interest on the above Sum from} Feby ct 1830 to may Caurt }	
		1831 one year & 3 months}	1..33
	1..05		19.07
		Ballance due the orphan her	18..02

Susannah x **WIGGINS**
mark

(101) 72 Elizabeth WIGGINS   her guard

          Dr Elizabeth WIGGINS orphan of Jashua WIGGINS decd A/c with Susannah **WIGGINS**

1831? To Cash paid Shff for Taxes /due/		**1831**	**Cr**
for 1829	..85	By this Amt due pr Last return made	
To Cash paid Clerk pr returns 2/	20	to Feby Ct 1830	17..74
To Articles furnished	28	By Interest on the above Sum from Feby} Court 1830 to May 1831 one Year &3 }	
		Months }	1..33
	1..33		19..07
		Ballance due the orphan her	17..74

Susannah x **WIGGINS**
mark

James WIGGINS   his gdn

1831   Dr James WIGGINS orphan of Jashua WIGGINS decd In A/c with Susannah **WIGGINS**

To Cash paid Sheriff for Taxes		**1831**	**Cr**
due for 1829	85	By this amt due pr last Return made} to Feby Caurt 1830 }	17..74
" Cash paid pr returns 2/	20	By Interest on the above Sum from Feby}	
To Articles furnished	28	Court 1830 to May 1831 1 Year 3 }	
		Months }	1..33
	1..33		19..07
		Ballance due the orphan her	17..74

Susannah x **WIGGINS**
mark

Mary WIGGINS   her guard

1831   Dr Mary WIGGINS orphan of Jashua WIGGINS in A/c with Susannah **WIGGINS**

To Cash paid Shff for Taxes		1831	
due for 1829	85	By this amt due pr last return made} to Feby ct 1830	17..74
" Cash paid Clerk pr returns 2/	20	By Interest on the above amt from Feby}	
To Articles furnished	28	Ct 1830 to May 1831 Say 1 Year &}	
		3 Months }	1..33
	1..33		19..07
		Ballance due the orphan her	17..74

Susannah x **WIGGINS**
mark

North Carolina }
Hertford County} May Caurt of Pleas &c 1831
These Accaunt was returned to Caurt on oath by Susannah **WIGGINS** Guard & ordered to be

(101) Mary WIGGINS (Cont.)
To Recorded   Test. L. M. **COWPER** clk

William **BOON**

1830   Dr William **BOON** orphan of Bird **BOON** decd In A/c With John **BARRETT** his Guardian

Augt ct To paid L M **COWPER** for return			Amt Brot up	54..869¼
& recpt	2..70			
" 3 yds Linen Brown @ 3/3 Shff of}			25/th/ E. S. **JEGITS** pr recept . . .	4..00
Sauthamptan pr recpt 1..07 }	3..69		1 pr Gloves Bot yaur Self 5/3?	87½
Octr 14th " paid Perry **BACKUS** for			one Book Arritimetic [sic] 3/	..50
making Cloths	[blank]		one pair Shaes 8/3 pair Socks 2/3	1..75
" 2 pair Shaes @ $1..12½	3..12½		March 23/d/ paid Clements **ROCHELLE**	
Decr " paid P **BACKUS** for making cloths	..93¾		pr recpt	3 12½
1831			June 1 pr Shaes 8/3 July quire paper 1/6	1..62½
Jay 4/th/ " paid L M **COWPER** pr recpt	9..13		July paid Penny **BACKUS** for making}	
" " " James **SCOTT** pr do	3 25		Clathes }	2 50
" " " Richard W **JOHNSON** pr do	13..22		Augt 1/st/ paid pr Richard W **JOHNSON**	
" " " John W **SAUTHALL** pr do	13..89		pr recpt	23..05
Feby? 21/st/ " " 1 hat Bot yaur Self	4..75		Amt Carried over	91..3_¾
Carred up	524..89¼			

(102) 73 William **BOON**

Dr William **BOON** orphan of Bird **BOON** decd In A/c with John **BAR____**   Cr

Amt Brot over	91..31¾	1830 Aug 25/th/ By Ballance due the Ward}	
3 & 4 To Cash $8 50 two yds Catton		this day on last return . . . . }296_..6_	
clath @ 10/¢/	8..70	1831	
19 " paid P **BACKUS** for making 1? Shirt		J Augt 1/st/ By Land rent due this day	10_00
& pantaloons . . .3/9	62½	Int on $10 land rent from 1/st/ Jay 1831}	
Wards Board from 21/st/ Feby 1830}		till 22 August 1831 . . . .}	..3_
till 22/d/ August 1831 with me @ }		Augt 24 By 12 months Ints on $2789..72	167..3_
$4 pr month }	72..00		
Augt 24 " Comissions on $302..59 @ 5 pct	17..62		
Ballance due the orphan	2949..92		
	3142 38		3142..38

North Carolina }
Hertford Caunty} August Caurt of Pleas &c 1831   John **BARRETT** Guard
This Accaunt was Returned to Caurt on oath By John **BARRETT** Guardian & ordered to be
Recorded   Test. L. M. **COWPER** c__

Newit **VICK**

Dr Newit **VICK** in acct Current With Benj/a/. **BRYANT** Guardian   Cr

To 20 /¢/ cets for returning the Act	20	By Cash	25..99
To 1 Hat at $2 50	2..50	By the Interest of? $25..99/¢/ for twelve}	
To Commissions on $4..29	21	months . . . . }	1..59
	2..91		27..58
	27..56		
	2..91		
Ballance due	·24..67		27..58

Cordia **VICK**

Dr Cordia **VICK** In Account Current With Benjamin **BRYANT** Guardian   C_

To To [sic] 20 /¢/ for returning this Act	20	By Cash	25..99
To 1 Hat at $2 50	2..50	By the Interest of? $25..99 for twelve}	
To Commissions on $4..29	..21	months . . . . }	1..59
	2..91		27..58

(102) Cordia VICK (Cont.)

	27..56		
	2..91		
Balance due	24..67		27.58
		B [sic]	Benjamin **BRYANT** Guard

North Carolina }
Hertford County} August of [sic] Pleas &c 1831
These Accounts were returned to Court on oath By Benjamin **BRYANT** Guard & ordered
to be Recorded   Test. L. M. **COWPER** clk

Rebecah VICK

Dr Rebecah **VICK** In acct current with Benjamin **BRYANT** Guardian			Cr
To 20/¢ for returning this acct	..20	By Cash.	25..99
To 1 Bonnet at 80/¢/	80	By the Interest on $25..99 for}	
To Commissions on $2..59	..12	Twelve months . . . . . }	1..59
	1..12		27..58
	27 58		Benjamin **BRYANT** Guardia_
	1..12		
Ballance due	26 46		

---

(103) 74 Rebecah VICK

Dr Rebecah **VICK** In A/c current with Benjamin **BRYANT** Guardian		Cr
Amt Brot forward	26..46	27..58

North Carolina }
Hertford County} August Court of Pleas &c 1831
This Account was Returned to Court on oath by Benjamin **BRYANT** Guardian & ordered to be
Recorded   Test. L. M. **COWPER** Clk

Etney VICK

Dr Etney **VICK** In A/c current with Benjamin **BRYANT** Guardian			Cr
To 20 for returning this Acct	20	By Cash	25..99
To Commissions on $1..79	.. 8	By the Interest on $25..99 for twelve}	
	28	months }	1..59
	27..58		27..58
	28		
Ballance due	27..30		27..58

William VICK

Dr William **VICK** In A/C Current with Benjamin **BRYANT** Guardian			Cr.
To 20 for paid returning this Acct	..20	By Cash	25..99
To Commissions on $1..79	8	By the Interest on $25..99 for twelve}	
	00..28	months }	1..59
	27..58		27..58
	28		
Ballance due	27..30		27..58

North Carolina }
Hertford County} August Court of Pleas &c 1831   Benjamin **BRYANT** Gudn
These Accounts were returned to Court on oath by Benjamin **BRYANT** Guardian & ordered to be
Recorded   Test. L. M. **COWPER** clk

Margaret WHITLEY

Dr Margaret **WHITLEY** in A/c with George **WHITLEY** her Guard			Cr
To amt paid Patrick **BROWN** pr bill	3..06	1831	
To Cash paid Clerk for bond & return}		Augt ct By amount due the ward on my}	
to August Court 1830 }	..70	last return at August Court 1830 }	8 39

(103) Margaret **WHITLEY** (Cont.)

To ditto for this return	20	To amt due from the Sales of l?ands}	
To 5 p cet Commissions on paid aut		which was Sold by the Clerk & master}	75..75
& recd	3..95		84..4
Ballance due the Ward	7..91		
To Aus?gt Caurt 1831 his	76 23		

George x WHITLEY
mark

David **WHITLEY**

Dr David WHITLEY in A/c with George WHITLEY his Guardian   Cr

To amt paid Patrick **BROWN** as pr bull	2..25	**1831**	
To making my return & renewing bond to}		augt ct By amt due the ward on my}	
August Ct 1830 . . . . }	..70	last return at augt ct 1830 }	8..89
To making this return	..20	To amt due from the Sales of }	
	3..15	land which was Sold by the clerk & master}	75..75
		Amt Carried forward	$76..64

---

(104) 75 David **WHITLEY** Dr David **WHITLEY** In A/C with George **WHITLEY** Guardian   Cr

Amt Brot forward	3..15		76.._
To 1 pr Shaes	37½		
To Commissions on the amt recd & paid	3..95		
	7..97		
Ballance due the ward to}		his	76..6 .
Augt Ct 1831 . . . .}	76..67	George x **WHITLEY**	
		mark	

North Carolina }

Hertford Caunty} August Caurt of Pleas &c 1831

these Accaunts were returned to Caurt on oath by George **WHITLEY** Guardian & ordered
to be Recorded   Test. L. M. **COWPER**

Jabez **WHEELER**

1830		Dr Jabez **WHEELER** In A/c with James **WORRELL** his Guardian	Cr
August 25 To Cash paid Clerk for }		**1831**	
returning Guardian bond & renewing}	1..90	Augt 23/d/ By Ballance due on last return	1399 .95
" Int on ditto 12 mo/s/	11	Int on ditto 12 months	83 .99
Decr 11 To Cash paid yau in MfrBoro [sic]	4..50		
1831 Int on ditto	18		
Jany 29 To do paid yau	20..00		
Int on ditto	68		
March 2/d/ To do paid yau	2..00		
Int an ditto	05		
May 15/th/ To do pd yau	2..00		
Int on ditto	02		
June 8 To ditto paid yau	3 00		
Augt 22/nd/ To 5 p cet coms on recpts &			
Expendatures amting to $718	5..90		
	40..34		
Ballance due the orphan	1443 60		
	1483 94		1483..94

James WORRELL Guardian

North Corolina }

Hertford Caunty} August Caurt of Pleas &c 1831

This Accaunt was returned to Caurt on oath by James **WARRELL** Guardian & ordered to be
Recorded   Test. L. M. **COWPER** clk

(104) ıCont.)

State oᴝ North Carolina} William H. WILSONs rect to John G. WILSON

Herᴝfoᴝd Caunty   } This day Settleed with John G WILSON my Guardian and recdved from him all my proportionable part of property by Which fell to me from my Farther George WILSON Decd and my Sister Rebecca WILSON Consisting of one Negro ᴣay SOLLOMON and eight hundred & twenty five Dollar/s/ and thirty five ½ cents which is in full of demands or ClaimsI have against the Said John G WILSON Guardian as before named June 1/st/ 1831

Witᴣess   William H WILSON

John HARRELL

North Carolina }

Herᴝfoᴝd Caunty} August Caurt of Pleas &c 1831

This Recept was proveed in open Caurt by the oath of John HARRELL the Subscribing witness

thereᴝo & ordered to be recorded   Test. L. M. COWPER clk

---

(105) ᴝ6 Rebecca P BRITT

      Dr Rebecca P BRITT orphan of James E BRITT decd In A/C with Henry L WILLIAMS guard

1830		1830	Cr
Feby? 23/d/ To Ballance due me from the last return	301..94	Sept 24 Recd of Carr DARDEN one nate against Thomas SHONE? & himself for $44..50	$ 44..50
Interest on $31..94 for 1 year }			
To Cash paid Clerk for Ishueing si fa} & renewing Bond . . . . . . .75}	1..85	Interest from 24 September 1830 to 22 Augt 1831	2..44
Interest from 23/d/ of August 1830 to } 22/d, Augt 1831 4½}	80	1831	
1831		Jany 13 Recd of Elias BRITT one nate for the hire of PONK for 1830	40..25
___ 19 Cash pd John W SAUTHALL as 1831 ᴘ bill	28..91	Interest from 13 of Janry 1831 to the 22 Augt 1831	1 40
Augt? 20 Cash paid Miss Phebe HILL} for dᴝessing Bonnet }	3..75		
To Commission on $33..46 cents being} the amount paid aut at 5 ct }	1..67		
To Commissions on 88 dallar/s/ & } 59 being the amount recd of Carr } DARDEN & Elias BRITT at 5 p cet}	4..42		
1831			
Augt 22/d/ Cash paid Clerk for making} this return . . . .}	40		
	72..74		
To Ballance due the Ward to 22/d/ Augt 1831	15..85		
	88..59	This return to August Caurt 1831	88..59
		1831	
		Augt 22/d/ Ballance due the Ward on this return 15..85	
		E E Henry L. WILLAIMS gd	

Norᴝh Carolina }

Hertford Caunty} November Caurt of Pleas &c 1831

This Accaunt Was returned to Caurt on oath by Henry L WILLIAMS Guardian & ordered to be Recorded   Test. L. M. COWPER clk

---

Samueᴝ F. MAGET

1828 Dr Samuel F. MAGET minor in A/c with his Guardian Jno WADDILLE			
Decr 1ᴝ/th/ To paid Doct BORLAND acct 13..50			Cr
Int compounded to Feby ct 1831}	2..74	By this Amt recd of Nicholas MAGET} Admr of John MAGET decd on the }	
1829 2 years & 2 months }		24/th/ may 1828 . . . . }	962..39
Decr 30 To paid Shff COWPER yaur} part of Land tax for 1827 & 1828 }	4..16	Int comp/d/ on this amt to Feby } Caurt 1831 2 year/s/ 7 moths [sic]}	164..84
Int comp/d/ to Feby ct 1831 2 years & 2 mc/s/	..72	By this amt for negro hire &c 1828	56..30

(105) Samuel F. MAGET (Cont.)

Oct? 12 To paid Coln **DARDEN**s fee for		
bill? in equity	8..95	
Int comp/d/ to Feby ct 1831-1 year 4½ mo/s/	..75	
Jay 17 To paid Coln **DARDEN** for Keep-}		
ing negro bay **MASES** the year 1828 }	15 00	
Int comp/d/. To Feby Ct 1831 2 ys 1½ mos	1..98	
Jay 1/st/ To paid Mr/s/ Mason **MAGET** for}		
Keeping Negro Ben **CHINA** & his Child . }	8..00	
Int comp/d/ to Feby Caurt 1831-2 ys 2 mo/s/	1..03	
1830		
Jany 1/st/ To paid Mr/s/ Mason **MAGET**}		
for Keeping Bay **BEN** 1829 . . . . . }	6..00	
Int Comp/d/ to Feb ct 1831-1 y 2 mo/s/	40	
To paid **MORGAN COWPER** & Co a/c	4..45	
Int comp/d/ Feby ct 1831	25	
	67..93	
Amt Carried forward		

Int Comp/d/ to Feb ct 1831-2 year/s/	
2 mo/s/	7..55
By this amt for hire of Negraes &c 1829}	
due 1/st/ Jay 1830 . . . . }	121 .41
Int Comp/d/ to Feb ct 1831-1 yr 2 mo/s/	8..35
By this amt for hire of Negraes &c}	
for 1830 due 1/st/ Jany 1831 }	131..74
Int to Feby ct 1831 2 months	1..31
	1452..89
Deduct	163 96
	1288..93
	1288..53
Amt carried forward	

---

(106) 77 Samuel F. MAGET Dr Samuel F MAGET minor in A/c with his Guardian Jno WA_____   Cr   1288..5_

1830 Amt Brot forward 67..93	
Augt 25/th/ To paid Sheriff **CAWPER**}	
yaur part of Land Tax for 1829 . . } 4..16	
Int to Feby caurt 1831 13	
1831	
Jany 14 To paid Mr/s/ Mason **MAGET** for}	
keepin bay **BEN** & girl **SARAH** for 1830} 12..00	
Int to Feby Ct 1831 06	
12/th/ To part Eli **CARTER**s A/c 87½	
Feby 24/th/ To paid Edw/d/ S. **JEGITTS** A/c 2 15½	
To 5 p ct Coms on $15..33 being the	
amt of receipts & Expendatures up	
to Feby Ct 1831 including the Int	
that has anneed? on the ballance due ward} 76..65	
163..96	
1288..93	
1452..89	

                    1288..93

North Carolina }
Hertford Caunty} November Caurt of Pleas &c 1831   due Ward to Feby ct 1831   1288..93
This Accaunt was returned to Caurt on oath by John **WADDILLE** Guardian & ordered   John **WADDILLE** Gua__
to be Recorded   Test. L. M. **COWPER** cl_

James MAGET

1828   Dr James **MAGET** minor in A/C with his Guardian John **WADDILLE**

Decr 18/th/ To paid Doct **BORLAND** act	2..50	
Int compd to Feby Ct 1831-2 year/s/}		
2 months . . . .}	..33	
1829		
Decr 20/th/ To paid Shff **COWPER** yaur}		
part of Land Tax for 1827 & 1828 . . .}	4..16	
Int Comp/d/ to Feby Ct 1831-1 year 2 mo/s/	30	
Oct 12/th/ To paid Coln **DARDEN** fee for}		
bill in Equity . . . . }	8..95	
Int Compd to Feby caurt 1831 1 year}		
4½ months . . . . }	75	

Amt Brot forward	40..89½
August 25/th/ To paid **mary WILLS** for}	
keeping Expensive woman & 2 children }	
in 1829	15 00
Int to Feby Caurt 1831	..90
1831	
Sept 3/d/ To paid Pelt **THAMAS** amt for	
yaur Board	20..00
Int to Feby Caurt 1831	60
Der 1/st/ To paid Doct **PEEL**s medical acct	5..00

(106) James MAGET (Cont.)

Jay 17 To paid Coln **DARDEN** for keeping		Int to Feby ct 1831	..08
Negro Woman **CHILA** in 1828	10..00	Jany 1/st/ To paid Mr/s/ Mason **MAGET**}	
Int comp/d to Feb ct 1831 2 year}		for keeping **STEPHEN** in 1829 }	6..00
1½ months . . . . . . }	1 25	Int to Feb ct 1831-1 year 2 mo/s/	..40
Jany 1/st/ To paid Mr/s/ Mason **MAGET** for}		1831	
maintenance of Negro **STEPHEN** in 1828}	5 00	Jany 1/st/ To paid Mr/s/ Mason **MAGET** for}	
Int comp/d/ to Feb ct 1831 2 year/s/ &		keeping **STEPHEN** in 1830 . . . . . . }	6..00
2 months	62½	In [sic]	03
1830		6/th/ To paid Mary **WILLS** for keeping }	
Augt 25/th/ To paid Shff **COWPER** for		**FEREBY** & 3 Children 1830	29..00
yaur part of Land Tax for the year 1829	4..16	Int	..25
Int to Feby Ct 1831	..13	Feby 12/th/ To paid Eli **CARTERs** act	2..00
May 1/st/ To paid **MORGAN** & **COWPER**		" 21/st/ To paid mis **CASE?** for yaur board	31..80
& co ac	2..61	" 24/th/ To paid Edw/d/ S **JEGITTS** act	2..15
Int to Feby ct 1831	..13		160..11
	40..89½		
Amt Carried forward		Amt carried forward	

---

(107) 73 James MAGET

Dr James **MAGET** minor in account with his Guardian John **WADDILLE**			Cr
Amt Brot forward	$160..11	By this amt Recd of Nicholas **MAGET**}	
To 5 p cet Coms on $1675 26 being the}		Admr of John **MAGET** decd on the }	
amt of recepts & Expenditures }		24th may 1828 }	962..39
up to Feby Caurt 1831 including }		Int Comp/d/ on this amt to Feby }	
the Interest that has anneed on the }		Caurt 1831 2 year/s/ 9 months }	164 964
Ballance due ward }	83..76	By this amt for Negro hire &c 1828	57..25
	243 87	Int from 1/st/ Jany 1829 to Feby ct 1831}	
Amt of receipts with Interest	1425..26	Comp/d/ . . . . }	7..70
Amt of Expenditures & Coms	243 87	By amt for hire &c /in/ 1829 . . .	119..91
Amt due ward at Feby ct 1831	1182..39	Int to Feby Ct 1831	8..39
		By this amt for hire &c in 1830	103..75
		Int to Feby ct 1831	1..03
North Carolina }	1182 39		1425..26

Hertford Caunty} November Caurt of Pleas &c 1831
This Accaunt was returned to Caurt on oath by John **WADDILL** Guardian & ordered to be
Recorded　　　　　　　　　　　　　　　　　　　　Test. L. M. **COWPER** clk

William **PARKERs** Receipt to William B **WYNNS** November Court 1831.
Received of William B **WYNNS** Guardian to my wife Elizabeth formely Elizabeth **BROWN** the Sum of one hundred and eighty Two dallar/s/ and Seven cents in full for all demands that I have against Said **WYNNS** as Guardian and I do here by descharge and aquit the Said **WYNNS** as Guardian from all Suit or Suits Either in law or Equity that I have or Cauld have or any person Claiming under me In witness I have hereunto Set my hand and Seal this 26 day of September 1831
Witness　　　　　　　　　　　　　　　　　　　　William **PARKER** (Seal)
M H **JERNIGAN**
North Carolina }
Hertford Caunty} November Caurt of Pleas &c 1831
This receipt was proved in open Caurt by the oath of Miles H **JERNIGAN** the Subscribing
Witness thereto & ordered to be Recorded　　　　　　　　Test. L. M. **COWPER** clk

---

William **WARDs** Receipt to A **BARDWELL** November Court 1831.
This day Settled all Accounts with A **BARDWELL** my Guardian and faund due A **BARDWELL** the Sum of $720..50 for which I gave him my Note October 5? th 1830
John **ALEXANDER**　　　　　　　　　　　　　　　William **WARD**
North Carolina }

(107) William **WARD**s Receipt (Cont.)
Hertford Caunty} November Caurt of Pleas &c 1831
this receipt was acknoledged in open Caurt by William **WARD** & ordered to be Recorded
Test. L. M. **COWPER** clk

John **MAGET**

1830	Dr John MAGET In act Current with Jacob HARE his Guardian		Cr
Sept 1/st/ To Cash paid R. G. COWPER}		1830	
Taxes on Land for 1829 . . . . . .}	4..16	augt 24/th/ By Ballance due last return	1032..56
Int up to 24 august 1831	..24	Int on ditto up to 24 augt 1831	61..95
3 To paid James SCOTT &c amt of act	3..12½	By hire of Negro JACQB 1830	30 00
Int on ditto up to 24 augt 1831	..17	" " WILES	46..30
To Cash paid William P MORGAN act	5..25	" " CROFFORD . . .	31 50
	12..94½	" " MIKE	26..75
			1229. 06

---

(108) 79 John **MAGET** Dr John **MAGET** In A/c current with Jacob **HARE** his Guardia_

	Amt Brot forward	12..94½		Cr	
	To Int on ditto to 24 Aug 1831	..30		1229..06	
Novr 6 To paid Mr/s/ Mason MAGET for}			**EDITH**	2..75	
keeping Negro CLARA & Child ANNIS &}			rent of 1/3 of Land to Mr/s/ MAGET	7..33	
EDITH the year 1828 let out by N MAGET}			rent of Land BATTON field to Benja BEAL	1 66	
Admr . . . .}	11..00		Int from 25/th/ Decr 1830 to the 24/th/}		
Int on ditto up to 24 Aug 1831	..50		Augt 1831 . . . .}	5..85	
8 To Cash paid John W SAUTHALLs act 29..93					
Int on ditto	1..41				
1831					
Apl 1/st/ To pd Mr/s/ N. YANCY for Board 15..50					
Int on ditto	36				
To 5 p cet com/s/ on recepts & expenditures					
amounting to 286$	14..30				
Augt 24/th/ To Ballance due the orphan	1160..40				
	1246..65			1246. 65	

North Carolina }   Novr 27/th/ 1831   Jacob **HARE** Guardiar
Hertford Caunty} November Caurt of Pleas &c 1831
This Account was returned to Caurt on oath by Jacob **HARE** Guardian & ordered to be
Recorded   Test. L. M. **COWPER** clk

Emily **ASKEW** Dr Emily **ASKEW** orphan of David **ASKEW** decd In act with Aaron **ASKEW** Jur

				Cr
to recording this Account	..40	By this amt due the orphan at my }		
To Cash paid John ASKEW admr of}		return to Feby Caurt 1831 . . }	260..52	
David ASKEW yaur farther on act }		Int on ditto up to Feby Caurt 1832	15..63	
of a refunding bond given Said Admr}		By yaur half of Negro hire for 1831	60 12½	
when I took the property aut his hands}		Int on ditto from 1/st/ Jany 1832 to this}		
as pr recept . . . .}	60..00	return	60½	
Int on ditto from the 21/st/ of July 1828	12 90	By yaur half rents of Land for 1831	7..00	
1830		Int on ditto	07	
Jay 1/st/ To Cash paid David & Marcus			343 95	
RYON	7..02½	1832		
Int on ditto	06½	Feby 27/th/ By Ballance due the orphan	249..62	
1831		deduct from the above Balance }		
Sept 9/th/ To Cash pd William D		pd Clerk to renew Guardian bond}		
VALLINTINE	2..50	Natice & return to Augt co/t/ 1831.}	1..57	
Int on ditto	06	Due the orphan	248..05	

(108) Emily **ASKEW** (Cont.)

July 27.th/ To Cash pai [sic] R G **COWPER**		
Shff for Taxes	1	40
Sept 20'th/ To Cash paid Lewis		
BOND Shff for do	1..	45
Int on ditto		03
To 5 p cet commissions	8..	46
To Ballance due the orphan	249..	62
	343..	95

Aaon O. **ASKEW** Guardian   Cr

Levina **ASKEW** Dr Levina **ASKEW** orphan of David **ASKEW** decd In act with Aaron **ASKEW** Jur gu___

Cr

To recording this acct	40	By Ballance due the orphan at my}		
To Cash paid John **ASKEW**		return to Feby Caurt 1831 }	264..	66
administrator of David **ASKEW** yaur		Int on ditto up to Feby caurt 1832	15..	87
farthar [sic] on Account of a refunding		By yaur half of Negro hire for 1831	60..	12½
Bond given Said Admr when I took the		Int on ditto		60½
property aut of his hands as		By yaur half of rents of Land for 1821 [sic]	7	00
pr receipt	60..00	Amt carried forward	348	26
	60..40			

---

(109) 80 Levina **ASKEW**

Dr Levina **ASKEW** orphan of David **ASKEW** decd In A/c with Aaron **ASKEW** Jur Guardian   Cr

Amt Brat forward	$ 60	40		348..	26
Int on ditto from the 21/st/ of July 1828	12..	90	Int on ditto		..07
To Cash paid Richard G **COWPER**}			1832	348	33
Sheff for Taxes . . . . }	1..	40	Feby 27 Ballance due the orphan	256	16
Int on ditto		04?	deduct from the the Above Ballance		
1831			pd clerk to renew Guardian Bond Notice		
Sept 9/th/ To Cash paid William D			& return	1..	57
VALLENTINE	..50		Due the orphan	254..	59
20 Tc Cash paid Lewis **BOND** Sheriff					
for Taxes	1..	45			
Int on ditto		03			
1832					
Jany 1/st/ To Cash paid D & Marcus **RYON**	7	02½			
Int on ditto		06½			
To 5 p cet Commissions	8	36			
To Ballance due the orphan	256..	16			
	348..	33		254..	59

Aaron O.**ASKEW** Guardian

North Carolina }

Hertford County} February Court of Pleas &c 1832

These Accounts were returned to Court on oath by Aaron O. **ASKEW** Guardian & ordered to be

Recorded   Test L. M. **COWPER** clk

James H **BRITT**

1831   Dr James H **BRITT** orphan William D **BRITT** In a/c with E. D. **BRITT** Guardn

_vr 26 To Cash paid yau when yau started}			1831		Cr
to New Orleans . . . . }	125..	00	Feby 28/th/ By Ballance due on las [sic]		
---- /th/ To 3 mos Int on ditto	1..	87	return	66..	35
Dec 24/th/ To Cash paid Taxes on Land	2..	40	12 mo Int on ditto	3..	98
1832			Nov 30 By 1/5 part of the bal of Sales of}		
Feby 27/th/ for " for Guardian return	40		Land Sald by R G **COWPER** Shff }	61..	16
To 5 p cet Com/s/ on receipts and }			3 mo/s/ Int on ditto	..91	
Expenditures amounting to $222.18/¢/}	11..	10	1832		

(109) James H BRITT (Cont.)

To Ballance due the orphan	18..09	Jay 1/st/ rent of Land for 1831	26..20
	158..86	2 mo/s/ Int on ditto	26
			158..86
		Feby 27 By Ballance due the orphan	18..09

1831   E. D. **BRITT** Guardian

Novr 27 Recd of Elisha D **BRITT** my Guardian one hundred & twenty five dallar/s/ which I promise
to Acct for in our Settlment

Witness   J H **BRITT**

Geor M **MULLEN**

North Carolina }

Hertford Caunty} Febyary Caurt of Pleas &c 1832

This Account was returned to Caurt on oath by Elisha D **BRITT** Guardian & ordered
to be Recorded   Test. L. M. **COWPER** clk

Rebeckah **BRITT**   guardian

Dr Rebeckah **BRITT** orphan of William D **BRITT** decd In a/c with Davis **BRYANT**

1832 To Cash paid Clerks fee	30		Cr
Jay 2 To Cash pd Taxes on Land	2..40	By rent of Land	26..20
18 To Cash pd Richard **JOHNSON**s a/c	25..45	Feby 27 By amt of Sales of Land}	
To Cash " John **SAITHALL**s do	9..35	with Inst to this date . . . . }	62 07
Feby 16 To do pd Board to			88..27
Henry **BARRETT**	20..00		67..81
To amt due me Feby 1831	2..88	Ballance Due the ward	20..46
To Commissions on $148 65/¢/ at 5 pct	7..43		
	67..81		

---

(110) 81 Margaret BRITT Dr Margaret **BRITT** orphan of William D **BRITT** decd in a/c with Davis **BRYA__**

1832 To Cash pd Clerks fee	30	By amt due the ward	63..83
Jay 2/d/ To Cash pd tax on land	2..40	Feby 27 By Int on $63..83 for one year	3..8_
18 To Cash paid Richard **JOHNSON**s a/c	6..00	By rent of Land	26..20
To Cash paid for Schooling	6..00	By amt of Sale of Land and Int to ths date	62..07
To Cash paid John **SAUTHALL** a/c	87½		155.9_
Feby 16 To Cash paid Henry **BARRETT**			53..75
for board	31..25	Ballance due the ward	$102..11?
To Commissions on $132..92 @ 5 p ct	6..94		Davis **BRYANT** Guard
	53 76½		

North Carolina }

Hertford Caunty} February Caurt of Pleas &c 1832

These Accounts were returned to Court on oath By Davis **BRYANT** Guardian & ordered to be
Recorded   Test. L. M. **COWPER** clk

Alexander **BRITT**

1831   Dr Alexander **BRITT** orphan of William D **BRITT** in act with E D **BRITT** gu___

Feby 28/th/ To Cash paid for return	20	1831	Cr
Sept 17 To Cash paid Richard W}		Feby 28 By Ballance due on last return	52..32
JOHNSON for Shaes . . . .}	1 00	12 mo/s/ Int on ditto	3..14
Decr 24 To Cash pd Taxes on Land	2..40	Nov 30 1/5 part of the bal of Sales of Land}	-
Jany 19 To Cash R W **JOHNSSTON**s [sic]		Sold By R G **COWPER** Shff . . . . .}	61 66
acct	6..98	" 2 mo/s/ Int on ditto	91
" " do pd J W **SAUTHALL**s A/C	1..62	1832	
" " do pd Patrick **BROWN**s do	1..75	Feby 27 By rent of Land 1831 (1/5 part)	20..20
" " do paid James **SCOTT**s do	1..25	" " 2 mo/s/ Int on ditto	.26
" " do paid James **WORRELL** for			143..99
Tuition	15..00		

(110) Alexander BRITT (Cont.)

" " do paid for making Shoes	..37½
" ' 12 mo/s/ Board at 4 pr mo . .	48..00
Feby 27 To 5 p cet Commissins on recpts &}	
Expenditures amounting to $170	8..50
To Ballance due the orphan	56..92
	143..99

143..99

By Ballance due the orphan 27/th/ of}

North Carolina }

Feby 1832 . . . .} 56..92

Hertford County} February Court of Pleas &c 1832

E. D. BRITT Guardian

This Account was returned to Court on oath by Elisha D BRITT Guardian & ordered
to be Recorded

Test. L. M. COWPER. clk

═══════════════════════════════

William BEVERLY

Dr William BEVERLY orphan of William BEVERLY dec in act current with Jas YE____

1831 To Cash paid E. WILLIAMSON				Cr
for tuition	10..40	By Ballance due him augt term 1830	84..94
May 25th/ To Commissions on $94	4..70	Interest up February Term 1832	7..64
Feby term To paid Clerk fees . . .	60		
To Balance due the Ward}			
February Term 1832 . . }	76..88		
	92..58	E E given under my hand this February	92..58

North Carolina }

Term 1832 James YEATES Guardian

Hertford County} February Court of Pleas &c 1832

This Account was returned to Court on oath by James YEATES & ordered
to be recorded

═══════════════════════════════

(111) 82 Martha BEVERLY

Dr Martha BEVERLY orphan of William BEVERLY ded In a/c current with James YEATES

1830? To Cash paid Clerks fees	60	By Amt due her August Term 1830	83..52
___ Term To Commissions on $91..36	4..56	Int on ditto	7..66
___ Term To paid Clerk for this present			
return	..60		
To Balance due the ward	85..48		
	91..18	E E given under my hand this	91..18

North Carolina

February Term 1832 James YEATES Guardian

Hertford County February Court of Pleas &c 1832

this Account was returned to Court on oath by James YEATES Guardian & ordered to be Recorded

Test. L. M. COWPER clk

═══════════════════════════════

George BAKER

1831 Dr George BAKER orphn of John BAKER ded In a/c with James RAWLS gdn

___ 12/th/ To recording this Account	40	By this amt due the orphan at my	Cr
To Cah pd Jas L GRIMES	1..50	return to February Caurt 1831	146..52
Int on ditto	07	Int on ditto up to February Caurt 1832	8 79
nov To Cash paid Jas L GRIMES	75	By yaur half of Negro hire & rent of	
To yaur half of mid wifes fees to}		Pine baxes for 1831	25 00
Negro MILY . . . . . . }	75	Int on ditto up to this return . . .	24
To yaur half of Scifa [sic] to renew			
guard bond	..30		
To Board & Clothing for the year 1831	30..00		
To 5 p cet commision	3..89		
To Ballance due the orphan	142..89		
	180..55	1832	180..55
		Feby 27/th/ By Ballance due due [sic] the orphan	142..89

(111) George BAKER (Cont.)

James **RAWLS** Guardian

John BAKER

1831   Dr John **BAKER** orphan of John **BAKER** ded In a/c with James **ROWLS** guard

_ul? 8/th/ To recording this Act	40	By this amt due the orphan at my}	Cr
" To Cash pd Jos L **GRIMES**	2..50	return to February Court 1831 }	151..38
Int on ditto	12	Int on ditto up to Februay Court 1832	9 .08
July 22 To Cash pd Jas L **GRIMES**	3..00	By yaur half Negro hire and rents	
Int on ditto	..20	of pine boxes for 1831	25..00
To yaur half of mid wifes fees to negro **MILY**	75	Int on ditto up to this return	[blank]
To yaur half of Scifa to renew guard bond	..30	Int on ditto up to this return	24
To Board & clothing for 1831	30..00		
To 1 hat	..75		
To 5 p cet commisions	3..56		
To Ballance due the orphan	145..22		
	185..70	1832	185..70

February 27/th/ By Ballance due the orphan 145..22

North Carolina }

James **RAWLS** Guardian

Hertford Caunty} February Court of Pleas &c 1832

These Accounts were returned to Court on oath by James **RAWLS** Guardian & ardered to be Recorded

Test. L. M. **COWPER** clk

---

(112) 83 Ann BRITT Dr Ann **BRITT** orphan of Etheldred **BRITT** dec in act with Elizabeth **BR___** /her/ _____

1830		1831	
Decr 24/th/ To amt pd Doct Thomas		Decr 25/th/ By hire of Negro man	
BORLAND as pr rect	9..17	**BRISTER** this year	$12 0_
1831		Rent of Land this year	3..50?
Jany 4 " amt John W **SAUTHALL**s " rect	9..52	1832	
1832		Feby 27/th/ By amt Ballance due the ward}	
Feby 13? " amt pd Doct Isaac **PIPKIN**		as pr former Act made the 22 Augt }	
as recept	4..50	1830 and returned . . . . . 277..73 }	
" 13 " amt John W **SOUTHALL** as recet	16..72	amt Interest on $277..73 from 22/d/	
Feby 27 By amt due the ward this day	278..55	Augt 1830 to 27 Feby 1832 inclusive 25..23)302..9_	
	318..46		318..46

Mary BRITT

her _____

1831   Dr Mary **BRITT** orphan of Etheldred dec in act with mrs Elizabeth **BR___**

Decr 3/d/ To amt pd Doct Thos		1831	
BORLAND act	11..91	Decr 25 By hire of Negro bay **JACOB** }	
1832		this year . . . . }	25..00
Feby 13 To amt " John W **SOUTHALL** act	3..31	Rent of Land this year	3..50
" To " " Isaac **PIPKIN** do	3..50	By amt ballance due the ward }	
" " " " Patrick **BROWN** act	7..97	as pr former act made 22/d/ Augt 1830}	
" Cash pd for returning former		and returned to 21..71 }	
act current	77½	Amt Interest on $21.71 from 22/d/ }	
" amt board the last year	15..00	Augt 1830 to 27/th/ Feby 1832 inclusive}2..00 23..71	
Feby 27 By amt due the ward this day	9..75		52..21
	52..21½		

Permelia BRITT

her gu__

1831   Dr Permelia **BRITT** orphan of Etheldred **BRITT** dec in a/c with mrs Elizabeth **B_____**

Decr 3 To amt paid Doct T. **BORLAND**s		1831	
act	7..83¾	Decr 25/th/ By hire of Negro woman **PHILLIS**}	
1832		with 2 children . . . . }	5..00

(112) Permelia **BRITT** (Cont.)

Feby 13 To Amt paid Patrick **BROWN**s act	6..00		rent of Land this [sic]	3..50
" " To amt pd John W **SAUTHALL**s act	4..18		1832	
To Board for one year 1831	15..00		Feby 27 To amt due the Guardian	85..08
To pd for returning former act				
act current	..77			
27 To amt due the Guardian in former}				
act returned & Interest . . . . }	59..79			
	93..58			93..58

Elizabeth **BRITT**   her gu__

1832   Dr Elizabeth **BRITT** orphan of Etheldred **BRITT** decd In act with mrs Elizabeth B____

Feby 13 To amt paid John W			1831	
SAUTHALL act	1..17		Decr 25 By hire of negro woman **VIOLET**	25..00
To 1 pr Shoes @ 7/6 prinel?	1..25		rent of Land this year	3..50
" 1 pr ditto Leather @ 6/-	1..00			
To Board for Last year	25..00			
To pd for returning former Act	77½			
Feby 27 To Amt due the Guar/n/ pr former			Feby 27 To amt Ballance due the	
return . . . . 19..16			Guardian this day	21..60
To Int on $19 16 cents up to 27/th/				
February 1832 . . . . . . 1 75	20..91			
	50..10			50..10

North Carolinea }

Hertford County} February Caurt of Pleas &c 1832

This Account was returned to Court on oath By Elizabeth **BRITT** Guardian & ordere_

to be Recorded   Test. L. M. **COWPER** clk

Elizabeth **BRITT** Guard

---

(113) £4 Henry **COTTON** Dr Heny **COTTON** orphan of James **COTTON** dec in a/c with James d **WYNNS** gdn

1832   Cr

Feby 27 To this amt paid ward in cloths &c	4..68		By this amt due the ward on Setts [sic]	52..00
To amt due the ward	52..00		Interest on the Same up to this day	
			Say one & half year/s/	4..68
	56..68			56..68

North Carolina }

Hertford County} February Caurt of Pleas &c 1832

This Account was Returned to Court on oath by James D **WYNNS** Guardian & ordered to be

Recorded   Test. L. M. **COWPER** clk

E E Feby Term 1832   James D. **WYNNS** guard

Daniel **DEANS**

__31   Dr Daniel **DEANS** orphan of James **DEANS** decd In act with Isaac **CARTER** g/d/n

__by 26 To Cash paid clerk for Sci fa &			1832	
return	1..30		Feby 27 By Ballance due on return to	
' 12 mo/s/ Int thereon	08		Feby Caurt 1831	$ 321..38
__t 26 To paid **REA & CAMP**	1..63		12 mo/s/ Int thereon	19 28
Shff Taxes 1830	..68		1831	
Int thereon	..05		Novr 21/st/ By this amt recd of	
To paid clerk this return	..40		James **DEANS**	98..00
Commrs on $123 @ 5 p cet	6..15		Int thereon up to this time	1..58
Ballance due	429..95			
	440 24			440..24
			By Ballance due this 27/th/ Feby 1832	429..95

North Carolina }

Hertford County} February Caurt of Pleas 1832

This Accaunt was returned to Court on oath by Isaac **CARTER** Guardian & ordered

E E Isaac **CARTER** Guardian

(113) Daniel DEANS (Cont.)
to be Recorded

Test. L. M. **COWPER** clk

Dr The orphans of William Mills **DAUGHTERRY** In A/c current with Titus **DARDEN** gdn		Cr	
1832 To amt pd Lewis M **COWPER**		1832	
for returns	80	By hire of Negro man **JIM**	50..00
Int on Same from 28 Feby 1831 till}		Int on Same from 25 Decr 1831 till}	
27 Feby 1832 . . . . }	04½	27 February 1832 . . . .}	..50
To amt Henry W **SKINNER** as p rect	7..00	By hire of Negro **JACOB** . . .	38..00
Int on Same from 12 augt 1831 till		Int on Same from 25 Decr 1831 till}	
27 Feby 1832	22½	27 February 1832 . . . .}	..38
To amt pd Mary M **DAUGHTERY**}		By hire of Negro woman **VIOLET**	3 00
in Cash . . . .}	4..00	Int on Same from 23 decr 1831}	
Int on Same from 18 July 1831 till}	14	till 27 February 1832 . . . .}	..03
27 Feby 1832 . . . .}		By hire of Negro girl **RACHEL**	16..25
To amt paid **DAUGHTERY & WEBB**}		Int on Same from 25 decr 1831}	
as p rect . . . .}	89..93	till 27 February 1832 . . . .}	16¼
Int on Same from 1/st/ Novr 1831 till}		By hire of Negro woman **CREECY**	13..00
27 February 1832 . . . . . , }	1 79½	Int on Same from 25 Decr 1831}	
To amt paid Lawrence S **DAUGHTERY**}		till 27 February 1832 . . . .}	13
in Cash . . . . }	15..00	By hire of Negro girl **MILLY**	2..00
Int on Same from 19 Jany 1832		Int on Same from 25 Decr 1831 till}	
till 27 February 1832	..08	27 February 1832 . . . . }	02
To amt paid Mary M **DAUGHTERY**		By hire of Negro girl **MANERVA**	17..25
in Cash	..84	Int on Same from 25 Decr 1831 till 27}	
	119..85½	of February 1832 . . . .}	17¼
Amt carried forward			140..89½

(114) 85 Dr The orphans of William Mills **DAUGHTERY** In a/c current with Titus _____

To Amt Brot forward	119..83½	~~By hire of Negro girl **ELIZUR**~~	140..89_
Int on Land from 1/st/ February		By hire Negro girl **ELIZUR**	3..00
1832 till 27 February 1832	[blank]	Int on Same from 25 Decr 1831 till}	
To amt pd Mariah A **DAUGHTERY** in Cash	..84	27 February 1832 . . . . . . }	.._
Int on Same from 1/st/ Feby 1832 till 27		By hire of Boy **ABRAM**	3..0_
February 1832	[blank]	Int on Same fram 25 Decr 1831 till}	
To amt pd Edw/d/ K **JEGITTS** for }		27 February 1832 . . . . . . }	15?
keeping Negro woman **CLARISSA** &}		By rent of **PORTER** plantation	65..00
three Children . . . . }	20 00	Int on Same from 25 Decr 1831}	
Int on Same from 7 Feby 1832 till		till 27 February 1832 . . . .}	..6_
27 February 1832	07½	By rent of Manor plantation	40..00
To amt pd Jas J **BARNES** as p rect	15 00	Int on Same from 25 Decr 1831}	
Int on Same from 18 Feby 1832 till		till 27 February 1832 . . . .}	..40?
27 February 1832	02½		253..16½
To Amt pd William G **DAUGHTERY**}			
as p rect . . . .}	63..88		
Int on Same from 18 Feby 1832 till			
27 February 1832	12		
To Amt pd R. G. **COWPER** for Taxes	8..23		
To amt pd R W **JOHNSTON** as pr rect	19..56		
To amt pd R W **JOHNSTON** as do	7 02		
To amt pd America **HUTCHINGS** for}			
Keeping negro woman **CHERRY** & }			
three Children . . . .}	27..75		
To Keeping Negro woman **VINEY** &}			
2 Children for the year 1831 . . . }	5..00		

(114) The orphans of William Mills **DAUGHTERY** (Cont.)

Int on Same from 25 Decr 1831 till

27 February 1832   05

To Boarding Mary **DAUGHTERY** fram}

28 February 1831 till 27 Feby 1832   }   48 00

To Boarding Mariah A **DAUGHTERY** from

28 February 1831 till 27 Feby 1832   [blank]

By Ballance due according   382..40½

to returns rendered 28 Feby 1831   109..53

Int on Same from 28 Feby 1831 till}

27 February 1832 . . . .}   6..57½

To 5 p cet commissions on $25?3..16½/¢/   12..50

                      511..01   253..16½

North Carolina }   Titus **DARDEN** Guardian

Hertford caunty} February Caurt of Pleas &c 1832

This Account was returned to Caurt on oath by Titus **DARDEN** Guardian & ordered to be

Recorded   Test. L. M. **COWPER** clk

===

Pennina **EVANS** Dr Pennina **EVANS** orphan of Noah **EVANS** dec in A/C current with

1831   Luke M **GLORHAN** Guardian

To paid Clerks fee returns &c   80

                             Amt carried forward

===

(115) 86 Dr Pennina **EVANS** orphan of Noah **EVANS** decd in act current with Luke /M/ **GLORHAN**

Amt Brat forward	80	1831		
Board with Guardian	10..00	May 19th By this Sum Recd of Wm }		
To 1 Book	37½	DAWNING Admr as former Guardian .}	66 66	
To paid E G **RIDDICK** for Tuition	2 90	" Int up to Jany 4/th/ 1832	1..08	
To do Watson **LEWIS** Act	10..12	Hire of Negroes 1831	26..50	
To do Jno A **ANDERSON** Act	1 37½			
1832 Commissions on $25..57	1..27			
Jay 4 To A Ballance due the ward	65 40			
	92 24	1832	92..24	
		Jany 4/th/ By A Ballance due the ward	65..40	

North Carolina }   Return by Luke M **GLORHAN** guardn

Hertford Caunty} February Caurt of Pleas & 1832

This Account was returned To Caurt on oath by Luke M **GLANGHAN** Guardian & ordered to be

Recorded   Test. L. M. **COWPER** clk

===

Alfred & J. **GRIFFITH**   present gd

1831   Dr Alfred & John **GRIFFITH** in a/c With Mat J. **GRIFFITH**

Decr 20.th/ To Guardian Bond . . .	60	By Cash	545 28¼
To goods bot of M & H D **GRIFFITH**	1..50	Int on ditto from the 14/th/ of Decr 1831}	
Ballance due the orphans pr contra	549..84	until February 27-1832 . . . . . . }	6..66
		By Ballance due the orphans p debit	551..94½
	549..84	Ballance due the orphans Feby term 1832)	549..84

                                          Mat J **GRIFFITH** Guardian

North Carolina }

Hertforc Caunty} February Court of Pleas &c 1832

This Account was returned to Court on oath by Mat J **GRIFFITH** & ordered to be

Recorded   Test. L. M. **COWPER** clk

===

Jesse Y **HARRELL** Dr Jesse Y **HARRELL** orphan of Joseph **HARRELL** decd In ac ct with

'1831   Abner **HARRELL** Guardian

Fe?by 15/th/ To 1 Hat	30	1831	
" To Cash paid Seth **DEANS** for Shoes 11/3 1	12½	Feby 28 By ballance due the Ward}	
25 To 1 Arithmetick 3/9	..37½	pr my return . . . .}	69..92

(115) Jesse Y HARRELL (Cont.)

1832			1832	
Jay 16 To Cash Lawrence **BEVERLY**	2 31¼		Feby 28 By Interest on on [sic] the above	
" To Cash pd **VALENTINE** for tuition	7..37½		to this return	4..19½
" To Cash pd **HARRELL M & BEVERLY**	6 62½		" " By 2/3 of the hire of the Negroes}	
Feby? 19 To 1 pair Shoes 16/3 and paid			" " for the year 1831 . . . . . .}	26 65½
for mending	1 62½		By Interest on the above to this return	27
27 To Cash paid pr this return	..20			
" To Cash pd Noah **HARRELL** for Support}				
of Negro **AMRUT?** }	3 33½			
" To Board of Jesse y **HARRELL** this year	20..00			
" To Commissions on $74..60 in mony}				
" recd & Expended . . . . }	3..73			
28 To This Sum due the ward	53..84¾			
	101..05		1832	101..05
			Feby 28 By Ballance due the ward	53..84¾

North Carolina }

Hertford Caunty} February Court of Pleas &c 1832 · · · · · · · · · · · · · Abner **HARRELL** Guardian

This Account was returned to Count on oath by Abner **HARRELL** Guardian

& ordered to be Recorded · Test. L. M. **COWPER** clk

---

(116) 87 Dr Sindy Rina & Malichia **HOLLOMON** orphans of Jacob **HOLLOMON** dec in act with Miles H. J_____

1832			1831	
Feby Caurt To Cash to record this Account	..60		Feby 25 By this amt due the orphans	58..0_
1831 To Cash pd yaur Mother Milly			Int on ditto up to Feby co 1832	3..4_
HOLLOMON for Clothing	2..50			
To Commissions on the money Expended}				
& Interest recd . . . . }	32			
To Ballance due the orphans	58..02			
	61..50		1832	61..50
			Feby 27/th/ By Ballance due the orphans	58..02

North Carolina }

Hertford County} February Court of Pleas &c 1832 · · · · · · · · · M. H. **JERNIGAN** Guardian

This account was returned to court on oath By Miles H **JERNIGAN** Guardian & ordered to be

Recorded · Test. L. M. **COWPER** clk

William **HOLLOMON**

1831			Dr William **HOLLOMON** orphan of Samuel decd In act with James **HOLLOMON** G____	
Feby 28/th/ To Cash paid Penelope			By this amt due the orphans at my}	
HOLLOMON	1..25		return to February Caurt 1831 }	251..27
March 29? To Int on ditto up to this return	07		Int on ditto up to this return	15..07
To Cash paid Alexander O **ASKEW**	2..00			
Int on ditto	11			
Dec 13 To pd Watson **LEWIS**	8 27			
Int on an [sic] ditto	..19			
30 To Cash pd Jason **HOLLOMON**				
for Boad	9..25			
Int on ditto	..09			
To recording this Account	..40			
To 5 p cet Commissions	1..83			
To Balleance due the orphan	242..88			
	266..34		1832	266..34
			Feby 27 By Ballance due the orphans	242 88
			James **HOLLOMON** Guardian	

Jacob **HOLLOMON**

1831 · · · · · · · · · · · Dr Jacob **HOLLOMON** orphan of Samuel decd in acct with James **HOLLOMON** g____

(116) Jacob HOLLOMON (Cont.)

Feby 29 To Cash paid Penelope			By Ballance due the orphan at}	
HOLLOMON	1..12		my return to Feby Court 1831 }	267..44?
Int on ditto	..07		Int on ditto up to this return	16..04
March 29 To Cash paid Alexander O				
ASKEW	2..10			
Int on ditto	..11			
Dec: 15 To Cash paid Watson **LEWIS**	9..27			
Int on ditto	..10			
30 To Cash pd Jason **HOLLOMON**	9..25			
Int on ditto	..09			
To recording this Account	..40			
To 5 p cet commissions	1..92			
To Ballance due the orphan	259..05			
	283..48		1832	283..48
			Feby 27 By Ballance due the orphan	259..05

North Carolina }
Hertford County} February Court of Pleas &c 1832
     James **HOLLOMON** Guard

     These Accounts were returned to Caurt on oath by James **HOLLOMON** gua__
& ordered to be recorded   Test. L. M. **COWPER** Clk

---

(117) £8 Starkey HARRELL

Dr Starkey **HARRELL** orphan of of? Starkey S **HARRELL** decd In acct current

__vr 3C? With John **WINBORNE** Guardian				Cr
__ To Guardian bond	..30		1832	
__3:			Jany 5/th/ By yaur part negro hire year 1831	54 62½
__y 5 To yaur part Spirits use negro hire	12½		By this Sum recd of Thomas B **SHARP**}	
" paid Doct **BARDWELL** bill for doctoring}			Admr of yaur farthers Estate it being }	
yaur negro **TILLIE**? . . . .}	13..00		yau distribute a Share of his Estate }	3..75
" paid Thos B **SHARP** act	1..30			
" paid Benj C **HANON**? acct	37½			
" paid Elizabeth **HARRELL** acct	10..40			
" Spirits use negro hire & yaur part	..07			
" paid Henry B **VANPELT** Hawling}				
tole corn . . . . }	1..50			
" Commissions on $27..27	1..36			
5 ' A Ballance due the orphan	29..74½			
	58..37½			58..37½
			1832	
			Jay 5/th/ By A Ballance due the orphan	29..74½

North Carolina }
Hertford Caunty} February Caurt of Pleas &c 1832
     John **WINBORNE** Guardian

    This Account was returned to Caurt on oath by John **WINBORNE**
Guardian & ordered to be Recorded   Test. L. M. **COWPER** Clk

---

Mary HARRELL

Dr Mary **HARRELL** orphan of [blank] Starkey S **HARRELL** decd In acct Current

1830 With John **WINBONE** Guardian				Cr
_ovr? To Guardian bond yaur part	30		1832	
1831			Jay 5th By yaur part Negro hire 1831	$54 62½
Jay 5 To yaur part Spirits use negro hire	12½		By this Sum recd of Thas B **SHARP** }	
21 " paid Abner **HARRELL** act	42 15		admr of Starkey S **HARRELL** decd it }	
Int on ditto up to Jay 5/th/ 1832	2 41		being yaur distributed Shaire of }	
_6 " l pr Shaes	1..25		Yaur Farther/s/ Estate referance to }	
_832 " paid Doct **BARDWELL** in bill			to [sic] be had from return novr term }	
yaur part	50		1831 }	3..75

(117) Mary HARRELL (Cont.)

Jay " do Watsan **LEWIS** act	7..86	A Ballance due the Guardian	19..20
" do Thas. B. **SHARP** act	17..35		
" do Benj C **HUSON** do	37½		
" " yaur part Spirits use negro hire	07		
" paid Henry B **VANPELT** Hawling}			
Tole corn yaur part . . . . . .}	1..50		
Commissions on $73 88/¢/	3..69		
1832	77..57 ½		77..57½
___y 5/th/ To Ballance due Guardian	19..20	John **WINBORNE** Guardian	

North Carolina }
Hertford Caunty} February Court of Pleas &c 1832

This Account was returned to court on oath by John **WINBORNE** Guardian
& ordered to be Recorded   Test. L. M. **COWPER** clk

William P JENKINS   gdn
1831   Dr William P **JENKINS** orphan of Charles **JENKINS** decd In act with Michael **DEANS**

Decr To Cash paid for the orphan	5..00	By the amt due the orphan Feby eet}	
To do paid the clerk for return}		Caurt 1831 . . . . }	151..52
to February Caurt 1832 }	40	By Interest . . . .}	9..07
To Commissions	..27	By hire of Negro girl to Self	14 00
	5..67	Amt carried forward	174..59

---

(118) 89 William P JENKINS
Dr William P **JENKINS** orphan of Charles **JENKINS** decd
In Act with Michael **DEANS** his Guardian _____ 174..39

Amt Brot forward	5..67		
	174..39		
	168..72	Ballance due the orphan Feby caurt 1832	168..72
		Michael **DEANS** gd_	

Charles S. JENKINS
Dr Charles S **JENKINS** orphan of Charles **JENKINS** decd In acct
with Michael **DEANS** his Guardian

T [sic] To Cash paid for the orphan	47..60	By the due the orphan Feby caurt 1831	175..15
To Cash paid the clerk for return}		By Interest	10..50
To February Caurt 1832 . . . }	..40	By the hire negro man to Samuel}	
	48..00	**GATLING** . . . .}	37..50
	223 15		223..15
	175..15	Ballance due the orphan Feby}	

North Carolina }   Court 1832 . . . .} 175..15
Hertford Caunty} February Caurt of Pleas &c 1832   Michael **DEANS** Guard

This Account were returned To Caurt on aath by Michael **DEANS** Guard
& ordered to be Recorded   Test. L. M. **COWPER** Clk

Winborne JENKINS   guardia_
1831   Dr Winbon **JENKINS** orphan of Benjamin **JENKINS** ded in a/c with Henry D J_____

Sept 3/d/ To Cash paid **REA & CAMP** $ 38 .		1832	
Decr 22/d/ To do paid Robbt **COBB** for		Feby 27 By Ballance due last return	63..92
tuition	8..86	12 mo/s/ int thereon	3..86
1832		By hire of **NAT** for 1831	41
Feby 22/d/ To do " L M **COWPER** his act	13	" " **EVRITT**	8..25
" " " " Patrik **BROWN** do	3..05	" " **EDITH**	16..06
To 12 mo/s/ board	50.00	rent of Land/ nec?k feild [sic]	8..13
" 1 pr Shaes 1.00 6 yds mixed cloth		" " Do Hause & feild	24..05

(118) Winborn JENKINS (Cont.)

	2..25	3..25	
" making Coat 75/¢/ Lining 18¾		94	
" making vest & pantaloons		38	
" 5 yds cloth @ 75/¢/ 1 pr Socks		4..00	
" making Jacket pantaloons & vest		75	
" 2¼ yds Cloth @ 25/¢/ 1 pr Shaes 1..25		1..81	
1832 " making pantaloons		..25	
Feby 27 To Cash paid clk this return		40	
" Commissions on $176..44 @ 5 p ct		9..22	
" Ballance due		83..14	
		166..16	

Negroes CELIA MARY & WILLIAM even
Int to 27/th/ Feby 1832   ..91

                                                                166..16
By Ballance due Feby 27/th/ 1832   83..14

North Carolina }
Hertford County} February Caurt of Pleas &c 1832   E E Henry D. JENKINS Guardi__
This Account was returned to Caurt on oath by Henry D. JENKINS Guardian & ordered
to be recorded   Test. L. M. COWPER clk

Penelope JENKINS

Dr Penelope JENKINS orphan of Benjamin JENKINS dec in act with
1831 Henry D JENKINS Guardian

		1832	
Decr 22/d/ To cash paid Robt COBB tuition	9..18	Feby 27 By this amt due last return	508 10
1832		12 months Int thereon	30..00
Feby 22 To do James SCOTTs acct	..50	?? Amt carried forward	538..10
	9..68		

---

(119) 90 Penelope JENKINS

Dr Penelope JENKINS orphan of Benjamin JENKINS dec In Acct
with Henry D JENKINS Guardian   **Cr**

Amt Brot forward	9..68		538..10
To paid REA & COMP act	7..90	Hire JERRY	35..00
" " Lewis M COWPER do	5..08	TONY	27..05
" " P BROWN . . . do	8..50	LUCY	37..75
" 12 months Board	50..00	Int to 27 February 1832	..90
" making 3 dresses	1 00		
" 1 Slide 12½ 1 pr Shaes	1..37½		
" 1 pr Shoes 1 00 1 bonnet $3..50	4..50		
" paid J WESTON for keeping BETH	5..00		
" clerk this acct	40		
" Comms on $218 84 @ 5 p ct	10..94		
" Ballance due	528..68		
	633..28		633..28

By Ballance due Feby 27/th/ 1832   528..68

North Carolina }
Hertford County} February Caurt of Pleas &c 1832   E E Henry D. JENKINS Guardian
This Account was returned to Court on oath by Henry D. JENKINS Guardian & ordered
to be recorded   Test. L. M. COWPER Clk

Charles E KNIGHT   **guard**

1831   Dr Charles E KNIGHT orphan of Sally KNIGHT decd In act with Clements ROCHELLE

May To amt paid Clerk for Guard bond	60	1832	
1832		Feby 27 By amt recd of James MAGET}	
__ by 27 " pd James MAGETs act for board}		Exr of Sally KNIGHT decd }	
Clothing and Schooling up to}		this conditionaly legacy of twelve }	
1/s/ January 1832 . . . .}	139..47	hundred dallar/s/ payable on his }	
for returning this act to this ct	..60	arrival to lawfull age . . . . }	1200..00
		By amt recd for Interest on Same }	

97

(119) Charles E KNIGHT (Cont.)

from the death of Said decd (31/st/ May } 1829) until 27 Feby 1832 agreeable } to the Consent and acreetion? of the kin? }	198 .00
By amt recd of Said Exr Said } orphans proper time of the residual } Estate of Said Sally KNIGHT decd }	352..42
amt Interest on Same from 25/th/ } august 1831 to 27 of Feby 1832 . . . }	10..69

1240..67

1761..12

deduct amt Expenditueres 140 67

The amt due the ward this day is 1620..45

Sixteen hundred & twenty dallar/s/ & forty five cert

Feby 27/th/ 1832   Clements ROCHELL gdn

North Carolina }
Hertford Caunty} February Caurt of Pleas &c 1832
This Account was returned to Court on aath by Clements ROCHELLE Guardian & ordered
to be recorded   Test. L. M. COWPER clk

A & M LIVERMON

1831   Dr Adamant & Martha LIVERMON In acct with Mat J GRIFFITH present gdn   Cr

Feby 27 To Guardian bend return	..20	By Cash	121..87
Adamant LIVERMON To Cash	1..87	" Interest from 27 of Feby 1831 until	[blank]
	2..07	Amt Carried forward	121..87

---

(120) 91 A & M LIVERMON

Dr Adamant & Martha LIVERMON In a/c with Mat J GRIFFITH Present g__

1831 Amt Brat forward	2..07		121..87
Martha LIVEMON		the 27 of February 1832	7..31
LIVERMON [sic] to Cash	1..87	Ballance due the orphans pr debit	129 18?
Ballance due the orphans pr contra	126..24	Ballance due the orphans at Feby Term 1832)126..24

North Carolina }
Hertford Caunty} February Caurt of Pleas &c 1832   Mat. J. GRIFFITH Gu___
This Account was returned to Court on oath by Mat J GRIFFITH Guardian & ordered to be
Recorded   Test. L. M. COWPER C_

Richard **MOORE**

Dr Richard MOORE in acct current with Alfred DARDEN next friend

1829   and Admr of John MOORE decd   Cr

Oct 9 To Cash paid James SCOTT for Spelling book	17	Novr To amt of yaur proportionable } part of yaur farther/s/ Estate as pr return}	
1830 To Cash paid REA & CAMP for goods pr act	2..15	to Nov Caurt 1831 . . . .}	326. 57
16? To Cash William d CLARK for Shaes	1..00	Int from 28 Novr 1831 till 28 Feby 1832	3. 26
Int from 9/th/ Oct 1830 til Nov 28 1831	28	By amt due yau for Land rent for	
Decr 25 To Cash paid Robt B COBB for} Schooling (1830) . . . .}	10..00	the year 1830	65. 00
		Int from 25 decr 1830 till Feby 28/th/ 1832	4. 55
31/st/ To board makeing & Washing} Cloths (1830) . . . .}	530..920	By Land rent due Decr 25 1831	31..00
Int from 31/st/ decr 1830 till Novr} 28 / 1831 . . . .}	3 20	Int from Decr 25/th/ 1831 til Feby 28/1832	..32
			430..64
To yaur part negro expences for 1830	5..71		170 94
To 5 p ct Commissions for Services	6..87		
amt of Int up to 28 Nov 1831	79 38		
1831 To Int from Novr 28 1831 till Feby 28 / 1832	79		

(120) Richard **MOORE** (Cont.)

Decr 31? To paid **REA & CAMP** pr acount 14..87

To paid yaur baard making & Washing}
for 1831 . . . . } 50..00

To paid R B **COBB** for
Schooling (1831)   10..00

" yaur proportionable part of $7..34}
for Clerks fees &c . . . . . . }   1..48

Int from 31/st/ decr 1831 til Feby
28/1832   ..74

To this amt due **HODGES**? in division}
of Negroes . . . . }   5 80

To paid yaur part of Negra Expences}
for 1831 . . . . }   1..05

To paid Henry **HERMAN** for Winter
Shaes   1..00

To 5 p cet commissions for Servises   5..83

       amt of debits   170..94   amt Still due Richard **MOORE**   259?70

North Carolina }   A. **DARDEN** Guardian

Hertford Caunty} February Court of Pleas &c 1832

This Account was returned to Court on oath by Alfred **DARDEN** & ordered to be

Recorded   Test. L. M. **COWPER** Clk

=====

(121) 92 A W **MOORE** Dr A W MOORE in act current with Alfred **DARDEN** as his next friend & as adm/r/ of J

__32   **MOORE** /ded/   1832   Cr

__3/d. To yaur proportionable part of}

the expense of the Negraes for the year 1830}   5..67   Jany 3/d/ By amt of yaur proportionale part}

Int from 25 decr 1830 till 25 decr 1831   ..34   of yaur farther/s/ Estate as pr Settlement }

To yaur proportionable part of}   retuned Novr 28th 1831   }326..56

expenses for 1831 . . . . }   98   Int from 28 Decr 1831 till 3/d/ Jay 1832   1 90

To this amt paid L M. **COWPER** and Jas   By this amt due yau for Land}

SCOTT Since the Settlement of the Estate   1 08   rent for the year 1830   }   33..00

To 5 pr Cet Commissions on $8..07 cts   ..43   Int from 25 decr 1830 till 25 decr 1831}   1 98

To this amt due from yau to the }   By amt of rents for 1831 due now   40..00

Stock in the division of Negroes}   6..00   403..44

To 5 p Cet Commissions on the rents of}   62..25

Lands for the year/s/ 1830 & 1831   }   3..75   341..19

To 7 1/2 months board for Self & Wife}   A. **DARDEN** Guardian

at Six dallar/s/ pr month . . . . . }   44..00

North Carolina }   62..25

Hertford County} February Court of Pleas &c 1832

This Account was returned to Count on oath by Alfred **DARDEN** Guardian & ordered to

be Recorded   Test. L. M. **COWPER** Clk

=====

A. E. **MOORE** Dr Adolphus E **MOORE** in a/c current with Alfred **DARDEN** /as/ next

1830   friend and Admr of John **MOORE** decd

_ay 7 To Cash paid **REA & CAMP**   Amt Brat up   117..55

for Shaes   75   Int from 1/st/ Jany 1831 till 28th Feby 1832   24

Oct 9 To Cash pd ditto for goods as pr act   4..09   1832

16 To Cash pd William D **CLARK** pr Shaes 1..00   Feby 27 To this amt paid dread **WARREN**}

Int from 16/th/ Oct 1830 till Nov 28/1831 ..39   for board & Clothing last year 1831   } 84..32

Decr 21 st/ For boarding and making cloths   To 5 per cet Coms for services   5 45

for the year 1830   50..00   amt of debits   207..56

To **REA & CAMP** for Hat p act   5..00

To paid Mr/s/ **PARKER** for 2   1831   Cr

(121) A. E. MOORE (Cont.)

Jackets @ 2/3	..75
To paid R B **COBB** for Shooling 1830	. 10..00
Int from 31/st/ Jay 1831 till Nov 28/1831	3 34
To Cash paid James **SCOTT** for}	
Spelling book . . . . . .}	17
To his part of Expense for Keeping}	
Negroes . . . .}	5 71
Int from 31/st/ Decr 1830 til Nov 28/1831	30
To 5 pr cet commisons for Services	9..60
To paid P **BROWN** for Shaes	1..00
Int and amt up to 28 Novr 1831	92..10
Int from Novr 28-1831 till Feby 28-1832	92
1831	
Jany 1/st/ To this amt paid **REA & CAMP**	
p act	16..20
To paid yaur proportion of Negro}	
expencs for 1831 . . . . . .}	1..05
Ta yaur proportion in? 1/5 part of }	
$7..34 for clerks fees &c }	1..48
To this amt due from yau to **HDGES** by	
division of Negras	5..80
Amt carried up	117..55

Novr 28 By amt of yaur proportionable part}	
of yaur farther/s/ Estate as pr Settlement}	
to this Caurt . . . . }	326 50
1832?	
Int from Novr 28/1831 till Feby 28/1832	3..26
By rent of orchard feild **ROBERTS**}	
Neck and the feild be hind [sic] the }	
Barn due the 25 Decr 1830}	5?0 00
old & new Neck feilds to Jet **DARDEN**	60..C0
Int from 25 Decr 1830 till 28 Feby 1832}	7..77
1831	
By rent of hause & orchard ve?	40..00
" do New Neck feild to R G **COWPER**	70..25
Int from 25 decr 1831 till 28 Feby 1832	1..10
Amt of credits	558..89
do of debits	207 56
Amt Still due Adophus	351..33

North Carolina }   A. **DARDEN** Guardian

Hertford Caunty} Febyuary Courts of Pleas &c 1832

this Account was returned to on [sic] oath by A. **DARDEN**

& ordered to be Recorded Test L. M. **COWPER** clk

---

(122) 93 Miss Mary Ann **MOORE** Dr Mary Ann **MOORE** in a/c Current with Alfred **DARD__**

1830   as next friend & Admr of John **MOORE** decd . . . . Cr

Apl 24/th/ To Cash paid for 4 Lemons		1831	
While Sick	25	Novr 28/th/ By amt of yaur proportionable }	
March 20 To Cash paid Doct T. **ODWIRE**		part of yaur Farthers Estate as pr Settlement}	
pr bill	28..00	returned to Novr Court 1831	} 326..50
" Int from March 20-1830 till		Int from 28 Novr 1831 til 28 Feby 1832	3..26
Novr 28/th/ 1831	2..75	amt debits deducted	222..56
Apl 24 To Cash paid J W **SOUTHALL** for			107..21
a book	50		
Oct 9 To Cash paid **REA & CAMP**			
fot goods pr acct __ __ __ __	8 21		
16 To Cash paid W D **CLARK** for a}			
pair Shaes . . . .}	1..00		
Int from 9/th/ Octr 1830 till Nov 28			
1831 __ __ __ __ __ __ __	60		
Der 31/st/ To paid Cash for Yaur board}			
" the year 1830 . . . . }	50..00		
", To Cash paid R B **COBB** for tuition			
" 1830 __ __ __ __ __ __ __	10..00		
" To Cash paid for yds [sic] Silk at			
85/¢/ pr yd	7..65		
Int from 31/st/ Decr 1830 till Nov 28/1831	3..38		
To yaur part of Expense for Negro/es/			
for 1830	5..71		
To 5 p cet Commissions on the	5..90		
expenditureres			
" amts and Interest up to 28 Nov 1831	123..95		
Int from Nov 28/1831 til Feby 28-1832	1..23		
1831			
Decr 25/th/ To **REA & CAMP** for goods	23..60		

(122) Mary Ann **MOORE** (Cont.)

To yaur proportion of Negro expense} for 1831_ _ _ _ _ _ _ _	1..05	
To yaur proportionable part of $7..34 for Clerks fees &c	1..48	
Int from 25/th/ Decr 1831 till 27 Feby 1832	,.26	
To Cash paid for yaur board this year (1831)	50..00	
Int to 27 Feby 1832 _ _ _	..50	
To this due from yau to **HODGES**} in the division of Negroes }	5..80	
To 5 p cet commissions on $83 92/¢/ for services	4..19	
To pa [sic] R B **COBB** for this year/s/ Schooling 1831_ _ _ _ _	10..00	
To 5 p cet Coms on 10 dallar/s/ for Schaaling as above	50	
	222..56	Leaves a ballance due Mary of 107..21

North Carolina   }

Hertforc Caunty} February Court of Pleas &c 1832

This Account returned to Court on oath by Alfred **DARDEN** & ordered to be Recorded

A **DARDEN** Guardian

Test. L. M. **COWPER.** Clk

Miss E. P. C. **MOORE**

Dr Miss Elizabeth P C **MOORE** in act current with Alfred **DAR___**

1830 as her next friend and Admr of John **MOORE** decd   Cr

Feby 20 th/ To Cash paid John A **ANDERSON** fo [sic] Shaes   1..50

amt carried forward

---

(123) 94 Miss E. P. C **MOORE**

Dr Elizabeth P C **MOORE** in current [sic] with Alfred **DARDEN** as her next friend and Admr of John **MOORE** deced

amt Brot forward	1..50	1831		
To Int from Febry 20-1830 til Nov 28/1831	16	Novr 28 By amt of her proportionable part} of her farthers Estate as pr Settlement } at Novr Term 1831 . . . .}	326..51	
Apl 15/t)/ To Cash paid Thas **SHAW** pr act	2..68			
Int fro [sic] 15 Apl 1830 til Nov 28/1831	..25	Int fro?m 28 Nov 1831 til 27 Feby 1832	3..26	
___ 10/t)/ To Cash paid Miss Phebe **HILL**} for bonnet bow . . . .}	4..00	By this amt due yau in the division of the Negroes . . .	29..00	
To Cash paid John W **SOUTHALL**} pr acct for goods . . . . . .}	16..41	amt of credits . . .	358..71	
Int from July 10-1830 til Nov 28/1831	1..37	amt debits	217..15	
Oct 9 To Cash paid **REA & CAMP** pr act	15..69	This ballance due Elizabeth . .	141..56	
W? Cash paid **MORGAN & COWPER** for} Tuck Comb . . . .}	5..00	A. **DARDEN** Guardian		
Int from Oct 9/1830 til Nov 28/-1831	1..27			
___ 23 To Cash paid Jno W **SOUTHALL** pr act	6..43	amt Brot up . . . Dr	119..37	
Int from Novr 23/d/ 1830 till Nov 28/ 1831	..37	To Int on $119..37 from Novr 28-1830 til Feby 27/th/ 1832	1..19	
___ r? 31 To Cash paid for 11 yds Silk @ 85/¢/ yd	9..35	1831 Decr 31/st/ To paid J W **SOUTHALL** pr } act for merchandise . . . .}	9..81	
1831 Tc Boarding her a part of the year	37..50	To paid Miss Phebe **HILL** for milliny	11..37	
___ 1/st/ " 1 bunch puffs 88/¢/ 1 Trunk 25/¢/	1..13	To paid Richard **JOHNSON** pr act} for merchandise . . . .}	7..50	
		To paid **REA & CAMP** for Mdse pr act	57..02	

(123) Elizabeth P C MOORE (Cont.)

To Cash 25/¢/ mending Shaes 25/¢/	..50	Int from 31/st/ Decr 1831 till Feby 27-1832	85
" paid 50/¢/ at Circus	..50	To paid H T SMITH pr act	2..37
To muslin 38/¢/ to yds		To yaur 1/5 part of $7..34 on Sundry act	
damesticks @ 9/d/	..92	Clerks tickets &c	1..48
To Int from Jany 1/st/ til Novr 28-1831	2..67	To paur proportionable part of Negro	
To her part of the expence of keeping}		Expence for 1831	1..05
Negraes 1830 . . . .}	5..71	Int from 27 Decr 1831 till 27 Feby 1832	..49
Int fro [sic] 25 Decr 1830 til Nov 28-1831	31	To 5 p ct Commissions on $95..13	4..65
To 5 pr cet Commision for Services	5..65		217..?3
amt carried up		[No signature]	
Amt & Int up to 28 Novr 1831	119..37		

North Carolina }
Hertford Caunty} February Caurt of Pleas &c 1832
This Account was returned to Caurt on oath by Alfred DARDEN & ordered to be Recorded

Test. L. M. COWPER Clk

The heirs of John MOORE

Dr The heirs of John MOORE decd in acct current with Alfred DARDEN his admr
for the hisrls [sic] of the Negraes that was left by the will to be hired aut for the mutual benifit of
1830 Alfred Elisabeth Adolpus Mary Ann and Richard MOORE

Decr 27/th/ To Cash paid Eli HARRELL }		1831	
for keeping negroes TOM & VENUS the year (1830)}	29..90	Negro BEN to William GRIFFITH	
Int fro 27 Decr 1830 to 27 Feby 1832		hired for	3 50
To Cash paid E. R. DARDEN for keeping}		Decr 25/th/ ANNIS & child Thas	
CHINA & 4 children this year 1830 }	22..79	P LITTLE for	7..10
Int from Decr 27-1830 til Feby 27/1832		HARRY to Samuel MOORE for	30.?5
To Cash paid Alfred W MOORE for		SAM to Alfred DARDEN for	30.00
keeping HANNAH & 2 children		RACHEL to Edward K JEGITTS for ..30	
this year (1830)	20..00	Int from Decr 25/1830 til Feby 27/th/ 1832 ..	
	72..69	1831 Decr 25 ANNIS to Johnson	
		VAUGHAN for	4..00
		RACHEL to A DARDEN for . .	3.00
		BEN to Allen MOORE for	11_50
		Amt carried forward	89..55

---

(124) 95 The heirs of John MOORE Dr The heirs of John MOORE decd in acct current
with Alfred DARDEN his admr for the hire of the Negraes that was left by the will
to be hired aut for the mutual bennefit of Alfred Elizabeth Adofpus Mary Ann and Richard MOORE

amt Brat forward	72..69		89..6_
Int from Decr 27-1830 till Feby 27/1832		SAM to Alfred DARDEN . . .	30..00
To Cash paid Thamas BRITTON for keeping}		HARRY to do do do	30..00
HASTY and Child this year .1830. }	12..99	CHISICK to John BAKER	2..30
Int from Decr 27/1830 til Feby 27/1832		Int from Decr 25?/th/ 1831	
To Cash paid W. A. WYNNS for keeping		til Feby 27-1832	
LOTTY & Child this year (1830) . . .	4..99		
Int fro Decr 27/1830 til Feby 27-1832 . :			
1831			
Dec 27 To Cash paid for keeping Negraes		By reference to their respective act	
TOM & VENUS	30..00	currents with me the Children	
Int fro Decr 27/1831 til Feby 27-1832		will find that they have Credits	
To Cash paid for keeping CHINA & 3 Children .	30..00	for for [sic] Land rent up to the time	
Int fro Decr 27/1831 til Feby 27-1832		of this return February Term 1832	
To Cash paid for keeping HASTYs child	7..00	A. DARDEN Guardian	
Int fro Decr 27/1831 til Feby 27-1832			

(124) The heirs of John **MOORE** (Cont.)

To Cash paid for keeping **HANNAH**}

& 4 Children . . . .}   18..00

North Carolina }

Hertford County} February Court of Pleas &c 1832

This Account was returned to Court on oath by Alfred **DARDEN** & ordered to be

Recorded   Test. L. M. **COWPER** Clk

Amon OVERTON

Dr Amon **OVERTON** orphan of Elisha **OVERTON** ded in acct with Miles H **JERNIGAN** gd_

		1831	Cr
To recording this Acct	40		
To 5 pr cet Commissions th [sic] Int &c	77	Feby 25 By Ballance due the orphan	253 21
To Ballance due the orphan	267..23	Int on that Sum up to Feby}	15..19
	268..40	Court 1832 . . . . . .}	268..40
		1832	
		Feby 27 By Ballance due the orphan	267..23

Know all men by these presents that I Amon **OVERTON** dath for and In consideration of the Sum of Two hundred and Sixty Seven dollar/s/ and twenty three cents to me in hand paid by Miles H **JERNIGAN** my Guardian have remised released and for ever quit Claimed for me my heir/s/ executor/s/ and administrator/s/ and by these presents do remise release and forever quit Claim unto Miles H **JERNIGAN** my Guardian aforesaid and his heir/s/ executor/s/ and administrator/s/ of all and all manner of action and actions Cause and Causes of actions what Soever that I have or Cauld have ar any person or persons Claiming under me against the Said **JERNIGAN** as Guardian either at Law or equity as this is a final discharge from the th beginning of the world up to the present date of all demands that I have against him In witness whereof I have here unto Set my hand and Seal this 27 day of Februay one thausand eight hund___ and thirty S Two

Witness   Amon **OVERTON** (Seal)

R. G. **COWPER**

---

(125) 9€ Amon **OVERTON**   Cr

Dr Amon **OVERTON** orphan of Elisha **OVERTON** In acct with Miles H **JERNIGAN** guardian

North Carolina }

Hertford County} February Court of Pleas &c 1832

This Account was returned to Court on oath by Miles H **JERNIGAN**-at the same time the receipt from Amon **OVERTON** to Miles H **JERNIGAN** was praveed [sic] by the oath of Richard G **COWPER** the Subscribing witness thereto & ordered to be Recorded   Test. L. M. **COWPER**. clk

---

Aron OUTLOW   gdn

1831   Dr Aron **OVETLOW** orphan of Aron **OUTLOW** decd in act current with John **DAWNING**

		1831	
Feby To return act current to court	$ 20	Jay 4 By a ballance due the ward	140..09
1832		1832?	
_ay 4 To A Ballance due the ward	175..34	Jany 4 " Int 12 months on ditto . . .	8..45
		" Negro hire 1831	27..00
	175..54		175..54
North Carolina }		By a ballance due the ward	175..34

Hertford County} February Court of Pleas &c 1832   John **DAWNING** Guardian

This Account was returned to Court on oath by John **DAWNING** Guard & ordered to be Recorded   Test. L. M. **COWPER** clk

---

Mary Jane PERRY   gdn

1831   Dr Mary Jane **PERRY** orphan of John W **PERRY** decd in act with William **SLAUGHTER**

Apl 8 To Cash paid William L **GRIMES**}		By yaur half of Negro hire for the year}	
for tuition . . . .}	2..50	1831 . . . .}	37..12½
Int on ditto up to this return	13	Int on ditto up to this return	..35
_ly 22 To Cash paid Wm L **GRIMES**	3..00	By yaur half of rents of Land for 1831	12 12½
Int on ditto	10	Int on ditto	12

(125) Mary Jane **PERRY** (Cont.)

___ 11 To Cash paid William L **GRIMES**	2..50		**1832**	
Int on ditto	..04		Feby 27 By Ballance due the Guardian	104..02
To ballance due the Guardian on}				
my return to Feby caurt 1831 }	90..59?			
Int oh ditto up to this return	5..43			
To yaur half keeping negro				
PEGGY & 4 children negro woman}				
RACHEL & children for 1831 . .}	19..50			
Int on ditto up this [sic] return 4 Jany	..18			
To recording this acct	..40			
To board & clothing for 1831	24..00			
To 5 p cet commissions on $107..50/¢/	5..37			
	153..74		**1832**	153..74
			Feby 27 By Ballance due the Guardian}	
			as above Stated of . . . . }	104..02

North Carolina }
Hertford Caunty} February Caurt of Pleas &c 1832   William **SLAUGHTER** gdn
This Account was returned to Caurt on aath by William **SLAUGHTER** Guardian & ordered
to be recorded   Test. L. M. **COWPER**. clk

William **PERRY**   gdn

1831   Dr William **PERRY** orphan of Jno W **PERRY** ded in act with William **SLAUGHTER**

April 8/th/ To Cash pd William L **GRIMES**			By yaur half of Negro hire for 1831	37 12½
for tuition	2..50		Int on ditto up to this return	..35
Int on ditto up to this return	..13		Amt carried forward	$ 37..47½
	2..63			

---

(126) 97 William **PERRY**

Dr William **PERRY** orphan of John W **PERRY** decd In act with William **SLAUGHTER**

Amt Brot forward	2..63			37..47
July 22/d/ To Cash paid William L **GRIMES**	3 00		By yaur half of rents of Land for 1831	12..22?
Int on ditto	10		Int on ditto up to ditto	..._
To Cash paid W L **GRIMES**	2..50		**1832**	
Int on ditto	04		Feby 27/th/ By a ballance due the Guardian	87..5_
To ballance due the Guardian in }				
my return to February Caurt 1831}	75..06			
Int on ditto up to this return 1832}				
February Court . . . .}	4..50			
To yaur half of keeping negro woman}				
PEGGY & 4 children Negro woman}				
RACHAL & Children for the year 1831}	19..50			
Int on ditto from 4 Jay 1831 up to this}				
return	18			
To recording this acct	40			
To board and clothing for 1831	24..00			
To 5 p cet Comms on $106..57	5 32			
	137..23			137..23

North Carólina }
Hertford Caunty} February Court of Pleas &c 1832   By a Ballance due the Guardian as then?   87..50
This Account was returned to court on oath by William **SLAUGHTER** Guardian & order [sic] to   William **SLAUGHTER** guard
be Recorded   Test. L. M. **COWPER**. clk

Jane **PARKER**

1830   Dr Jane **PARKER** orphan In acct with David **PARKER** Guardian   Cr

Novr 1/st/ To yaur part of bond   20   1830

(126) Jane PARKER (Cont.)

"	"	To Cash this amt	4..00	Augt 27 By this amt recd of L **PARKER**	
"	"	Interest thereon	31	Exor	72..37?
"	8	To paid J **SCOTT** acct	19..44	12 months int thereon	4 34
		Interest thereon	1..52	Int from 27 august 1831 up to this time	2..30

1831

M/r/ch 30 To paid L M **COWPER** . .   3..63

    Interest thereon . . . .   '23

1832

Feby 27 To To [sic] Clk for this act   20

    Coms on $. [sic] @ 5 p cet   5..42

    Ballance due . . . . . .   44..08

       79..03   79..03

North Carolina }   By Ballance due Feby 27-1832 . .   44..08

Hertford County} February Court of Pleas &c 1832   E E . . . . David **PARKER** Guardi__

This Account was returned to Court on oath by David **PARKER** Guardian & ordered to be

Recorded   Test. L. M. **COWPER**. Clk

Lemuel PARKER

1830   Dr Lemuel **PARKER** orphan In act with David **PARKER** Guardian   Cr

Feby 9 To yaur part of Guardian bond   20   1830

" '   To Cash gave yau   5..00   Augt 27 By this amt recd of L **PARKER** }

    ditto paid Clerk for this return   20   Exor . . . . }   72..39

    Comms on $ @ 5 p ct   4..20   12 months Int thereon   4 34

    Ballance due   69..43   Int from 27 augt 1831 to this time   2 30

                   79 03   Amt carried forward   79..03

---

(127) 93 Lemuel PARKER

       Dr Lemuel **PARKER** orphan In acct with David **PARKER** Guardian   Cr

    Amt Brot forward   79..03   79..03

                          By Ballance due 27 Feby 1832 . . .   69..43

North Carolina }   E E . . David **PARKER** Guardian

Hertford County} February Court of Pleas &c 1832

This Account was returned to Court on oath by David **PARKER** Guardian & ordered

to be recorded   Test. L. M. **COWPER**. clk

Robert PARKER

       Dr Robert **PARKER** orphan In Account with David **PARKER** Guardian   Cr

    To yaur part of Bond   20   1830

1832   aug 27/th/ By this amt recd L **PARKER** Exor   72..39

Feby 27/th/ To Cash paid Clerk this return   20   12 months Intererest [sic] thereon   4..34

    Comms on $ @ 5 p ct   3..97   Int from augt 27-1831 up to this time   2..30

    Ballance due   74..66

                   79 03   79..03

North Carolina }   By Ballance due Feby 27-1832.   74..66

Hertford County} February Court of Pleas &c 1832   E E . David **PARKER** Guardian

This Account was returned to Court on oath by David **PARKER** Guardian & ordered

to be recorded   Test. L. M. **COWPER**. Clk

James PERRY

__1   Dr James **PERRY** orphan of Freeman **PERRY** decd In acct current With John **WINBORNE** gdn

__ 28 To Clk fee return acct   ..40   1831   Cr

    ' paid do Cast Suit Jas **WARD** for negro}   Jay 5 By a Ballance due the Ward}

    ANDREW . . . .}   2 00   from last returns . . . . . . }   189..68

    ' Irt up to January 5/th/ 1832   ..13   Int up to Jay 5-1832   11..38

(127) James PERRY (Cont.)

____ 16/th/ To paid William **HAYS** on Jugment	8 30
" do Lewis **DERVISON?** act doctoring Negro girl **AZETTE** yaur part }	1..66 2/3
Guardian finding Sheet Coffin &} Burreing [sic] Sd **AZETTE**}	1..16 2/3
Int up to January 5th 1832	..52
__ 32	
__t 22 Cash Sent the orphan by Mr John} **BEAMAN** at Boro . . . . . }	5..00
To Int up to Jany 5th 1832	11½
Feby? 5 To Cash given yau when going to} Murfreesboro in opresence of Harrell } B **VANPELT** }	5..00
To paid John G **WILSON** act	2..87½
To paid Henry B **VANPELT** Support} old man **YARKE** 1831 . . . . . }	8..33 1/3
To paid Jas **WHITE** Support **ANUST** do	3..00
Brandy use negro hire	07
Comms on $38.57	1..92
A Ballance due the Ward	220..84
North caralina }	261 32 2/3

1832

Jany 5 By yaur part negro hire rent Corn Land pine baxes Tole brandy &c 1831	60	26 2/3
	261	32 2/3

1832

Jany 5/th/ By A Ballance due the Ward   220..84
Return February Term 1832 By

                    John **WINBORNE** Guardian

Hertford Caunty} February Court of Pleas &c 1832
This Account Was returned to Court on oath By John **WINBORNE** Guardian & ordered
to be recorded   Test. L. M. **COWPER**. Clk

═══

(128) 99 Joseph PERRY

1831   Dr Joseph **PERRY** orphan of Freeman **PERRY** decd In act current with John **WIN____**

Feby To this amt paid Lewis M **COWPER**} cast Suite Jas **WARD** avs the heirs of } Freeman **PERRY** decd for negro } **ANDREW** . . . . }	2..00	Aamt Brot up	70..8_
Int up to January 5th 1832	..10	To paid Watson **LEWIS** on act	13.._
Clerk fee Sesdn? act return to ct	20	" Expence yaur part old **YORK** &} **ANUST** 1831 ____ . }	11..3_
making 2 Sheets at home	..50	To paid Henry E **BLANCHARD** for} Tuition . . . . }	1.._
March 4 To paid John P **MITCHEL** for Tuition	1..38	To yaur part Spirits use negro hire	..0_
Apl 16 To do William **HAYS** on Judgment	8..38	To 1 pr Shaes made at hame and} finding Leather . . . . . . }	1..2_
" do Lewis **DERVISON** for attending on negro girl **AZETTE** When Sick & dide 13 days	1 66 2/3	To Sarah **PARNAL** makin 1 over Jacket}	5 0?
Guardian for finding Sheet coffin & burring Said Negro **AZETTE**	1 66¾	Commissions on $98..34	4 91
Int up to Jany 5th 1832	55	1832	
June 10/th/ To making 1 vest 20 2 yds cloth} and making 1 pr Trawser/s/ }	1..20	Jany 5 To a ballances} due the Guardian	103..25 19..7_
To paid Sarah **PERRY** makin 1 over Jacket and 1 vest	..56¼	1831 Jany 5/th/ By a Ballance due the Ward} return Novr Term }	Cr 21..97
Augt 31/st/ To making 3 Shirts at hame @ ¾	1..00	Int up to Jay 5-1832	1..31
Octr 4 To 2 pr Woolen Sacks @ 40/¢/	80	1832	
To making 1 pr Trawser/s/ 30/¢/ finding Cloth makin Vests 50/¢/	80	Jay 5 By yaur part negro hire rent Lands} rent Pine baxes & Tole brandy 1831 }	60..25?
1832		A Ballance due the Guardian	19..70
Jay 2/d/ To board with Guardian from 20 of			103..25

                    John **WINBORNE** Guardian

(128) Joseph **PERRY** (Cont.)

Janue?ary 1831	50..00
amt Carried upt	70..80¾

North Carolina }

Hertford County} February Court of Pleas &c 1832

This Account was returned to Court on oath by John **WINBORNE** Guardian and

ordered to be Recorded   Test. L. M. **COWPER** Clk

William **PERRY**

1831?   Dr William **PERRY** orphan of Freeman **PERRY** decd In act current with John **WINBORNE**

Feby 28 To paid Lewis **COWPER** cast }			Dr
Suit Jas **WARD** for negro **ANDREW**}	2..00	Amt Brot up	16..48¾
To paid do cast return to Court}	20	July 10/th/ To paid Elisha B **NORFLEET**}	
Guardian acct . . Int }	.11	for tuition . . . . }	5..00
Apl 16 To paid William **HAYS** on		Int up to Jany 5-1832	..19
Judgment Int	8..30	To making 1 vest 20 1 do Shirt 30	..50
" paid Lewis **DEVERSON** for		Decr 19/th/ To pad Edward **HARDY** goods	17?
attendance on Negro **AZETTE** when		To making 1 vest & making	..50
Sick & dide [sic]	1..66 2/3	1832	
To Guardian for finding Sheet Coffin &}		Jany To paid Watson **LEWIS** on acct	10..53
burreing Sd Negro **AZETTE** }	1..66 2/3	To do James **WHITE** Support}	
To making 1 p Trawsers & finding buttons	..30	**ANUST** 1831 . . . . . . }	3..00
" Int up to Jany 5/th/ 1832	.68	To paid Henry B **VANPELT** do old mon	
To 2 yds home Spun Clothing finding }		**YARK** do	8..35?
thread buttons & making 1 pr trawsers}	1..00	To paid Henry B. **VANPELT** board}	
July 1/s/ To paid Sarah **PERRY** making}		yaur Self 1831 . . . . }	50..00
1 over Jacket 2? vests . . . . . . }	56¼		95..31½
	$16..48¾		

---

(129) 100 William **PERRY**   gdn

          Dr William **PERRY** orphan of Freeman **PERRY** decd in a/c current with John **WINBORNE**

Amt Brat forward	$ 95..31½	1831	
To paid Elisha B **NORFLEET** for tuition do	3..00	Jay 5 By a Ballance due the ward}	
" do Sarah **PARNAL** making over}	..50	from last return . . . . . . }	48..44
Jacket . . . . }		By Interest up to Jany 5th 1832	2..90
To yaur part brandy use negro hire & [sic]	..07	1832	
To Coms on $99..88/¢/	4..99	Jay 5/th/ By yaur part negro hire rent Lands}	
To making 3 Shirts @ 33 1/3/¢/	1..00	rent pine baxes Tole brandy & Sold }	
To Ballance due the orphan	6..73	James **WARD** . . . . }	60..26½
	111..60		111..60
		By A Ballance due the Ward	6..73

North Carolina }

Hertford County} February Court of Pleas &c 1832   John **WINBORNE** Guardian

This Account was returned to Court on oath by John **WINBORNE** Guardian & ordered to be

Recorded   Test. L. M. **COWPER**. clk

Jacob **SHARP**   gdn

1831   Dr Jacob **SHARP** arphan of Jacob **SHARP** ded In ac With Elish [sic] H **SHARP**

____ 18 To paid E B **NORFLEET** }		1831	
Support **CHERRY** & **TAMER** yr pt}	2..50	Jay 4/th/ By this Sum due the Ward this}	
____ 27 To Edward S **JEGITTS** acct	12..25	day . . . . }	912..00
____ 26 To paid William **NIEL**		By Int on the above Sum 12 months}	
Tuition act	31..50	up to Jany 4/th/ 1832 }	54..72
____ 29 To paid Patt **BROWN** act $55 00 &}		By yaur part Negro hire for 1831	
Eli **CARTER**/s/ acct ----	14 62½} 69..62½	an demand Jany 4/th/ 1832	64 38
To paid R B? **PARKER**/s/ a/c $6. Edwd}			1031..10

(129) Jacob SHARP (Cont.)

S-JEGITTS S JEGGITTS a/c $3 }	9..00	
To paid Jas SCOTT $3..50-1over Caat $17	20..50	
____ 31/st/ To paid Dact WARD a/c		
doctrg SAWYER	38	
1832		
Augt? 4 To paid E B NORFLEET		
Doct TAMER &c	..50	
To paid Mr/s/ YANCY board act	48..00	
To Cloths for negro SAWYER 50/¢/}		
return . . . .}	90	
Coms on $313..85/¢/	15..69	
due Ward this day	820..26	
	1031 10	

1832   1031..10

Jay 4/th/ By this sum due the Ward}

this day   } 820..25

Elisha H SHARP Guardian

Elizabeth SHARP   gdn

1831   Dr Elizabeth SHARP orphan of Jacob SHARP ded in act with Elisha H SHARP

Fe?by 28 To paid Samuel HARRELL

tuition a/c	2..95	amt Brot up	127..82½
" do E B NORFLEET Support		To paid James SCOTTs act	4..01
CHERRY & TAMER y	2..50	To do Miss Pheby HILL acct . . .	7..12½
" Pianar musick [sic]	62½	" do Eley CARTERs acct	..37½
Sept " 1 pr Shaes	1..25	31/st/ To do Doct WARDs acct Doctr	
Oct 6 To 6 yds flannel @ 75 of ANDERSON	4..50	SAWYER	..33
Decr 28 " paid PRUDEN & DARDEN acct	4..25	1832	
___ 29 " paid Mr/s/ H w J BANKS act	91..00	Jay 4 To paid E B NORFLEETs act Doctr}	
" " paid Patrick BRAWNs act	20..75	TAMER yaur part . . . .}	..50
	127..82½		140..21½
amt carried up		Carried forward	

---

(130) 101 Elizabeth SHARP Dr Elizabeth SHARP orphan of Jacob SHARP decd In a/c wi__

1832	E. H. SHARP Guardian		1831	
Jay 4	Amt Brot forward	140 21½	Jay 4 By this Sum due the Ward	846.._
	To paid Mr/s/ E BISHAPs acct	5..87½	By Int on the above 12 months}	
	Cloths for negro SAWYER your part	..50	up to Jay 4 1832 - is --- }	52.._
	" To paid Jno A ANDERSON ac	3 12½	By yaur part negro hire for 1831}	
	To 4 months board ending this day	20..00	on demand Jany 4-1832 }	64.._
	This return	40		
1832	Coms on $286..49	14..32		
Jany 4 To this Sum due the Ward this day	798..81		
		983..24	1832	983..2_
			Jany 4 By this Sum due Ward this day	798..8_
			Seven hundred and ninety eight dollar/s/	
			81/100.	

North Carolina }

Hertford County} February Court of Pleas &c 1832   Elisha H SHARP Guard

This account was returned to Court on oath by Elisha H SHARP Guardian & orderded [sic]

to be Recorded   Test. L. M. COWPER clk

Livinia SIMONS

1831   Dr Livinia SIMONS orphan of John SIMONS in act current with John WINBO___

Jany 5/th/ To a ballance due the Guardn}

in Settlement . . . .}	30..94	Amt Brot up	106..12

(130) Livinia SIMONS (Cont.)

Int up to Jany 5th 1832	1..86	
" To paid Clk fee return to caurt y pt [sic]	20	
To paid John P **MITCHEL** for tuition	1..30	
Mch 5 " do Sarah **PERRY** making 1 Frock	..50	
" do Eliza **NORFLEET** repairing 1 leg}		
horr bonnet . . . . }	2..75	
" do John G **WILSON** act 1 pr Shaes	1..50	
" do Henry B **VANPELT** yaur}		
part repairing fence . . . . }	3..54	
Int up to Jany 5th 1832 . . .	..47	
June 2/d/ To paid Guardian for baling aut}		
Tole Corn and delivering the Same at }		
SCULLs Landing} . . . . . . }	4 32½	
To pad Hariet B **VANPELT**}		
making 1 Frock . . . . . }	37½	
" 1 Skeene Silk & Inst up to		
Jay 5/th/ 1832	22¼	
Augt 22/d/ To paid John A		
ANDERSON acct	3..12½	
To yaur part Taxes in Hertford Caunty	1..34	
To paid do do do Bertie	..24	
Int up to Jany 5th 1832	8	
Novr 14 To paid Edward **HARDY** act	1 40	
25 yaur part Guardian bond	[blank]	
1832 Hauseing tole Corn Recd S **SMITH**	66	
Jay 2/d/ board with ditto 12		
months @ 4 16 2/3	50 00	
To paid Harriet B **VANPELT**}		
making 1 Frack . . . . . }	..75	
	106..12	

amt carried forward

To paid Watson **LEWIS** Guardian for}	
Sarah **SIMONS** in division of negroes}	
yaur part . . . . }	6..99
To paid John **MOORE** 1 pr Shaes	1..50
To do Henry E **BLANCHARD** for tuition	1..83?
To do Watson **LEWIS** acct	46..44?
To do Freeman **EVANS** yaur part}	
5 days worke hauseing Tole Corn }	
at Henry B **VANPELT**s . . . }	..21
To paid Jas **RUSSEL** layin of **URIAH**}	
when delived Child **JOE** }	8_
To do John **BIRD** do **PHILLIS** chid **EAN**?	..66
To do William **VALENTINE** do **CELIA** do}	
do **LUCY** . . . . }	66
To yaur part Spirits use negro hire	..25
To paid Lewis **DEVERSON** doctoring}	
negro **PHILLS** . . . .}	30?
Comms on $160. 22	8..00
A Ballance due the Ward	156 47
	324..74
1831 By yaur part Toles Tole [sic] Corn}	
Sold Watson **LEWIS** Decr 16-1830 on }	
demand June 16th 1831 at 2..30 pr BBl . }	70..14
By this Sum Omited [sic] in fodder}	
last returns . . . . . . }	54
	70..68?

---

(131) 102 Livinia SIMONS   gdn

Dr Livinia **SIMONS** orphan of John **SIMONS** In ac current with John **WINBORNE**

Amt Brot forward	324..74	70..68
16 Jany		
By Int up to Jay 5th 1832		2..34
1832 Novr 25 By 1/7 part of your Farthrs}		
Estate		154..80
By Int up to Jany 5-1832		1..02
Jany 5 By 1/6 part Negro hire rent pine		
baxes Sale Fish & rent gin house 1831		45..96¼
By 1/5 part negro hire pine baxes		43..27
By 1/6 part Sales 20 BBls corn		
Sold Henry B **VANPELT** @ $2 pr bbl		6..66½
	324..74	
1832		324..74
Jany 5/th/ By a ballance due the Ward		156..51

         John **WINBORNE** Guardian

North Carolina }
Hertford County} February Court of Pleas &c 1832
This Account was returned to Court on oath by John **WINBORNE** Guardian & ordered to be
Recorded   Test. L. M. **COWPER**. clk

Mary SIMONS   gdn
1831   Dr Mary **SIMONS** orphan of John **SIMONS** decd In act current with Jno **SIMONS**

(131) Mary SIMONS (Cont.)

' 28 To this Sum pd Clrk return to court	20		

		Amt Brot forward	94..17½
Mch 4 To paid John P MITCHEL for tuition	1 30	To John BIRD do PHILLIS do child ROSE	66 2/3
To do Henry B VANPELT repaird fence	3..54	To do William VALENTINE do CELIA do	
Int up to Jany 5th 1832	23	do LUCY	66 2/3
2/d/ To Guardian for baling? aut Tole}		To do Spirits use negro ~~hire~~?	25
corn & delivering yaur part at SCULLs }		To paid Lewis DEVORSON Doctoring	
Landing . . . . }	4 32½	PHILLIS	30
To paid Harret B VANPELT making}		Comms on $96..16	4..83
1 Frock . . . .}	50		353..69
Int up to Jany 5th 1832	..16	To A Ballance due the Ward	252..86
Augt To yaur part Taxes 1830 in Hertford Cty	1..34		
Oct? 19 ditto ditto in Bertie do	24	1831	Cr
Board With Guardian from Jany 1/st/} 1831 . . . .}	36..11	Jany 5 By a ballance due the Ward	27..32
Int up to Jany 5th 1832	1..15	Int on up [sic] to Jany 1832	1..63
yaur part expences hauseing Tole Corn}		June 16 By 1/6 part Tole corn Sold Watson}	
1832 recd of Sipha SMITH by Guardian }	66 2/3	LEWIS . . . . }	70 14
Jany 2/d/ To pd Watson LEWIS Guardian		this Sum omitted in fodder last returns	54
for Sarah SIMONS in division of negras		By Int up to Jany 5th 1832	2..34
yaur part	6..98	Novr 25 By 1/7 part yaur Farther/s/ Estate	154..86
To paid Elizabeth HARRELL a/c board		Int up to Jany 5th 1832	1..12
from 19 Sept 1831 up to Jay 5-1832	13..89	1832	
To pd Henry E VANPELT for tuition	1..63	Jany 5/th/ By 1/6 part negro hire rent pine}	
To do Watson LEWIS act	20..90	baxes Sale fish & rent gin hause /1831/ }	45..96¼
To do Freeman EVANS 5 days hausing}		By 1/5 part negro rent [sic] pine boxes 1830	43..27
Tole Corn recd Tole Corn recd Henry }		By 1/6 do Sales 20 Bbls Tole corn Sold	
B VANPELT 1831 . . . . . . }	21	Henry B VANPELT	6..66 2/3
To paid James RUSSEL /Layin of }			353..69
URIAH/ When delivered Child JOE}	80		
amt carried up	94..17¼		

---

(132) 103 Mary SIMONS

Dr Mary SIMONS orphan of John SIMONS decd In acct current
with John WINBORNE Guardian

Amt Brot forward	353..69	1832	353..69
		Jany 5 By A Ballance due the Ward	252..86

North Carolina }
Hertford County} February Court of Pleas &c 1832
This Account was returned to Court on oath By John WINBORNE Guardian & ordered to be
Recorded   Test. L. M. COWPER. Clk

John WINBORNE Guar____

Edward SIMONS

Dr Edward SIMONS orphan of John SIMONS decd In ac current With
1831 John WINBORNE Guardian   Cr

Feby 28 To this Sum paid clk fee return to court	..20	1831	
March To paid John MOORE 1 pr shaes	1..10	Jany 5 By a ballance due the Ward} from Last return . . . . . }	48..27
To do Henry B VANPELT repairing fence	3..54	Int up to Jay 5th 1832	2..89
" Int up to 5 Jany 1832	..23	June 16 By 1/6 part Tole corn Sold Watson} LEWIS	70..16
June 2/d/ To do Guardian for baling aut Tole corn and delivering the Same		By this Sum omited in fordder	54
		Int up to Jay 5th 1832	2..34

(132) Edward SIMONS (Cont.)

at SCULLs Landing	4..32½	
To do Harret B VANPELT making		
over Jacket 1 pr Trawser & 3 Shirts	1..00	
To paid yaur part Taxes in Hertford cty	1..34	
To do do do Bertie County . . .	..24	
To ' 1 pr wooling Stockings found}		
by the Guardian . . . .}	37½	
Int up to Jany 5-1832	14	
Novr 25 To " Guardian hauseing Tole}		
1832 corn recd S SMITH . . . .}	66½	
Jany To " pd Harret B VANPELT}		
making Cloths . . . .}	1..25	
" do Watson LEWIS Guardian for }		
Sarah SIMONS in division of Negraes}	6..98	
" paid Watson LEWIS a/c for gods?		
in Store	14..30	
" do Freeman EVANS housing Tole}		
Corn recd Henry B VANPELT }	21	
" do James RUSSEL layin URIAH}		
When delivered Child JOE }	80	
" do Jemmia VANPELT board from		
1/st/ day of Jany 18321 up to 1/st/		
Jay 1832	50..00	
To yaur part Spirits use negro hire	25	
To " 1 pr Wooling Stockings	30	
To do William VALENTINE layin}		
CELIA When deliverd Child LUCY}	66 2/3	
To do John BIRD do PHILLIS do ROSE	66 2/3	
To do Lewis DEVORSON Doctoring		
PHILLIS	30	
Comms on $88..77	4..43	
A Ballance due the Ward	282..70	

Nov 25		
By 1/7 part yaur Farther/s/ Estate reforance}		
to be had from return Novr Term 1831 }	154..80	
1832		
Jay 5 Int up to Jay 5 1832	1..02	
" " By 1/6 part negro hire rent Pine baxes}		
gin hause & Sales fish 1831 }	45..96½?	
By 1/5 part negro hire rent pine baxes do	43..27	
By 1/6 do Sale 20 BBls Corn sold}		
Henry B VANPELT . . . . .}	6..66 2/3	
	375..90	

1832	375..90	
Jany 5 By a Ballance due the Ward	282..70	
return by John WINBORNE guardian		
to February Term-1832		

North Carolina } February   375 90 Caurt of Pleas &c 1832

Hertford County} This Account was returned to Court on oath by John WINBORNE guard & ordered to be Recorded

Test. L. M. COWPER. clk

---

(133) 104 Sarah SIMONS   gdn

1831   Dr Sarah SIMONS orphan of John SIMONS decd in acct current with John WINBORNE

__by To this Sum paid clk for return to court	20	
To paid Henry B VANPELT repairing		
fence	3..54	
To Int up to Jay 5th 1832	15?	
June /2d/ To guardian for baling aus?t Tole}		
Corn and delivering the Same at }		
SCULLs Landing . . . .}	4..32	
Int up to Jay 5th 1832	14	
To " Taxes 1830	1..34	
" " yaur part hausing Tole Corn by the}		
Guardian S. SMITH . . . . .}	..66 ½	
" " Watson LEWIS Guardian for yaur }		
mother in division of negraes }	6..98	
" " Freeman EVANS hausing Tole corn}		
recd Henry B VANPELT . . . . .}	..21	
" " yaur part Spirits use negra hire &c	15	

1831		
Jany 5 By this Sum due the Ward from}		
last return . . . .}	39..66	
Int up to Jay 5 1832	2..37	
June 6 By 1/6 part Tole Corn Sold Watson}		
LEWIS . . . .}	70..14	
Fodder omited last returns	..54	
Int up to Jay 5-1832	2..52	
Novr 25 By 1/7 part yaur Farther/s/ Estate	154..80	
Int up to Jay 5th 1832	1..02	
1832		
Jany 5 By 1/6 part negro hire rent pine boxes}		
& gin hause & Sale Fish at Liberty Hill }	45..96¼	
By 1/6 part 20 Bbls Tole Corn Sald}		
Henry B VANPELT . . . . . }	6..66 2/3	

(133) Sarah **SIMONS** (Cont.)

" " William **VALENTINE** layin when delivered child LUCY . . . . . .}	..66 2/3		
" " John **BIRD** do **PHILLIS** do **RASE**	..66 2/3		
" Comms on $19..99	96		
" A Ballance due the Ward	303..51		
	323..50	1832	323..50
		Jay 5 B ablance [sic] due the Ward	303..5:

North Carolina }
Hertford County} February Court of Pleas 1832

Return by John **WINBORNE** Guardian
Feby Term 1832

This Account was returned to Caurt on oath by John **WINBORNE** Guardian & ordered to be
Recorded

Test. L. M. **COWPER**. Clk

Elizabeth **SIMONS**

Dr Elizabeth **SIMONS** orphan of John **SIMONS** decd In act current
1831 With John **WINBORNE** Guardian

				Cr
__ by 28 To yaur part Clk fee return Court	..20	Amt Brot up		13/Dr/23
March To paid John P **MICHEL** for tuition	1..26	To " Int up to Jany 5 1832		..06
To " Sarah **PERRY** for making 1 Silk Frock	..50	To yaur part hauseing Tole corn} Recd of? Sipha **SMITH** . . }		65½
" John G **WILS** [sic] on 1 Intraduction	25	Decr 19 To pd Edward **HARDY** a/ct		1..50
" Int up to Jany 5 1832	..11	1832		
" pd Henry B **VANPELT** for repairing fence	3..54	Jany 2/d/ To board with Guardian 12 manths		50..00
June 2 To " Guardian yaur part baling aut Corn and delivering the Same at} SCULLs Landing . . . . . }	4..32½	To paid Watson **LEWIS** Guardian} for Sarah **SIMONS** in } division of negroes . . . . . }		6..93
Int up to Jay 5/th/-1832	27	To Henry E **BLANCHARD** for tuition		2..11
__ 16 To paid Harret B **VANPELT** making 2 frocks	62½	To paid Watsan **LEWIS** acct		29..73
Augt 22/d/ To Taxes in Hertford caunty 1830	1..34	To paid Freeman **EVANS** housing } " " Tole Corn recd Henry B **VANPELT**}		..21
To do do do Bertie caunty do	24	To paid Jas **RUSSEL** layin **URIAH**		
To paid Edward **HARDY** act 1 Hook?	37½	when delivered Child JOE}		
To Footing 1 pr Stacking [sic]	25	1/5 part 4$ . . . . . }		80
	13..28			105 33½
Amt carried up		amt carried forward		

---

(134) 105 Elizabeth **SIMONS**

Dr Elizabeth **SIMONS** orphan of John **SIMONS** decd In
acct current With John **WINBORNE** Guardian

			Cr
amt Brot forward	105 33½	1831	
To Spirits use negro hire &c yaur pt	..25	Jay 5 By a Ballance due the Ward	24..__
To 1 pr Wooling Stocking	62½	Int up to Jay 5th 1832	1..__
To paid William **VALENTINE** layin} **CELIA** child LUCY }	66 2/3	June 16 By 1/6 part Sales Tole Corn	70..__
To paid John **BIRD** do **PHILLIS** do **RASE**	66 2/3	By fodder omitted in last returns	__
To paid Lewis **DEVOERSON** doctoring **PHILLIS**	..30	By Int up to Jay 5th 1832	2..__
To Comms on $107..83	5..39	" 1/7 part yaur farther/s/ Estate referance} to be had from Return Novr Term /1831/}	154..__
To a Ballance due the Ward	237..67	" Int up to Jany 5th 1832	1 1_
		" 1/6 part negro hire rent pine baxes}	
		" Sale Fish & rent gin hause 1831 }	45..9_
		" 1/5 part negro hire rent pine baxes 1831	43..2_
		" 1/6 do 20 Bbls Tole Corn Sold}	
		Henry B **VANPELT** @ $2 pr bbl}	6..6_
	350..90	1832	350..90

(134) Elizabeth SIMONS (Cont.)

North Carolina }

Hertford County} February Court of Pleas &c 1832

This Account was returned to Court on oath by John WINBORNE Guardian & ordered to

be Recorded

Jany 5 By abblance [sic] due the Ward   237..67

John WINBORNE Guard___

Test. L. M. COWPER C__

John SIMONS

1831   Dr John SIMONS orphan of John SIMONS In a/c current With John WINBORNE Gua__

Feby 28 To clk fee return to court yaur part	..20		Dr
March 4 To paid John P MITCHEL for		Amt Brat f up	$ 66..35
tuition	92½	To paid Watson LEWIS Guardian}	
To do Henry B VANPELT yaur part}		for Sarah SIMONS in divii?sion }	
repairing fence 1831 . . . . . }	3..54	Negroes . . . . }	6..99?
To Int up to Jay 5 1832	23	" " Henry E BLANCHARD for tuition	2..11
June 2/d/ To paid Guardian for baling aut}		" " Watson LEWIS acct	12..51
Tole Corn and delivering the Same }		" " Freeman EVANS 5 days hausing}	
at SCULLs Landing . . . . . }	4..32½	" " Tole Corn recd H B VANPELT }	..21
" " Irt up to Jay 5 1832	..14	" " Jas RUSSELL layin URAH when}	
" " making 1 pr Trawser/s/	..25	delivered Child JOE . . . . .}	80
" pd Harret B VANPELT making}		" " yaur part Spirits use negro hire	..25
1 over Jacket	..25	" " John PARNAL a/c for making 1 Coat}	
augt 22/d/ " " Taxes in Hertford Caunty	1..34	" " & 1 pr Trawser/s/ . . . . }	1..00
" " do do do Bertie Caunty	24	" " 1 pr Wooling Stockings	..30
Ocbr " " 1 pr Wooling Stockings net at}		" " William VALENTINE layin CELIA	
Leaner? . . . . }	..50	When deliverd Child LUCY	66 2/3
" " making 1 pr Trawser/s/ at hame	25	" " John BIRD do PHILLIS do RASE	..66 2/3
" " Int up to Jany 5-1832	02	" " Lewis DEVOERSON doctoring PHILLIS	..30
" " Guardian hausing Tole corn}		" " Comms on $92..20	4..61
recd Sipha SMITH yaur part }	..66 2/3	" " a balance due the ward	[blank]
Decr 10 " " Edward HARDY act . .	1..60		
1832 " ' 1 pr Shaes made at hame	87½		
Jany 2/d/ " " making 1 pr Trawser/s/ at do	..25		
" " " " 12 months with Guardian	50..00		
" " " " Livinia SIMONS making 3 shirts	..75		
amt carried up . . .	66..35	amt carried forward	367..24

---

(135) 106 John SIMONS   gdn

Dr John SIMONS orphan of John SIMONS decd In a/c current With John WINBORNE

Amt brot forward	367..24	1831	
		Jay 5 By a balance due the Ward}	
		last Returns . . . . . }	40 10?
		By Int up to Jay 5 1832	2..40
		June 16 By yaur part Tole corn Sold}	
		Watson LEWIS	70..14
		By Int up to Jay 5 1832	2..34
		" fodder omit last returns	54
		25	
		N"ovr yaur part yaur Farther/s/ Estate}	
		after settleed . . . . }	154..80
		" Int up to Jay 5th 1832	1..02
		1832	
		Jay 5 By 1/6 part negro hire rent pine}	
		baxes gin Hause /&/ Sale fish 1831 }	45..96¼
		By 1/5 part negro hire rent pine}	

(135) John **SIMONS** (Cont.)

boxes . . . . }			43..27
By 1/6 do Sale 20 BBls corn Sold}			
		Henry B **VANPELT** @ 2 pr bbl }	6 66 2/3
	367..24	1832	367 24
		Jay 5 By A Ballance due the ward	270..43

This return made By John **WINBORNE** Guardian

North Carolina }
Hertford County} February Court of Pleas &c 1832
This Account Was returned to Court on oath By John **WINBORNE** Guardian & ordered to be
Recorded   Test L M **COWPER** Clk

The Childen [sic] of Elisha **SESSOMS**

Dr Perthena Ann **SESSOMS** William H **SESSOMS** Amgiad W **SESSOMS**
Aragimite M **SESSOMS** Assad S **SESSOMS** & Aronah S **SESSOMS** orphans of Elisha **SESSOMS** Guardian [sic] In ac
current with Elisha **SESSOMS** their Guardian

1832		1832	
Feby term To cash paid Lewis M }		Feby Term By this amt returned to}	
COWPER for return made }	20	Feby termTerm 1831 . . . }	47..72
		By Interest on the above Sum to . }	
		February Term 1832 . . . . }	2..87
			50..29
			29
		Ballance due the orphan [sic] up to this time 50..09	
		E E Elisha **SESSOMS** Guardn	

North Carolina }
Hertford County} February Court of Pleas &c 1832
This Account was returned to Caurt on oath by Elisha **SESSOMS** Guardian
& ordered to be Recorded   Test. L. M. **COWPER**. Clk

Hillery **SOWEL**

Dr Hilery **SOWEL** orphan of Christian **SOWEL** decd In ac current

1831 with John **DOWNING** Guardian			Cr
To return acct court	40	1832	
May To 1 pr Shaes	1..25	Feby 23/d/ By this Sum due the ward	143..55
Octr To 1 Trunk	2..50	" Cash	83
To 1 Book 62½ 1 quire paper 25	87½	" Int up to Feby 23-1832	8..61
1832 To Commis on $5..02½	25	" James **TODD** rent hause	3..00
Feby 23 To a balance due the ward	159 72½	" 6 Bbls Tole Corn @ 1..50/¢/	9..00
	165..00	Amt carried forward	165..00

---

(136) 107 Hilery [sic] **SOWEL**

Dr Hillery **SOWEL** orphan of Christian **SOWEL** In acct current

with John **DOWNING** Guardian			Cr
Amt Brot forward	165 00	1832	165..00
		Feby 23 By a Balance due the ward	159..7__

North Carolina }
Hertford County} February Court of Pleas &c 1832
This Account was returned to Court on oath by John **DAWNING** guar_
& ordered to be Recorded   Test. L. M. **COWPER** ___

Elizabeth **VANPELT**

Dr Elizabeth **VANPELT** /ded/ orphan of Daniel in ac current with

1831 Henry B **VANPELT** her Guardian			
May 23 To ninety cents p/d/ **COWPER**		1832	
Clerk	90	Feby 26 By amt due the ward and }	
Sept 12 To 1 Fancy handkerchief	1 25	return to May Term 1831 }	

(136) Elizabeth VANPELT (Cont.)

Octr 1/st/ To Miss Ann and Elisa NORFLEET}		without Calculated up to Feby 28-1831}	98..60?
for bleaching lining and dressing }		By Int on ninety eight dallar/s/ }	
one leghorn bonnet Towo dallar/s/}		60/100 up to February Term 1832}	5..91
50/100	2..50	" her part negro hire for the year of	
To Board with Guardian twelve}		1831 forty Six dallar/s/ 12½/¢/	46..12½
months up to Jany 1/st/ 1832 }	48..00	" Interest up to 5 day Jay 1832	..39
To Comms on forty Six dallar/s/}		1832	
12½'100 it being the her part of}		Jay 5 By this Sum due the ward	
negros for the of [sic] 1831 up }		in thes Division of Negroes	
1832 to Jany 1/st/ 1832 }	2 30	thirty Seven dallar/s/ and 50/100	37..50
Jany 10 To Elisha B NORFLEET		Int up to February term 1832	..31
for Schooling	8..00		188..83½
To Cash paid Lawrence BEVERLY	9..18¾		
To Ballance due the ward	116..69¾	H. B. VANPELT Guardian	
	188 83½		

North Carolina }
Hertford County} February Court of Pleas &c 1832
This Account was returned to Court on oath by Henry B VANPELT Guardian &
ordered to to [sic] be Recorded   Test. L. M. COWPER. Clk

The heirs of Jessee VANN

1830	Dr The heir/s/ of Jesse VANN To Kinsy JORDAN guard		1830		Cr
Augt 25 To Recording Guardian bond	1..00		Augt 25 By ballance due heir/s/		66..66
1831 To Int to 25 day Feby 1832	09		" Int up to 27 day Feby 1832		6 00
April 14 To Cash paid Jerry D ASKEW	1..50		1832		
" Int to 27 Day Feby 1832 . .	07		Jay 1/st/ " rent of plantation to John }		
May 27 To Taxes for year 1829 . . .	12 80		" " GAINES? for the year 1831 }		24..00
" Int to 27 day Fby 1832 . . .	70		" " " Int to 27 day of Feby 1832		..23
" 30 To Recording Coppy of Will}			" rent of Plantation Creek to}		
1832 of J WILLIAMS decd . . }	80		Allen HALL . . . . . }		20..00
Jay 1/st/ To Taxes for year 1830	8..65		By Int to 27 day of Feby 1832		10
" Int to 27 day Feby 1832	08		" rent of Plantation late Blue}		
To Commisions $52 @ 5 p cet	2..12		Water to Jerry D ASKEW }		8..00
1832 To Recording of the Same	..20		Interest		..04
Feby 27 To Balance due the Heir/s/	96 96		1832		125 03
	125..03		Feby 27 To Debtor		28 07
			Ballance due heir/s/		96 96

North Carolina }
Hertford County} Februay Court of Pleas &c 1832   E E Kinsey JORDAN Guardi__
This Account was returned to Court on oath by Kinsey JORDAN guadn [sic]
& ordered to be Recorded   Test. L. M. COWPER. clk

---

(137) 108 Sally M. WILLIAMS Dr Sally Miriah WILLIAMS orphan of Benj B WILLIAMS

1831 Int acct current with Depsey NAWEL Guardian

To the returns made to Feby Term	..40		1831	
To coctris [sic] for FILLIS	1 25		Feby 24 Returns made to Feby term	155..53
To 2¾ yds of Cloth	1 48		Int on $155 50?	3..33
To goods bought of Lawrence BEVERLY	32½		1832 By hire of negraes due	
To keeping FILLIS & 4 childen 1 year	25..00		5 day of Jay . . . . 56..00	
To goods Bought John WILSON	..84		" Int on $56 dollor/s/	..45
1832 To goods bought of Edward HARDY	6..68½			
To Tuition 27 days . . .	1..10			
" 12 months board . . .	42..00			

(137) Sally M WILLIAMS (Cont.)

" Comms on $221..31	11..06½	1832
" a balance due the orphan	130 56	Feby 27 returns made Feby Term	$130..56

North Corolina }
Hertford County} February Court of Pleas &c 1832
This Account was returned to Court on oath by Dempsey NAWEL Guardian & orderdererd [sic]
To be Recorded   Test. L. M. COWPER. clk

Melvill **WISE**

1831   Dr Melvill WISE in acct with Williams B WISE his Guardian   Cr

/25/ Decr To this amt paid for keeping negro}		1831	
woman & children for year 1831 }100..00		Decr 25 By rent of Land to David }	
To Interest on Same 25 decr 1831 to}		PARKER for the year 1831 . . }	50..00
T 28 February 1832 . . . . . . }	1..04	" Hire Boy JOE for 1831	5..00
To Cash paid clerk for Guardian}		" do negro woman SILVIA}	
bond . . . . }	80	& child SUSAN for 1831 }	10..00
To commisions on one hundred & }		" rent of hause & Lat in}	
Seventy eight dolls & 2¢? @ 2½ p ct}	4..47	Murfreesboro for 1831 }	10..00
		" Int on Seventy five dallar/s/}	
		from 25 decr 1831 to }	
		28 February 1832 }	..78
	106..71	Ballance due pr contra	30..93
			106..7.

the Follawing is a list of the property in my
hands beleonging to Melvill WISE to wit one hause & Lat lying in the tawn of
Murfreesboro one track Land in Hertford County suppased to contain acres [sic] more or
less one negro woman namded EDY & five children to wit JOE NELSON JULIA BARBARY
& MONGO also one negro woman named SILVIA & Child SUSAN

North Carolina }   William B WISE guardr.
Hertford County} February Caurt of Pleas &c 1832
This Account was returned to Court on oath by William B WISE & ordered to be Recorded
                                        Test. L. M. COWPER. clk

---

1829 Jaseph **YEATES**

Novr   Dr Jaseph YEATS orphan of Wm YEATS decd In acct Current with James YEAS Guardian

Term To Cash pd clk fees &c &c	1..60	1829	Cr
1831 " Int on ditto	..12	Novr By amt recd of Jesse YEATS decd}	
Decr 8 " To Abner HARRELL act	2..91¼	his former Guardian including }	
1832 Int on ditto	02¼	Interest up to this day for rent of }	29..72½
Feby 5 To repair/s/ on chimney . . .	1..00	Land 1830 }	
	6..25½		29..72½

---

(138) 109 Jasph [sic] **YEATS**

1832   Dr Joseph YEATS orphan of Wm YEATS decd In acct current with James Y____

Feby 5 Amt Brot forward	6 25½		29..7__
" 15 To paid David WEAVER for Shaes	1..25	By rent of Land and hire of negraes}	
To commissons on $134 dallar/s/	6..70	ANTHANY including Int for }	43.._
To Ballance due the ward	[blank]	the year 1831 . . . .}	
		By rent of Land and hire of negro }	
		ANTHOY due 8 of Jany 1832 Int}	
		included up to this day }	50..
	123..72½		2123..72_
		given under my hand this February	

North Carolina }   Term 1832   James YEATS Guardia_
Hertford County} ~~February~~ May Court of Pleas &c 1832
This accoant was returned to Court on oath By James YEATS Guardian & ordered to be

(138) Joseph YEATS (Cont.)
Recorded   Test. L. M. **COWPER**. c_

Robert **FLYNN**

1832	Dr Robert **FLYNN** in acct current with Samuel **MOORE** guardi__		Cr
		1831	
		may 23/d/ By this amt due yau in former}	
		Settlement . . . .}	373..50
		" Int from may 23/d/ 1831 til }	
		May 23/d/ 1832 . . . . }	22..41
North Carolina }		due the. Ward	$395..93

North Carolina }
Hertford County} May Court of Pleas &c 1832   Samuel **MOORE** Guardn
This Account was returned to Court on oath by Samuel **MOORE** Guardian & orderen?
To be Recorded   Test. L. M. **COWPER**. clk

Mary Jane **MONTGOMERY**

D [sic] Mary Jane **MONTGOMERY** orphan of John C **MONTGOMERY**
1832 In Account current with her Guardian G W **MONTGOMERY** for the year 1831 Feby 27-183_

Jany 1/st/ To keeping & furnishing one negro}		1832	
woman **ISABELA** and her Two children}		Feby 27 By her Interest in one negro	
" **VENUS & BITHA** during the year 1831}	10..00	Woman **ISABELA** & 2 children	
" 12 To $1..92/¢/ Cash pd Miles H		**VENUS & BITHA** supposed to be	
JERNGAN in full for her taxes due on}		twothisas?[worthless?].	[blank]
her Land for the year 1830 }	1..92	By 318½ acres of undrained?or	
Feby 27 To 40 cent cash pd clk for this		unimproved Land	[blank]
return	..40	Feby 27-1832 G. W. **MONTGOMERY** Guardian	
Comms	..60		
	12..92		

North Carolina }
Hertford County} May Court of Pleas &c 1832
This Account was returned to court on oath by G W **MONTGOMERY** gurdn
& ordered to be Recorded   Test. L. M. **COWPER**. clk

Priston **PERRY**

Dr Priston **PERRY** orphan of Jaseph **PERRY** decd In acct current
Agatha **PERRY** Guardian   Cr

1831 To 1 Hat 30/- 1 cap 10/- 1 pr		1831	
Shoes 15/-	5..50	Jay By a balance due the Ward	54..99
To paid William D **VALENTINE**}		1832	
for tuition . . . . }	2..40	Jany " 12 months Int on Same	3..29
	7..90	Amt carried forward	58..28

---

(139) 110 Priston PERRY   gdn
Dr Priston **PERRY** orphan of Jaseph **PERRY** decd in a/c current with Agatha **PERRY**

Amt Brot forward	7 90	Jany	58..28
To Clerk fees return to may term 1831	..35	yaur part Tole Corn & fodder Peas}	
1831? To Board Clothing &c . . do	24..36	brandy & negro hire &c 1831 }	29..32
8 To A Balance due the ward	54..99		
	87..60	8	87..60
		8 By a Ballance due the ward	54..99

her
Agatha x **PERRY** guadn
mark

---

(139) (Cont.)
Mary PERRY

Dr Mary PERRY orphan of Jaseph PERRY ded In act current
with Agatha PERRY Guardian

1831 To Court C/h/arges for returns	..35	**1831**		
" 1 bonnet 1 ban bax c& [sic]	5..62½	Jany By a Ballance due the ward	54..99	
" 4 yds Callico @ 65 1 belt Ribon 25	2..95	" 12 months Int on ditto	3..29	
" 5 yds ditto @ 25/¢/ 1 glaves? @ 50/¢/	1..75	" yaur part Tole Corn fodder }		
" 2 pr Shaes @ $1..37½	2..75	" Peas brandy & hire ngraes /1831/}	29..32	
" pd William D? VALENTINE for}				
1832 Tuition	1 00			
May 8 " A ballance due the Ward	54..99			
	87..60	Jany 8	87..60	
		By a balance due the ward her	54..99	

Agatha x PERRY Guardn
mark

Patrick PERRY   gdn
1831   Dr Patrick PERRY orphan of Jaseph decd in acct current with Agatha PERRY

Jany To clerk fee return to court	35	**1831**	
" pd William D VALENTINE}		Jay By A balance due the ward orphan	54..99
for tuition . . . . }	2..20	" Interest on ditto	3..29
1832 " 12 months board & clothing	30..00	" yaur part Tole corn fodder }	
May 8 " A balance due the ward	54..99	" Peas brandy & hire of ngraes /1832/}	29..32
	87..60	8	87..60
		By a balance due the ward	54..99

her
Agatha x PERRY Guardn
mark

Joseph PERRY   gdn
1831   Dr Joseph PERRY orphan of Jaseph decd in acct current with Agatha PERRY

May To Clerk fee return Caurt	..35	1831	Cr
To pd William D VALENTINE for		Jay By a balance due the orphan	$54..99
tuition	2..12	" 12 [sic] Interest on ditto	3..29
1832		" yaur part Tole corn fodder }	
Jay 8 To a balance due the ward	54..99	Peas brandy & negro hire 1831}	29..32
	87..60	8	87..60
		By a balance due the Ward	$54..99

her
Agatha x PERRY Guardian
mark

1831 Elizabeth PERRY
May   Dr Elizabeth PERRY orphan of Jaseph PERRY decd in act current with Agatha PERRY gdn

To Clerk fee return Court	35	1831	Cr
1832 To 12 months board & clothing	32..36	Jay By a balance due the ward	54..99
	$32..791	" 12 months Interest on ditto	3..29
		Amt corried forward	$58..28

(140) 111 Elizabeth PERRY

Dr Elizabeth PERRY orphan of Joseph PERRY ded in acct
Current with Agatha PERRY Guardian   Cr

1832 Amt Brot forward	$32..71	1832	58..28
Jany 8 To a balance due the ward	54..99	Jany By yaur part Tole Corn fodder }	

(140) Elizabeth **PERRY** (Cont.)

			Peas Brandy & negro hire 1831}	29..32
	87..60	8		87..60
			By a balance due the ward	54..99

her
Agatha x PERRY guar__
mark

John D. PERRY

1831   Dr John D **PERRY** orphan of Jaseph **PERRY** decd in act current with Agatha **PERRY** g__

may To clerk fee return court	35	**1831**	
1832 To 12 months board & clothing	32..26	Jay By a balance due the ward	54..99
Jay 8 To a balance due the ward	54..99	1832 " 12 months Int on ditto	3..29
		Jay 8 " yaur part Tole Corn fodder}	
		Peas brandy & negro hire 1831 }	29..32
	87..60		$87..60
		A Ballance due the ward	54..99

North Corolina }
Hertford County} May Court of Pleas &c 1832
This Account was returned to Court on oath by Agatha **PERRY** guardin &
ordered to be Recorded   Test. L. M. **COWPER** clk.

Margaret CURL

Dr Margaret **CURL** orphan of Anne **CURL** In act
    with Jethro **CURL** Guardian

1832 To 14 lbs bacon @ 10 1 bushel		By this amt due the orphan on last}	
meal @ 50	1..90	return }	25?..29
" cash pd Self 50 pad John **WEAVER**	1..56¼	" Interest	1 57¾
" Cash paid for returning this act	..20		3
" Commis an $3..66 at 5 p ct	18		
	3..84¼		22..96¼
		Ballance due the orphan 1/st/ day}	
		of Jany 1832 . . . .}	22..96¼

his
E E . . Jethro x CURL Guardian
mark

North Carolina }
Hertford County} Many Court of Pleas &c 1832
This account was returned to Court on oath by Jethro **CURL** Guardian & ordered
to be Recorded   Test. L. M. **COWPER** Clk

Barshaba JEGITTS

gd_

1830   Dr Barshaba **JEGITTS** orphan of John **JEGITTS** decd in acct with Edward K. **JEGIT__**

Augt 23 To board from 23/d/ Augt 1830 to 25 May}		**1830**	
1832 1832 making 1 year 9 months @}	52..50	Augt 23 By this amt due Barsha ba }	
30 pr year }		**JEGITTS** to this time as pr my }	
Feby 28 To Cash paid David **WEAVER**		return to Augt Court Court [sic] 1830}	317..89
1831 for Shaes	1 37½	By Int from 23/d/ August 1830 to}	
Novr? 23 " Cash paid Phebe **HILLs** acct	4..00	28 May 1832 . . . .}	35..14
1832 " Int to 28 May 1832	13		
May 25 " Cash paid Lewis M **COWPER**/s/			
acot	16..04		
" " " Cash paid John W. **SOUTHALLs**			
act	7..06		
" 8 " Cash pad Mat /&/ H. D **GRIFFITHes**			
act	1..00		
May 23 " Cash paid the Clerk making this			
return	..40		

(140) Barshaba **JEGITTS** (Cont.)

" Commis @ 5 p ct on $30 . . . | 1 50
|---|
| 84..00½ | 353..03

amt carried forward

---

(141) 112 Barshaba **JEGITTS**

1830   Dr Barshaba **JEGITTS** orpan of John **JEGITTS** decd In account

with Edward K. **JEGITTS** Guardian   Cr

amt Brot forward	84 00½		353..03
To Ballance due up to this day	269..02½		
	353 03	1832	353..03
		May 28 By Ballance due }	
		Barsha **JEGITTS**}	269..02

North Carolina }   E E   Edward K **JEGITTS** Guardian

Hertford County} Augt Court of Pleas &c 1832

This Account was returned to Court on oath by Edward K **JEGITTS** Guardian & ordered

to be Recorded   Test. L. M. **COWPER** clk

Jabez B. **WHEELER**

1831   Dr Jabez B. **WHEELER** in a/c With James **WORRELL** his Guardn

__ut? 22/d/ To Cash paid clk for returning		1831	Cr
Gd ac	75	Augt 22/d/ By Ballance due on last return	1443. 60
" Int 12 months/ 4 days	05	" Int 12 months	86. 61
__ct? 13 To Cash John W **SOUTHALL** s a/c	38 00		
do pd Rich/d/ W **JOHNSTON** do	11..01		
Int 11 months/4 days	2..86		
_ch 25 To Cash paid yau this amt @?	2..00		
1832 Int 10 months	..10		
__by 14 To Cash pd yau this amt	5..00		
Int 6 months 13 days	..16		
24 To Cash P **BROWN**	24..32		
Int 6 months 3 days	..73		
___ 1/st/ To Cash paid yau by J **WILLS**	100..00		
Int 5 months 26 days	2..90		
To 5 pr cet coms on recpts and			
1832 expenditures amtg to $275. 01	13 75		
_ugt 17 To Ballance due yau	1327 98		
	1530..21		1530..21

North Carolina }   James **WORRELL** Guardian

Hertford County} August Court of Pleas &c 1832

This account was returned to Court on oath by James **WORRELL** Guardian & ordered to be

Recorded   Test. L. M. **COWPER** clk

Margaret **WHITEY** [sic]

     Dr Margaret **WHITLEY** In a/c current with George **WHITLY** Guardian   Cr

To amt paid Patrick **BROWN** pr bill	2..40	1832	
To Cash paid Trial **WILLIOMSON**}		Augt ct By Ballance due the ward}	
for 1 pr Shaes . . . . }	1 12 1/3	on my last return at }	
To Comms on the amt pd aut @ 5 pr ct	..22	August Court 1831 }	76..23
By Ballance due the ward to}	76..36	" Int for one year	4..57
august court 1832 . . . }			
	$ 80..80	his	$80..80

     George x **WHITLEY** Gurdn

     mark

(142) 113 David WHITLEY Dr David **WHITLEY** in a/c current with George **WHITLEY** his Guardian

1832			1832		
To Cash paid Patrick **BROWN** as pr bill	7..40		augt ct By amt due the ward}		
" ditto pd clk for making this return	..70		on my last return at	}	
" Comms on the amt pd aut @ 5 pr ct	..40		August Court 1832	}	76..6_
To 1 pr Shaes of Trial **WILLIAMSON**	87½		" Int for one year		4..6_
" Balance due the ward }					
up to August Court 1832}	71 90				
	$81..27			his	$81..27

North Carolina }
Hertford County} August Court of Pleas &c 1832
These Accounts were returned to Court on oath by George **WHITLEY** Guardian & orderen
To be Recorded

George x **WHITLEY** gu___
mark

Test. L. M. **COWPER** clk

===

John MAGET

1831   Dr John **MAGET** in a/c current with Jacob **HARE** his Guardn   Cr

1831			1831		
Der 24 To Cash paid R W **JOHNSTON**,act	19..13		augt 24 By Ballance due the orphan		1160..01
1832 ' Int on ditto up to 24 august 1832	..76		1832		
Feby 2/d/ To paid Thos **O DYARE**s? act	2..00		augt 24 By hire of bay **JACOB**		30..00
" " Int to 24 august 1832	06½		" " " " **WILEY**		37..25
" 8 To do paid Ely **CARTER**s act	1..75		" " " " **CROFFORD**		40..00
" Int to 24 august 1832	06		" " " " **MIKE** . . .		35..37½
" 18 " pd Redmond **PARKER**/s/ act	14..00		" " Girl **EDITH** . . .		4..12½
" Int to 24 august 1832	..42		" rent of Land		9 00
March 1/st/ To paid John W **SOUTHALL**s			" Int on ditto from 1/st/ Jany 1832		6..07?
act	52 86				
" Int to 24 august 1832	1. 74				
May 23/d/ To paid R G **COWPER** Shff}					
Toxes on land	2..80				
" Int to 24 august 1832	14				
" 25 To pd Mr/s/ **BRITT** for Services					
rendered	2..00				
Int to 24 august 1832	..03				
" 28 To paid yau at winton	8..950				
Int to 24 august 1832	12				
July 28 To pd R W **JOHNSTON** acct	1..27				
1832 To 5 p cet comms on receipts &}					
and [sic] expenditures amtg to $338..49/¢/}	16..92				
aug 24 To Ballance due the orphan	1267..87				
	$1391..84				1391..84

North Carolina }
Hertford County} August Court of Pleas &c 1832
This Account was returned to Court on oath by Jacob **HARE** Guardian & ordered
to be Recorded

Jacob **HARE** Guardian

Test. L. M. **COWPER** clk

===

Dossey A OUTLOW [sic]

     Dr Dossey A **OUTLAW** orphan of George **OUTLAW** decd In

1830 with [sic] David O. **ASKEW** Guardin   Cr

Augt 15 To Cash paid Lewis **BOND** Shff					Dr
for Taxes	2..08		amt Brat up		16..34½
1830 Int on ditto up to? June 21/st/ 1832	22		Jany Int on ditto		..97
Augt 15 To Cash pd Lewis **BOND** for Taxes	2..48		16 To Cash pd James **RUSSELL**		24..00
Jany 15 Int on ditto up to ditto . . .	..12½		Int on ditto		2..06
To Cash pd Doct John R **HALL**	$11..45		Feby 15 To Cash Doct Thamas **BORLAND**		32..32
	16..34½		amt carried forward		75..69½

121

(143) 114 Dossey A **OUTLOW**   £dn

Dr Dossy A **OUTLAW** orphan of George **OUTLOW** ded in acct with David O **ASKEW**

Amt Brot forward	75..69	**1831**
To Int on ditto	2..63	Feby ct By Ballance du [sic] the orphan}
Mch? 15 To Cash sent yau by Lawrence		at my return to this Court } 92 80
BEVERLY	50..00	By Compound Int on ditto up}
" Int on ditto	3..65	to this Settlement } 7..22
May 17 To a draft on Henry **WARELL** & son	80..00	By hire of negrou?s for the year}
Int on ditto	5..24	1831 payable 16 of Jay 1832 } 273..65
July 13 To Cash paid at princetown &}		Int on ditto up to 21/st/ of}
" expence home }	70..35 00	June 1832 . . . .} 7..07
/Int on dito/ }	/3 92/	By hire of Negrous for the year
Nov? 28 To Cash pd Mss **TARPLY**	21 75	1832 payable 15 Jay 1833 $315
Int on ditto	70	deduct the Int so as make it
Decr 10 To Cash paid Watson **LEWIS**	3..75	due the 21/st/. of June 1832
1832 Interest on ditto	..12	leaves due 304..29
Jany 2/d/ To Cash advanceed yau . .	10..00	By Dassey A **OUTLAW**s note
Int on ditto	..27	given the 21/st/ of June 1832 for the
2 To Cash paid John **HORTEN**	19..87½	Ballance of this act 26..11
24? Int on ditto	55	711..44
16? To Cash Jere **OUTLAW** . . .	16..60	
Int on ditto	41	North Carolina }
26 To Cash paid Doct Jere F **WARD**	78..28	Hertford County} To all whome it may concern
Int on ditto	1 89	know ye that we David O **ASKEW** Guardian to
30 To Cash paid B J **MONTGOMERY**	25..00	Dassy A **OUTLAW** and Dassy A **OUTLAW** now
1832 Int on ditto	58	full age have this day Settled all accounts
Feby 8 To Cash paid **HARRELL** &		as relates to the Guardian Ship of Said Dassey
BEVERLY	76..71¼	and received a pay ment from each other
" Int on ditto	1..66¾	which Settlement we Bind aur Selves aur aur [sic]
" To Cash paid Lawrence **BEVERLY**	10..43¾	heir/s/ executor/s/ or administrator/s/ to Stand to
Int on ditto	22¼	and abide by & that we naw have not nor
May? 7 To Cash advancd yau	5..00	Shall have any Claim against each other
Int on ditto	03	in any manner whatsoever either in law or
14 To Cash advance yau	10..00	at Equity as this is a final Settlement
Int on ditto	06	from the beginning of the world up to
To Cash advance do yau	3..75	the day & date here after written In witness
Int on ditto	..02	we the said David O **ASKEW** and Dassey A
To Cash paid Ezekiel **AROCHER**	62½	**OUTLAW** have here unto Set aur hands and Seals
" " paid Susun **GREGORY**	1 00	this 21/st/ day of June 1832
To Cash paid E **BERRY**	1..87	Witness David O **ASKEW** (Seal)
To this amt is to pay for Keeping negraes}		Miles H **JERNIGAN** Dossey A **OUTLOW** (Seal)
for the year 1832 $70..50 }		
deduct the Int so as to make it due }		
the 21/st/ of June 1832 leaves }	67..90?	
To 5 pr cet coms on the many expended		
and received Saey on $1241.88	62..09	
	711..44	

North Carolina }

Herttford County} August Court of Pleas &c 1832

This Account was returned to Court on oath by David O **ASKEW** Guardn
at the Same time the receipt was proved by the oath of Miles H **JERNGAN** the
Subscribing witness thereto & ordered to be Recorded   Test. L. M. **COWPER** Clk

---

(144) 115 Sarah **SIMONS** Dr Sarah **SIMONS** daughter of of [sic] Watson **LEWIS** In a/c current with
1831   Watson **LEWIS** Guardian

(144) Sarah **SIMONS** (Cont.)

Feby 23 To Ballance due the Guardian	65..22
Mar 1 To Cash paid Court Charges on dowry	9..55
" 2 To ½ yd muslin @ 75/¢/ 2 Spools @ 12½	..63
" " 3 " Thread eging @ 12½	38
" 4 To Guardian a/c returned to Feby ct	..40
" 5 To 1 pr Shaes for **PAYTON** yaur order	1..50
" 14 To 2 oz Indigo @ 25	50
" " 5/lb/ Spun Cotton @ 35 ¢	1..75
" " 3 yds Cotton Cambrick @ 20/¢/	60
" 26 " " ¼ ditto Jackinett muslin @ 75/¢/	..18
" " " 5 ditto Collor cloth @ 12½	..63
" " " 1¼ ditto ditto @ 20/¢/	22
" " " 3½ ditto ditto	70
Apl 1/st/ " ½ ditto Callico 40/¢/	20
" 5 " ½ ditto Jackinett muslin	16
" 11 " Cash paid yau	5 00
" " " ditto Mr/s/ **SPELLING?**	2..80
" " " ditto part for Currug? bonets	20
" 23 " 2 Books 90 4 yds flannel @ 60/¢/	3..34
" " " 4 ditto Brade @ 6¼	..25
" " " 2 doz pearl buttons @ 25/¢/	50
" " " 15 buttons ditto @ 2¼	..31
" 26 " 3 yds Silk @ 70/¢/	5..60
" " " 1½ ditto Callico @ 25/¢/	..67
" " " hank Silk 6/¢/	06
" 29 " 1½ yds Checks @ 30/¢/	45
May 2 ' amt paid Catharine **SIMONS**	1..00
" " " 1 Fancy Shawl	1..25
" " " ½ Fig/d/ Swiss muslin @ $1	50
" " " 3 bunches tape @ 10/¢/	30
" " " 1½ yds Callico @ 40/¢/	60
" " " 2 pr Stockings 50 & 75	1..25
" 4 " 2½ yds grodonap? Silk @ 80/¢/	2..00
" " " 1 Crape Shawl	1..25
" 5 " 2 bunches Brade @ 20/¢/	..40
" " " 1 pr Shaes for **LINDER**	1..50
" 7 " 1 do morocco	1..50
" 18 " Cash	1..05
" 20 " 5¼ yds Callico @ 37/¢/	2..44
" " " 1 7/8 do Figd muslin 1½ do Blk? @ 25	2 78
" " " 2 Spools catton @ 12/¢/ 2 paper/s/ brade	..75
" 28 " amt paid **TONY**	..25
" " " 10 yds Cattons @ 30 Cash 75	3..75
June 10 " 1 pr White Silk gloves	38
" " " 1 yd Cambrick 20/¢/ 1½ thread /Lace/ $1?	2..70
" " " 3 do Catton Cloth @ 20/¢/}	..90
" " " 1 Bal? Catton 25/¢/ }	
amt carrie/d/ up of?	128..45

Amt Brot forward	128..45
13 To 1¼/lb/ Catton @ 25	..31
17 ' " 1 pr Childerons [sic] Shaes	..50
19 " Cash paid yau	2..00
24 " ½ yd white Crape	..37
28 " 1¼ " Cambrick @ 50/¢/	..62
" " ½ ditto book muslin @ $1	50
" " 2¾ ditto Catton cloth @ 20/¢/	..55
30 " ½ ditto B muslin	..63
July 11? Cash paid yau	[blank]
To 1 yd muslin 62 1 ditto callico 37	1..00
" 3 ditto Ribband @ 30/¢/	90
25 To 1 pr prunell Shaes	1..25
Augt 5 To Cash 1..25-1 yd Catton Clath 10	1..35
To ½ yd Lace @ 30 1 Hdff 88	1..03
6 To Hank Silk	06
9 To 2¼ black Silk @ 75/¢/	1..88
10 " 1 Battle preston Salts	..38
18 " Cash	3..00
" " pr Stockings Catton	..63
24 " Amt paid Taxes	4..03
" " 1 pr Shaes $1..25 1 Vail 75	2..00
30 " 2 yds Ribband	50
~~Sept 8~~ " knife	13
Sept 8 " amt paid Milly F **FLEETWOOD**	..75
14 " 3 yds Catton @ 20 1½ Callico 40	1..30
" " 1¾ ditto Callico @ 37½	..65
" " 1 Hff 25 1 do 37-3 yds Cattons	1..00
14 " Cash	2..00
28 " 1 doz needles 12½ 1 Spool Catton 12/¢/	..25
Octr " 12 yds Silk @ 75/¢/	9..00
" " making & Trimming	2 64?
" " Ballance on watch	5..50
25 " 1 Bead packit	3..25
" " 1 ditto Beoerce?	..50
" " 2 yds Catton @ 12½ 1 do Small towls?	..38
" " 3 belts? @ 25 .. 7½ yds Silk @ 1 05	8..62
" " 2 yds Lace @ 20/¢/ 1 Lecashin?} Shawl @ 2..25 . . . . . . }	2..65
" "1 under dress 1..50 7 yds Calico 37	2..63
" "2 yds pink ribband @ 20	..40
" "½ do Silk 30 2 bunches brade 12½	..56
" "1 Cake soap 25 2 pr glaves} 62 & 37 . . . . . . }	1..25
" "2 pr Small Shaes @ 31¼	..63
" "¾ yds lace @ 1 --- ---	..75
amt carried forward	$198..61

123

(145) 116 Sarah SIMONS   gdn

Dr Sarah SIMONS daughter of Watson LEWIS In act current with Watson LEWIS

Amt Brot forward	$198..61	Amt Brot up	274..85
31 To 1 Hdff 75.. ½ yd Catton @ 12½	..81	March 6 To 3 kegs white Lead @ 3	9..00
" 1 pr Indian rubber Shaes	1 75	" 1 lb Letherags	..25
Nov 2 To amt paid James ALSTON for}		To 5 Bbls Tar @ 1 $ 100/lbs/ Spanish	
9 Brandy BBls }	6..75	Brown 6$	11..00
" " ditto Nathan PINNER for cider}		" 6 paper/s/ Lampblack @ 12½/¢/	..75
mill . . . . }	10..00	14 " ½ yd muslin @ 75	38
8 " 1 hank Silk 6¼ 1 pr Shaes 1..25	1..31	" " ½ ditto Silk @ 50	..50
" 1½ yds Checks @ 25 ¾ ditto ginghay	2..63	21/st/ " 2 kegs white Lead @ 3$	6..00
" 6 fine hat for PAYTON	2..00	23 " 2½ yds Ribband @ 25	62½
" 2 yds futting @ 12/¢/	25	30 " 1 pr Shaes @ 1..50	1..50
14 " 1 Blanket $1. 1 pr Shaes 1..25	2..25	" " 1 work Barskett	..75
" " 2½ yds Corcashion @ 62½	1..25	" " 1 pr Shaes for LINDER . . .	1..25
" " 1¾ ditto Checks @ 25/¢/	..44	" " 1 do Side Combs	1..00
24 " 2 yds ribband @ 12½	..25	" " 1 do Stockings	..75
Decr 1 " 3½ ditto yellaw flannel	2..18	" " 2¼ yds Checks @ 20/¢/	..45
" " 1¼ ditto @ 30 callico @ 30/¢/	..25	" " 1 pr Side Combs	1..00
12 " ¾ ditto B Muslin @ 50/¢/	..38	Apl 23/d/ To 2 fancy Hffs @ 1 12½ 1 do 87	2..00
" Cotton Hdff 25 2 hanks Silk @ 6½	..38	" " " Cash $5 1½ yds ribband @ 20/¢/	5..25
" 1 yd Mitinett	12	" " " 7 yds Callico @ 40/¢/	2..80
" 1 ditto ribband	20	" 28 " ½ do Cottons @ 20/¢/	..10
" 1 ditto Linen	38	May 9 " ½ yd Has/d/? muslin @ 62½	31
" 1 doz hooks & eyes	12	" " " 1 Spool Catton	..13
17 " Cash	4..00	" " " ½ yd bobinett Lace @ 80/¢/	..40
23 " ditto	2..50	" " " 3½ ditto Callico @ 25	..88
24 " 1 Torter Shell Comb . . .	5..00	" " " 4½ ditto @ @ 20/¢/	..90
" " 5 ditto Callico @ 40/¢/	2 00	" 10 " amt paid Riddick LAWELL	15 00
" " 1 ditto blk Silk @	..88	" " " 7 galls Linseed oil @ 1.25	8 75?
" " 1 pr Catton Stockings	..75	" " " 3 yds Checks @ 20/¢/ 2 ditto	
" " 1 hank Silk	06	Cotton 12½	..85
31 " 2 yd ribband @ 6½	..13	17? " " 1 Bottle Snuff 30 1 pr Shaes 1..25	1..55
1832		21 " " " 3 yds Checks @ 20/¢/	..60
Jay 10 " this amt paid John WINBORNE }		22 " " 1 Spool Cotton 12½ 1½ yds} .	
" for hire girl VILOT for year 1831}	6..50	Ribband @ 12½ }	..32
14 " Cash	5..00	June 9 " Amt paid yau	1..00
23 " 1¾ yds Checks @ 25	..44	" 19 1 Silk Handff 1$ 1 ditto 75	1..75
Feby 4 " 1 dunstable bonnett	3..50	" " ¾ yds belt Ribband 20 Silk 6	..22
" " 1 Silk Handkerchief 75 work}		" " ¾ ditto Nankeens @ 30/¢/	..23
" Barsket . . . .}	1..50	23 " 1 ditto & Card Muslin @ 50}	
" " amt paid Sipha SMITH for		belt 25 . . . .}	75
Surveying land	3 00	24 ditto Cattons Cash 156 @ 12½	1..31
9 " 8 yds Catton Cloth @ 25	2..00	July 3 " To 5/8 yds Card Muslin @ 62½	..39
" " 3 ditto Callico 40/¢/	1..20	6 " Cash	6 00
" " 1 Bible 50/¢/ 1 yd Catton @ 12½	63	19 " " " Tune?ing Pianna Forte	2..00
19 " amt paid TOM	..20	29 " " " 1 pr Bronze prunel Shaes	1..50
" " 1 pr Shaes	1..25	" " " Cash 62½ 3/4 yds Catton cloth 1 20?	1 23
27 " 1 Blankett 1$ 1 ditto check 25	1..25	" " " 8 yds Checked muslin @ 62½	5..00
" " Cash 50/¢/ 1½ Cambrick 50/¢/	75	" " " To Cash paid Miles JERNEGAN	
	274..85	Taxes on land for 1831	4 00
" amt Carried up		amt Carried forward	374..32

(146) 117 Sarah SIMONS

Dr Sarah SIMONS daughter of Watson LEWIS in a/c current with Watson LEWIS guardian

(146) Sarah SIMONS (Cont.)

To Amt Brot forward	374..32	**1831**	
Augt 2 " 1½ yds Callico @ 30 . . .	..45	Apl 7 " By this amt recd of John}	
15 " Cash	3..37½	**WINBORNE**	105..68
18 " ½ yd Bobinet Lace @ $1	50	May 9 By 2133 herings @ 3$	6..40
" " 2 ditto Silk @ 89 6 do Swiss		" " " 14533 ditto @ 2 50	36..36
muslin @ 1	7..7?5	June 3/d/ By 52 bush Caw & Red Peas @ 40	20..80
Augt 23/d/ " Ballance due S. SIMONS	235..07	Novr 2/d/ " 9 BBls brandy @ 15	135..00
		Decr 1/st/ " 3836/lb/ fodder @ 50/¢/	19..18
	622..46	" 27 " 6 2/3 bush Caw Peas @ 40/¢/	2..53

Received of Watson **LEWIS**
Guardian Two hundred thirty five
dollar/s/ & Seven cents in full of the
against all [sic] Law & Court of
Equity August 23/d/ 1832
Edward D **LEWIS**   Sally W **SIMONS**

1832		
Jany 10 " this amt recd from John}		
WINBORNE admr of John }		
SIMONS decd due from the }		
Estate of Said decd }	45..48	
" ditto for division of negraes	41..88	
14 " 3 1/3 BBls Corn 1 25 . . .	4..16	
Feby 7 " hire of negro bay **PAYTON** for		
year 1831	30..00	
Aprl 6 " hause rent recd of Jas **ALSTON**	4..00	
9 " 1 pr Side Combs returned . .	1..00	
" 23 " ginghams returned	2..25	
May 10 " 16.666 herrings @ 2..50	41..66	
June 19 " 139 bushels Corn @ 45 . .	62..55	
Augt 20 " 117½ bushels Corn @ 48/¢/	56..22	
" " " 7 1/3 BBls ratton corn @ 1$	7..33	
	622..44	
Augt 23 By Ballance due S **SIMONS**	235..07	

North Carolina }
Hertford County} August Court of Pleas &c 1832
This Account was returned to Court on oath by Watson **LEWIS** Guardian at the Same time
the receipt was proved by the oath of Edward D **LEWIS** the Witness thereto & ordered to be
Recorded   Test. L. M. **COWPER** Clk.

Corda [sic] VICK

Dr Cordia **VICK** In a/c current with Benjamin **BRYANT** gdn			Cr
To 20 cents for returning this act	20	By Cash	$24..67
" medical aid	1..00	By Interest on the Same from august}	
" 1 pr Shaes	87½	term 1831 to august term 1832 }	1..48
" 4 yds of Clath @ 25	1..00		
" Comms on $4..35	..21		
" 5 months board @ 3 50 /¢/ pr month	17..50		
" Comms on $17..50/¢/	..87		26..15
	21..59		21..59
Ballance due to the Cr	4..56		4..56

North Carolina }   Benjamin **BRYANT** Guardian
Hertford County} August Court of Pleas &c 1832
This Account was reterned to Court on oath by Benjamin **BRYANT** Guardian
& ordered to be Recorded   Test. L. M. **COWPER**. clk

---

(147) 118 Rebecca VICK Dr Rebecca **VICK** in a/c current with Benjamin **BRYANT** Guardian

To returning this acct	20	By Cash	26..46
To 1 pr Shaes @ 1$ 25	1..25	By Interest on the Same from term [sic]}	
" 1 do prunel Shaes	1..87	1831 to August term 1832 }	1..58
" Comms on $4..80/¢/	24		28..04

(147) Rebecca VICK (Cont.)

3..56			3..5€
		Ballance du [sic]	24..48
			Benjamin **BRYANT** guₐn

William **VICK**

Dr William **VICK** In a/c current with Benjamin **BRYANT** guardn

To returning this Act	..20	By Cash	27..3C
To 4 yds of Cloth @ 25	1..00	By Interest on the Same from}	
To Comms on $2..83	..14	august term 1831 to august }	
		term 1832 }	1..03
	1..34		28..33
To Ballance due	27..59		1..34
			27..59
		Benjamin **BRYANT** Guardian	

Etna **VICK**

Dr Etna **VICK** In act current with Benjamin **BRYANT** Guardn

To returning this A/c	20	By Cash	27..30 /Cr/
" 1 pr Shaes [erased & illegible words]	1..66?	" Interest on the Same from }	
" Commis on $2..83	..14	August term 1831 to augt term 1832}	1..63
	1..34		28..93
To Ballance due	27..59		1 34
		Benjamin **BRYANT** gdn	27..59

Newet **VICK**

Dr Newet **VICK** In a/ct current with Benjamin **BRYANT** Guardian   Cr

To Returning this A/c	20	By Cash	24..67
To Commissions $1 68	08	By Interest on the Same from }	
		augt term 1831 to augt term 1832}	1..48
	28		26..15
To Ballance due	25..87		28
			25..87
		Benjamin **BRYANT** Guardian	

North carolina   }
Hertford County} August Court of Pleas &c 1832
These Accounts were returned to Court on oath By Benjamin **BRYANT** Guardiand
& order to be Recorded   Test. L. M. **COWPER** clk

Account Sales William **NAWEL**
Account Sales of negro man **STEPHEN** the property of William **NAWEL** Esqr dec
Sold the 30 day of July 1832 for Cash to Mr. **DARHAM** for $375.00   375 00
North Carolina }   A **THAMAS** admr
Hertford County} August Court of Pleas &c 1832
This Account Sales was returned to Court on oath by Abraham **THAMAS** admr
and ordered to be Recorded   Test. L. M. **COWPER**. clk

---

(148) 119 Account of Negroes hired out on thursday 29/th/ of December 1831
At the Hause of Hartnell **GRIFFITH** the negroes are nat to go the Sane

DAVID usual clothing	Samuel **MOORE**	51..50
WILLIS usual cothing To	David **CROSS**	41?..00
TOM usual`Clothing To	Jethro **CURL**	28 00
Do **BET** & Child to the Lawest under taker the	Widow	10..00
& **JONUS?** nat Hirred aut Staey with the	Widow	
North Carolina }		

(148) (Cont.)

Hertford County} ~~August~~ November Caurt of Pleas &c 1832

This Account of hire of Negraes was returned to Caurt on aath by James **PAWELL** ex? &

ordered to be Recorded   Test. L. M. **COWPER**. clk

Rebecca P **BRITT**

Dr Rebecca P **BRITT** orphan of James C **BRITT** decd In A/c

1832 current with Henry L **WILLIAMS** Guardian		1832	
Jany To Cash paid Elias **BRITT** acct}			
of Jas E **BRITT** }	25..44	Jany To amt Recd of Elias **BRITT** }	
Interest for 11 Months	1..37½	which was due from her farther/s/ Estate}	260..56
Feby 10 " Cash paid Jaseph **BRITT**		Interest on that Sum for 11 months	14..30
keeping little? Negraes	10..00	To Ballance due the ward on Cash	15..85
Interest for 10 months	[blank]	return	
To Cash paid **REA & CAMP** as pr bill	18..44	Int for 1 year on that amt	..95
Interest five? months	..09	To the hire of **FRANK** for 1831 to Elias	
" Cash paid John W **SAUTHALL**		**BRITT** for	40..00
as pr bill	29..30		331..66
Augt 25 " Cash paid Ely **CARTER** for Shaes	1..50		
" Cash pd Clk for this return	..40	this return to August Caurt 1832}	
" my Commissions on $87..05 being}		Ballance due the ward this return}	213..18
" the amt paid aut at 5 pr cet }	4..35	E E Henry L. **WILLIAMS** Guardian	
" Cash paid Elias **BRITT** for keeping}			
bay **WRIGHT** 1831	10..00		
Commissions on 10 dollar/s/ being			
the amt paid for keeping negro	50		
To Commissions on $331..66 at 5 pr ct			
being the amt recd	16..58		
	118..48		
By Ballance due the ward augt 27/1832	213..18		
	331..66		

North Carolina }

Hertford County} November Court of Pleas &c 1832

This account was returned to Court on aath by Henry L **WILLIAMS** Guardian

& ordered to be Recorded   Test. L. M. **COWPER**. clk

John **MAGETT**

Dr John **MAGETT** orphan of John **MAGETT** decd In act current

1832 with Jacob **HARE** Guardian			Cr
Augt 27 To Cash paid clk for Last	..75	1832	
" " paid yau at Winton	10..00	August 24 By Ballance due on last return	1267..87
" Interest on ditto up to 24 Novr 1832	..14	novr 26? " Interest on do up to 24	~~19..01~~
	10..89	November 1832	19..01
		amt Carried forward	1286 88

---

(149) 120 John **MAGET**   gdn

Dr John **MAGET** orphan of John **MAGET** decd In a/c current with Jacob **HARE**

amt Brot forward	10..89		1286..88
Octr 13 To paid Ely **CARTER** for Shaes			
& Boots	8..75		
Interest on ditto	..04		
" paid Mr/s/ Mason **MAGET** for keeping}			
"negro woman **CLARA** & Children for }			
the year 1831-- }	21..00		
Interest on ditto	13		

(149) John MAGET (Cont.)

Nov 23 " paid Doct Thomas J **HARPER**/s/}
    acts for board & medicin [sic]   23..50
    Nov 24 To Commissions on the above }
    expenditares amtg To $63..31½ @ 5 p ct} 3..16½
    " Ballance due the orphan 24 Nov 1832 1220..40
                             1286 88

To this amt paid Mason **MAGET** for   }
Keeping negro woman **CLARY** &   }
Two Children for the year 1832 as pr recpt} 20..00
" Commissions on hire of negraes   }
    & rent of Land Saey on $160..85 also}
    on $20 for keeping negro Waman   }
    & Children @ 5 pr ct   } 9..04
" Commissions on $19-01 which is}
    on Interest @ 5 prcet . . . .} 95
    Clerks fees . . . . 1..50
To Ballance due the orphan this 1/st Jay 1833 129..86
                             160..35

		1286..33
By hire of Bay **JACOB** due 1/st/ Jay 1833		30..00
" do " " **WILEY** due " "		40 00
" do " " **CROFFORD** " "		35..50
" do " " **MIKE?** " " "		37..25
" do " girl **EDITH** ." " "		1..10
" do " **AMUS** even " '		
" rent of Land at Mr/s/ **MAGET**s ½ pt		10 00

1832   160. 85
Novr 24 By Ballance due the orphan}
up to this day as Stated abve   } 1220..40
" " By Ballance due the Same 1/st/ Jay 1833}
    for hire of negroes & rent of Land   } 129..36
November 25 th 1832   Jacob **HARE** Guardian

North Carolina }
Hertford Caunty} November Court of Pleas &c 1832
This Account was returned to Court on oath by Jacob **HARE** Guardian & ordered to be Recorded
               Test. L. M. **COWPER**. clk

END OF BOOK

DECEDENT INDEX

Elizabeth Britt. Dr Elizabeth Britt as of Etheldred Brittin Act with Elizabeth Britt

Amt Brot forward $ 51.12½   Amt Brot forward $ 9..00
                    71 47-99   August 1830   54-13
22 August 1830 ___   13.20 By Rent of land this year due the
                                25 dver next   5..50
                              By hire of negro girl (Violet)
                              this year due that 25 dec next   18.00
                              By Amt due the guardian 22 May   19.14
              $ 135.79 $ 135.79

                                    Elizabeth Britt
                                        mark

North Carolina } August Court of Pleas 46 1830
Hertford County } Court an entry by Elizabeth Britt Guardian
This Account was returned to
& ordered to be Recorded   Test J M Crawford Clk

Martha Brown Dr Martha Brown orphan of Harvey Brown deceased in act with William B Wynns per Guardian

1830 To 1 lb Loaf Sugar & 2/6 lb Cotton   0. 5½   By Balance due the orphan $ 209.87
25 To 5 lb Loaf Sugar @ 3/4   1.25   Interest on do up to August Court 1830   6.36
   cash paid on entry for taxes for 1829   216.15
To 5 per Cent Commissions   August 25 By balance due the orphan 213.48
To Ballance due the orphan   213.48
                                         216.15   W B Wynns Guardian

Elizabeth Parker Dr Elizabeth Parker (or Brown) in act with William B Wynns Guardian
To 3 lb of Cotton @ 1/3 3 lb Sugar 3/4   By Ballance due the orphan
& to Chair   35   at my settlement Feby Court 1831   264.70
Interest up to August 1830   50   Interest on do up to August Court 1830 6.14
To Recording this act   12   271.04
To Cash paid Sheriff for taxes   6.75
To 5 per Cent Commissions   2.16   1831
To Ballance due the orphan   171.59   August 25 By Ballance due the orphan 171.59
                                       271.04
                                                    W B Wynns Guardian

Rebecca Bell

Dr Rebecca Bell orphan of James C. Bell deceased with Henry L. Williams

Feby 22d   Cash paid Lewis M Cowper for
1830   Lacy guardian Bond   £10

          Cash paid John W Southall
          for goods as pr bill   39.58

          Cash paid Clk for making this return   .10

          Commissions an on dollar 18 cents expps   74

1831   Amount due me from the wards pp   36.24
Aug 23d up to this time   30.24

                    Henry L Williams gud

North Carolina
Hertford County   August Court of Pleas &c 1830
     This Account was returned to Court & was sworn by Henry L Williams Guard
& ordered to be recorded
                                        Test L M Cowper Clk

William N Bonn

Dr William N Bonn orphan of Bonn Bonn deceased with John Barns his gu
1827
Jany 2d By hire from William Ferguson
          Estate this Amt
          To fee Clerk for guardian Bond   60
          paid Eaton Barclis Clk & master for copy
          of John Bonns proceedings in partn   3.16
          1 hat & bot of Morgan & Cowper   2.75
          14 yds Callico Cloth of   3.00
Feby 9th and Knit & 4 in Mar 31st pd H Long & prop 20.35
Apl 10th 1 pair Shoes 75 mending Shoes 55   1.30
          paid Edith Ferguson for Cloth for wrds   6.23
          little paid Anderson for schooling wds   3.31
May 22d   By recd from Suit Bell admt
          of John Bonn
          15 fee Clerk and master Expns
Jany 7th 1 clay Shirt buttons 7d
          making Clothes at 1 hemstds   3.34
          pd Sydlea Bell for Shirt 7/5   1.25
          To one hund Bot of Peter an Bonn of   3.33
          paid Benjamin Brown for schooling wds   11
1831
Jany 1   £33.1

                                                            £ 2739.03

FEMALE GIVEN NAME INDEX

Perthena Ann
   SESSOMS 55,
135
Phebe HILL 105,
123,140
Phebee HILL 41
Pheby HILL 86,129
Porthena Ann
   SESSOMS 87

R. HOLLOMON 78
Reany
   HALLOMON
   46
Reany
   HOLLOMON
   46
Rebecah VICK 57,
102,103
Rebecca P. BRITT
   36,105,148
Rebecca VICK 147
Rebecca WILSON
   104
Rebeccah BRITT 37
Rebeckah BRITT
   34,72,73,109
Renea
   HOLLOMON
   78
Rina HOLLOMON
   116

S. SIMONS 146
Sally BEVERLEY
   34
Sally BEVERLY 34
Sally KNIGHT 119
Sally M.
   WILLIAMS 60,
93,137
Sally Maria
   WILLIAMS 30
Sally Miriah
   WILLIAMS 137
Sally W. SIMONS
   146
Sarah (LEWIS)
   SIMONS 56,91,
92,144-146
Sarah M.
   WILLIAMS 30
Sarah PARNAL 128,
129
Sarah PERRY 83,

84,128,130,133
Sarah PERY 89
Sarah PORTER 52
Sarah SIMONS 56,
91,92,130-134,144,
145,146
Sidney
THOMPSON
   71
Sindy HOLLOMON
   78,116
Susannah WIGGINS
   100,101
Susannah WIGG___
   100
Susun GREGORY
   143